make over
your marketing

12 months of marketing
for salon and spa

For Single Chair Artist to Multi-Station to Chain Salon or Spa

A guide for how-to make over every aspect of your marketing:
and ideas, events and promotions for salon and spa
stylists • estheticians • therapists • managers • owners

Elizabeth Kraus

Owner/CEO, Be InPulse Branding Marketing & Design
www.12monthsofmarketing.net

For more on marketing, read my blog at www.savvystylist.net.
Branding and Marketing Workshops and branded, customized Distributor and Manufacturer
"12 Months of Marketing for Salon and Spa" publications available.

12 Months of Marketing for Salon and Spa

by Elizabeth Kraus

Owner/CEO, Be InPulse Branding Marketing & Design

12monthsofmarketing.net

Branded | Customized Distributor or Manufacturer "12 Months of Marketing for Salon and Spa," custom calendars, print and display materials, workshops and other resources available at www.12monthsofmarketing.net.

Read the author's blog at www.savvystylist.net with promotion, display and marketing ideas for salon and spa.

Author/Editor: Elizabeth Kraus

Cover and Interior Design/Lay out: Elizabeth Kraus (Be InPulse Branding, Marketing & Design)

Printing History: 2011 First Edition

ISBN-13: 9781456593384

To my parents, Jim and Sheryll Robinson
who always made me believe that everything is possible,
to my sister Carrie and my brother Craig,
who always cheer me on.

To my children, Amanda and Gavon, Eric and Laura,
Sarah, Sam, Noa and Rania

and to my grandchildren, Jaxon and Jaycee
whose possibilities are endless.

To my husband, Dan
who brought my heart back to life, makes me laugh
and makes sure I believe in myself.

Elizabeth

"It's not the dates on your tombstone that matter,
it's what you do with the dash in between."

Adapted, singer/songwriter Kevin Welch

contents

12 months of marketing for salon and spa
make over your marketing

Create a bigger, more influential role for your business in the lives of your clients:

Generate more referrals, increase the frequency of client contacts and entice your clients to join your "tribe."

Add new and even non-traditional services and products to meet more needs of clients.

Create incentives for loyalty, retail sales, service packages, multiple sales, double bookings and referrals.

Meet more needs of your clients: social, intellectual, ego, health, wellness, education, personal development, networking and more.

Create a haven, an oasis, a creative space, a third space, a social setting, a place to escape or a place to gather.

Be the facilitator for your clients within the community; link them with other businesses, community leaders, civic organizations, local government, specialty education and with schools and charity resources and great causes in your community.

Tap deep pools of potential clients.

Be the voice of change, conscience and progress in your community.

Grow your professional and personal ability to lead and influence others and strengthen your reputation in the community.

Have fun—and be a place where people have fun—listen to great music, laugh, eat, and escape from the doom and gloom of the rest of the media that bombards them!

january
make over your marketing
(and "everything is marketing")

My husband is a dentist and I wanted to help him with some marketing projects, but since I don't know a lot about how dental offices operate, I read the book *Everything is Marketing* by Fred Joyal, the founder of 1-800-Dentist. While at first glance you might not expect to find many correlations between salons and spas vs. dental practices and professionals, I was struck by several commonalities.

Like professionals in the beauty industry, dentists are primarily interested in and are most profitable when practicing their craft. Like you, they want to spend their time providing service to their customers. Like you, they invest a significant amount of time and money learning new skills and techniques and upgrading the equipment and tools needed to help them serve their clients better and faster. They are interested in the health, well-being and self-esteem as well as the physical appearance of their patients. Like you, the services they provide not only change the appearance of their patients, but also affect their attitude and self-confidence— all of which can also affect their personal, social and professional success.

And like salon and spa services, many dental services are paid for out-of-pocket with consumer's expendable resources, or "disposable dollars," if you will. It is an industry where procedures not covered by third party insurance are often viewed as unnecessary 'extras' and so are only done when 'extra' dollars are available to pay for them, and where clients perceive value in the expertise, advice and skill of the practitioner.

Even though (like you) these professionals just want to practice their craft; nonetheless (like you) they are responsible to manage many other facets of their business from marketing to employee relations, finance, vendor negotiations, landlord and leasing services, etc. Small wonder then that much of what I read in Fred Joyal's *Everything is Marketing* could apply equally well to the professional in the salon or spa. And the concept underlying the words of the title, "*Everything is Marketing*," resounded so strongly with me that it led directly to some of the development of this book.

Think about it: Everything is marketing.

Stop thinking that marketing is a verb—something that you should be, or should start, doing. Marketing is not a verb. A verb implies action that begins and ends. Just as when you make over a client you first have to remove other products and deconstruct old styling from the hair and skin to create a clean palette, to make over your business for success in the future you need to be willing to jettison old ideas, deconstruct preconceived notions, and the let go of the old ways of thinking about marketing and other areas of your business.

In point of fact, *everything* in and about your business is marketing. Or rather, every component and characteristic of your business (all of the "verbs" you have to do) like retailing, communications, training, advertising, holding events, making appearances, taking classes, managing staff and the culture of your business, cleaning, and merchandising—plus all of the characteristics—the words that you would use to describe your business, your staff, your skills, your specialties, your products; all of the verbs, nouns and descriptive adjectives that make up your business—all of these make up your marketing. Marketing messages are conveyed to your customers through both the direct and intentional as well as the indirect and unintentional. Everything and anything that impacts any part of your customer's experience, directly or indirectly, is part of your marketing.

I probably don't need to tell you that the stylist behind the chair delivers messages to clients in a way that directly impacts the customer experience, and is therefore part of marketing. But what about the other messages a client receives? The conversation they overhear in the break room while they are at the back bar or going to the rest room. What about the state of the break room as the client walks past and catches a glance, the haircolor mixing area or the back bar itself? Do you have problems with your building that are "not your fault" or that your landlord is truly responsible to correct? Sorry—despite any disadvantages of your facility that are actually the responsibility of your landlord, it's *not* your landlord's responsibility to create and manage your client's experience, it's yours.

How about the workstation next to you, left a dusty, mucky mess by your co-worker? Boxes half unpacked and left on the counter or by your retail shelves? The dust on your slow-moving retail products? The mish-mash and disarray of the left over products you tossed into your "Everything in this basket $5" basket? (Not to mention, what do you think *that* says to your clients about the value of the products you sell?) Your menu with X'ed out pricing or text? How you communicate negative policies in your signage? The appearance of your staff? Their attitude? Their conversations with other employees or clients themselves?

Everything and anything that impacts any part of your customer's experience, directly or indirectly, **is marketing.**

Everything is marketing. Everything about your business works together to paint a picture in the client's mind about who and what you are —and if you are honest, you have to admit that sometimes the picture painted is not what you hoped or intended it to be.

Everything—advertising, scripting, signage, web site, e-mail, phone conversations, answering machine messages, menu, pricing, financial policies, salon policies, merchandising, retail, your check out and payment procedures, your check in and appointment procedures, your presence in the community, your personal development, skills, tools, equipment, facilities, technology, environment, ambiance, interior, exterior, staff appearance and conversations, all of your communications—*everything is marketing.*

In order to spend the most time possible practicing your craft, and to do so most profitably, you need to run every aspect of your business as though you truly believe that everything is marketing.

This is true no matter what business you are in, and no matter how small (or big) your business is. In fact, it is arguably *more* important for you to understand this concept if your business is small, because this will give you the best chance of growing and creating an engaged, highly loyal, friend-referring client base. Viewing and operating your business from the standpoint that everything is marketing is the best insurance policy against a slow economy, unstable conditions and cost increases, and in order to ensure the perpetuity of your business into the future.

If you subscribe to the philosophy that everything is marketing, and you design and manage every aspect of your business from end-to-end with this in mind, you stand the best chance of building a business that can support you now and that you will be able to grow to the next level, move to a larger market, pass on to the next generation, or sell in order to retire and enjoy financial independence into your golden years. Changing the way you do business to reflect a sincere conviction that everything is marketing represents both a short term and a long term win-win-win scenario for you, staff and clients.

As you read the coming chapters, resolve to honestly evaluate, explore and commit to making over each and every area of your business, in whatever ways are needed. This will require honest self-evaluation and may even result in a few hits to your ego when long-held perceptions are challenged and disillusioned, the discomfort or dissatisfaction of staff has to be confronted, and the need for real, fundamental, meaningful change is revealed. Resolve to do so not just because it will improve your business (and it will) but also because it's the right thing to do for yourself, for your staff and for your clients —as well as for your business itself.

Ideas for January Promotions

In keeping with the spirit of reflection and being open to honest self evaluation and improvement, January's promotions focus on identifying some of the areas which need to change, and laying out plans to change them.

Lay the Foundation for Success

You might come off as cliché if you use "New Year," "New You" or other variations of these phrases in the promotions you design for January unless you create promotions that genuinely support the types of New Year Resolutions to which your clients may have committed.

Whether your goal is to make your clients or your business (or both) the best they can be for the coming year, you need to lay a foundation that can sustain the changes and growth you have planned. Accordingly, you can construct free add-on service and/or product promotions, sampling and combination treatments designed to:

- Fortify, strengthen and repair
- Clarify
- Deep condition
- Be skin or scalp reparative
- Identify problem areas
- Provide a professional skin, hair or scalp analysis / consultation

Honest Exposure

You cannot change what you do not acknowledge. Key for you as well as for your client's resolve for a healthier, more beautiful new year is honest exposure. Help clients create an honest "before" picture in order to set and measure goals in the coming year.

Partner with a photographer, nutritionist, physical trainer or fitness expert, counselor, dentist, orthodontist or even a physician or cosmetic surgeon to provide clients with a consultative "before" picture event for the areas that concern them. These professionals should be invited to provide your clients with a special offer, samples or literature. Their clients should be invited to participate along with your own. As your part of the "before" picture for all attendees, do scalp or skin analysis, color consultations, offer mini versions of your services, samples, and extend a bounce-back offer.

Provide prescriptive plans for participants that include a time line of measurable, achievable goals and interim milestones and incentives. Working with your marketing partners, help your clients lay out a game plan that can take them from 'where they are' to 'where they want to be,' step by step. Plan get-togethers along the way to measure, report, celebrate and reward participants for interim gains.

A salon-spa "prescription" form featuring common areas where you might prescribe services or products is available for download on the 'Resources' page of my website at www.12monthsofmarketing.net. You can also choose to purchase pre-printed pads of prescription forms in multiple styles, including an option for having the prescription pad customized for your business.

Create on-going working marketing partnerships with photographers in your area. They can be an asset to you by working with you on photo shoots, attending and photo-documenting events, photographing your work for use in your marketing or to create your own look book.

Photographers can be a source of referrals for bridal parties, anniversaries, corporate events, school and senior pictures, proms, graduations and other events that they are hired to record. In turn, you can provide them with personal services and/or products in trade, referrals from among your clients, referrals to bridal parties and other big events for which you are providing services and general client referrals for family or holiday photos.

Some of the projects for which you could create combined package deals with a photographer-marketing partner:

- Family photos, Christmas card photos, anniversary parties, family reunions

- Engagement, wedding and reception photos

- Special event preparation and photography (holiday parties, corporate events, conventions, graduation, prom, etc.)

- School photos, senior photos

- Head shots, photo shoots

- Social media profile photos

- Corporate blog and web site photos, professional corporate publication photos

- Before-and-After photos for makeovers or to document major life external transformation projects (such as restorative or cosmetic surgeries, weight loss programs, etc.)

Milestones and Achievable Goals

To seriously support your client New Year Resolutions over the course of a new year, create a system to record not only their final goals but one that is broken down to add the shorter term goals which must be reached in between to help create milestones and achievable goals. For instance, the idea of losing a total of 50 pounds may sound impossible to one of your clients, but losing a pound a week over 50 weeks might sound far more achievable; plus, no matter how the goal is stated, either way the client achieves their goal before the end of the year. Other items to consider putting on a New Year's Resolution time line are marathons, reunions, fitness competitions, performances or recitals, vacations and other points in time before which clients want to achieve their goals.

Systems and Celebrations

Set up a way for your clients to track their progress against goals and celebrate the small wins as well as the big ones at a monthly "happy hour" social event. Encourage participants to bring a friend to these events and allow them to register and track their goals as well (in other words, let people start their 'New Year' resolutions at any time during the year). Invite businesses that work with you (or desire to) as marketing partners to attend as well as their customers and make sampling, consultations and bounce-back offers part of the event. Create a dedicated web page, blog site or Facebook page for this group:

- for participants to interact with and encourage one another
- to post encouraging quotes and relevant statistics and tips
- to share links to related articles about health, fitness, nutrition, etc.
- to post recognition as participants reach short and long-term goals
- to post "after" pictures or results of those that achieve their goals or pass a milestone; invite your photographer to attend and help track intermediate progress
- you should not use this page as a forum for hard selling, but you can still make readers aware of the benefits of products and services you sell that can help them reach their goals

From the Inside, Out

Include employees in your New Year Resolution goal setting and tracking, and be brave enough to make your own goals public. We all do better when we share our goals with others, track progress, and hold ourselves accountable by participating in support groups. Ask some of your marketing partners to extend free or reduced price options for your employees (and extend similar offers to theirs).

Just imagine what would happen in the years to come if each year your salon or spa were able and publicly known to have helped 5, 10, 20 or even more people to meet their New Year Resolutions relative to weight loss, health, fitness, education, or professional or personal development. How much would you be expanding the role of your business in the lives of your clients? How would it change client perception as to the role that your business plays in their lives? How could it impact your retail and service sales, or even impact the composition of your retail and service offerings? How would it impact your ability to attract new clients?

Bundled Convenience

Create specially-priced bundled series packages to offer to your clients for a 3, 6, or even 12 months schedule of pre-paid, pre-booked service appointments at a frequency appropriate to their specific salon or spa services (such as every 6 weeks for women's hair services, every two weeks for manicure, every week for massage, etc.) This will help to prevent clients from extending the time between their service appointments and help to ensure that they don't have a reason to look to another business to fulfill these needs. To avoid diluting the perceived value of your services that can occur with special pricing, create messages that word promotions with added value rather than discounted-cost language.

Dynamic Duos

Create packages pairing retail products with services to entice clients to experience other services offered by your business throughout the year, through seasonal makeup palettes, through changing hair color, through common seasonal or detrimental environmental conditions and resulting hair or skin needs, etc.

The Tip of the Sales Iceberg

Before the New Year begins, create a salon or spa-branded 12-month wall or desk calendar as a gift for clients to distribute in December and January that includes:

- Seasonal hair and skin care tips

- Styling tips

- Professional photos of your work, or before-and-after styling, makeup or skin care photos

- Product and/or service benefits

- Suggested schedules for services (such as 6 weeks for women's hair services, more frequently for precision or short styles, 3 weeks for men's hair services, etc.)

- Recommended product listings to address specific hair or skin conditions

- Combined makeup palette/product suggestions for seasonal wear or to complement hair and/or eye colors

- Makeup how-to and application tips (such as creating a smoky eye, making eyes look bigger, minimizing flaws, makeup tips to maximize or minimize face shape, etc.)

- An 'offer of the month' for each calendar month

Or work with your cross and cooperative marketing partner/s to create a larger combined-business calendar, sharing space and including offers specific to each month redeemable by code word or cut-out to be distributed to their clients as well as yours.

When you work with other businesses on events and projects your resources go further because you share expenses and you extend a much broader reach. Plus, your marketing will be specifically directed toward your "ideal" prospects (individuals who fall naturally within some of your desired target markets). Create this calendar prior to the beginning of the calendar year for distribution either as a holiday gift to clients in December or early in the New Year, or create a semi-annual or even quarterly version of your calendar so that you are reaching out to clients and prospects more frequently for re-distribution.

Visit www.12monthsofmarketing.net and click on 'Resources' to download a blank calendar template and/or for a quote or information to find out how to get a calendar or other projects (such as your business menu, postcards, bag stuffers, event collateral, etc.) created and printed.

If you are excited about doing a calendar of your own but you missed out on New Year timing, you can create a 16-month 'school year' calendar for distribution mid-year instead. Include your calendar's 'offer of the month,' product or service of the month and other information in your monthly e-mails, on your web site, or use it to create postcards for monthly mailings to clients and prospective clients, for distribution at your point of purchase, and for distribution by the businesses with whom you work on shared marketing projects.

Pay it Forward

Create a quarterly or semi-annual local makeover and gift package contest. Soliciting nominations from within your client base and the greater community, choose a deserving individual from within your community to honor with a day of pampering as well as additional prizes donated by businesses who want to partner with you on this worthy cause. Write a press release to publicize beforehand and to report results afterward, including photos of this deserving individual at the salon or spa and the other activities (such as dining, entertainment, or other destinations that are part of your prize package). Inspiration for this idea is due to Claire Koutsouros of *Hair by Claire* in Doylestown, PA. For details on the program she initiated called "Make Over My Hero" go to www.makeovermyhero.com. (With thanks to Jessee Skittrall, national educator, platform artist, and with partner Marcus Edwards co-owner of Absolut Hair, a complete hair and makeup bar located in Everett, Washington (www.absoluthair.net) to passing this idea forward!

Your prize packages can even work to build cross referrals with cross-over prizes (meaning that one of your clients would win a prize from the business of one of your marketing partners, and the prize that you donate would be awarded to a customer of one of your marketing partners in order to create a scenario where both/all participating businesses have an opportunity to win new clients).

January Month-Long Observances

January is National Blood Donor Month

Contact your local blood bank and offer to help host or promote a blood drive.

Reward donors (those who participated in your blood drive, or any who have recently donated blood) with a salon or spa-branded tchotchke (such as a nail kit, travel mug or water bottle, t-shirt or tank top, etc.), product sample or complimentary add-on service or product.

January is National Hobby Month

Partner with a local hobby or craft store or instructor for cross or cooperatively marketed offers.

Hold a hobby workshop on a topic that would interest your customers (such as scrap booking, photography, do-it-yourself repair or decorating, cooking, sport or game league, knitting or crochet, etc.)

January is Hot Tea Month

Set up a beverage station in your waiting area and sample gourmet teas to clients at appointments. Purchase unique teacups, travel mugs, gourmet teas, etc. for retail sale in your salon or spa.

Feature "did you know" tidbits of information about the health benefits of various types of teas on bag stuffers, in posts on your Facebook or blog page, etc. Hold a drawing for a tea-inspired gift basket at the end of the month.

Partner with a caterer, tea shop or restaurant and hold a real "tea party" to teach clients about the traditions of the tea party and how they can construct their own tea party luncheon, bridal or baby shower. Demonstrate tea party hair styling, makeup application, manicures and pedicures.

January Week-Long Observances

The First Week of January
is Home Office Safety and Security Week

Partner with personal safety experts or safety product sellers to provide special workshops or cross or cooperative offers for customers. Hold a self-defense workshop for clients and encourage them to bring friends and/or reach out to local colleges and high schools to invite female students to attend.

Include personal safety tips (such as safety and security in the home, parking lots, garages and other public places) on bag stuffers and feature them in posts on your Facebook page.

Host a workshop on personal safety and security to help ensure that your employees and all employees in your business park, mall or general area feel safer.

The Second Week of January
is Women's Self-Empowerment Week

Partner with a local counselor, life-coach or motivational speaker for a special workshop or cross/cooperatively marketed offers.

January Holidays and Observances

January 3 is Fruitcake Toss Day

No offense to people who actually enjoy eating Fruitcake, but there is a reason that this holiday staple is the butt of jokes; most of us don't. In fact, many of us receive unwanted, tacky, and other tasteless gifts during the holidays, so for the sake of this idea, let's classify any poorly chosen, unwanted gift as a 'Fruitcake.' Let your clients exchange any of these so-called "Fruitcakes" received during the holidays for retail product or service discounts, gift cards, for salon-branded merchandise like pens, nail files/nail tool kits, lip balms/glosses, mirrored compacts, t-shirts/tank tops, or a special goodie bag combining branded items with retail sample size products. Create bigger gifts for exchange by partnering with local businesses for additional freebies, gift cards or coupons.

January 4 is Trivia Day

Partner with local businesses to create a local trivia contest for clients; prizes could include freebies and/or special offers from all participants.

Hold a 'Trivial Pursuit' contest at a local bar or restaurant with door and winner's prizes and bounce-back offers from participating businesses. Collect attendees' contact information for addition to your contact database.

January 13 is Make Your Dreams Come True Day

Partner with a local life coach, counselor, retirement/financial planner or similar expert to hold an in-salon motivational seminar for clients or cross promote services to both sets of clients.

January 14 is Dress Up Your Pet Day

Partner with a local veterinary office, animal groomer, pet store or another pet-related business to create combo owner-pet grooming offers or cross promoted services.

Add pet "bling," specialty or boutique collars, leashes, bowls or other accessories or pet coat care products to your retail.

Distribute manufacturer's foil pack samples or cross-sell hair or skin care products and extend bounce-back offers in the business of a local pet professional.

Donate a percentage of sales for pet-related (or other specified) retail products to a local animal shelter or local animal emergency services provider. Publicize your efforts on your web site and Facebook page. Write a press release beforehand to increase awareness in your community and afterward to report results.

January 15 is National Hat Day

Purchase spa or salon-branded hats or visors for client gifts, employee wear, gift-with-purchase, contest prizes, incentives, rewards or retail.

January 19 is Popcorn Day

Have some fun! Partner with a local party/equipment rental company and rent an old-fashioned popcorn cart for the week (or month) so you can treat clients to popcorn during or after their appointment.

Contact nearby businesses and provide them with coupons that their clients and/or staff can bring in to exchange for free popcorn and a bounce-back offer for your salon; offer to book an appointment upon redemption.

January 23 is Measure Your Feet Day

Partner with a local shoe retailer or clothing/shoes boutique for cross marketing.

Or work together to create a local fashion show to build business and/or to benefit a local charity (such as a local children's services organization or shelter, or in combination with 'Dress Up Your Pet' day, create an event or donate a percentage of combined sales to a local animal shelter or emergency services provider).

Reward clients with a salon or spa-branded tchotchke, a special offer, gift card for future use or another thank you gift when they bring new children's shoes in with them to their appointment. Donate the shoes to a local children's charity, mission or shelter. Publicize your efforts with a press release beforehand to raise awareness for your chosen charity and afterward to report results. Post updates on Facebook, your web site, blog or other social media site.

National Chili Day is in January

Set a date in mid-January to hold an official "Chili Day." Join forces with a local caterer, restaurant, build-a-dinner organization or similar business and cross market a special lunch or other event to both sets of clients to give away a free "Cup of Winter Chili" in the salon. Extend the spirit of winter chill-i by holding the event each week, or throughout the month. Promote a discount for services to "heat up" your client's look for the rest of the winter.

Spouse's Day is in January

Since you probably have clients whose spouses receive salon or spa services elsewhere, create a special couples or family offer for clients. Book appointments together or in conjunction with a special couples' day or event. Treat couples to extra-special add-on pampering that might include mini-manicure or pedicures, mini-massages, wine and chocolate, etc.

Create bigger packages to celebrate Spouse's Day by partnering with other area businesses for a special event, to create a date night out, or for cross or cooperatively-marketed offers.

January 28 is Fun at Work Day

A healthy, happy business begins from the inside out. Partner with local businesses to create special goodie bags for all employees including samples, coupons, and special offers designed specifically for, and offered only to, employees and their families.

Surprise employees on Fun at Work Day with special on-the-spot surprise thank you notes, group recognition and/or rewards. Include client kudos and raves in your employee and client communications.

Partner with a local business to provide lunch for employees or with a local restaurant to hold a special 'happy hour' for employees after work.

Have a No Pressure De-Stresser

January is a perfect month for low-key social mixers. People need some time to enjoy themselves after the holidays without pressure and they are missing the busier social schedule that provided them with a constant stream of good times with family and friends. For a twist, set up a "mixer" with other stylists and salon professionals in your community to brainstorm solutions, share ideas and socialize. Or treat staff (and yourself) to massages or another de-stressing service.

January Planning and Tasks

Working with staff and distributor sales consultants, order from manufacturer's January-February promotions to support the client events and promotions you plan to hold in March and April.

You probably have more than one Distributor Sales Consultant who visits your salon or spa each month (or even more frequently) who continually offers you the ability to tap their expertise as well as corporate and additional manufacturers' resources and support—take them up on it!

Distributor Sales Consultants may be able to provide personnel, supplies, product samples or representatives to assist you at events or demonstrate products to customers in the salon. They may be able to provide you with support such as downloadable print collateral for postcards, invitations, or even for web and e-mail graphics. Your distributor and manufacturer's representatives should be ready and willing to help you obtain marketing collateral and imagery to assist in promoting retail sales.

Put the finishing touches on January and February events including a Valentine's Day gift certificate sales plan.

Begin publicizing Valentine's Day gifts and specials early in January (as well as other February events and promotions).

Put a healthy framework around March events and solidify responsibilities delegated to staff, vendors and marketing partners.

Order postcards, flyers, and artwork needed for February and March promotions, charitable endeavors and events.

Lay out at least some general plans for April and May events now, identifying needed partners in order to have enough time to plan and publicize your coming promotions and events.

Communicate in January

Items to include in your e-mail or print newsletter, web site, Facebook and blog posts and in direct mail communications this month:

- Remind clients that this is the last chance for January events, expiration dates of promotions and RSVP deadlines.

- Solicit contest or drawing entries due in January.

- Introduce, pre-sell and highlight coming promotions and events for February, for Valentine's Day and all those occurring in the next 6-8 weeks (all the way into March). Give more weight in communications to those promotions that you feel will be the most enticing to customers. Make sure that those items are front and center in advertising, not lost in a long list of items.

- Alert clients to openings on the books for those whose locks are too long (and who forgot to pre-book).

- Create an offer to extend to those who might need help preparing for a special night out or those whom you have not seen in a while.

- A spotlight product, service and/or staff member of the month.

January Calendar / Suggested Communications and Tasks Schedule

SUN	MON	TUE	WED	THU	FRI	SAT

1st week of Month

1st of January—Merchandise for January

1st of January—Begin collecting entries for January contests

SUN	MON	TUE	WED	THU	FRI	SAT
		Order from manufacturers retail promotions for products to support February - March marketing plans; design related signage			Send January Newsletter with coupons, announce contests and winners, new products and services, coming events, openings still on the books, events and promotions	

2nd week of Month

SUN	MON	TUE	WED	THU	FRI	SAT
Begin promoting and selling Valentine's promotions and Gift Certificates		Order in gifts, salon-branded items, impulse buy and other items for February			Write press releases for any events/results reporting or future events / charitable focus	

3rd week of Month

SUN	MON	TUE	WED	THU	FRI	SAT
		Finalize, review and lay out plans for February - March - April events and promotions			Send January "last chance" promotions and openings on the books e-mail and/or direct mail	

4th week of Month

Last day of January—Take down any January-only promotions

Last day of January—Draw January contest winners

SUN	MON	TUE	WED	THU	FRI	SAT
		Order event supplies, postcards, gifts and salon-branded items needed for March promotions			Send February focus e-mail / direct mail	

January Worksheets

$_____ Retail Sales Goal

Promotions_____

_____

_____

_____

_____

$_____ Avg. Retail/Client

$_____ Retail Sales Results

$_____ Service Sales Goal

Promotions_____

_____

_____

_____

_____

$_____ Avg. Service/Client

$_____ Service Sales Results

$_____ Event Revenues Goal

Events _____

_____

_____

_____

_____

#_____ Attending Event/s

#_____ Apts/Booked at Event

$_____ Event/s Sales

$_____ Total Event/s Results

$_____ Charity/Fund Raising Goal

Charity Events _____

_____

_____

_____

_____

#_____ Attending Event/s

#_____ Apts/Booked at Event

$_____ Charity Event/s Sales

$_____ Total Charity Results

January Marketing Summary

Marketing Partners: _____

_____

_____

_____

Marketing Collateral Needed (or Used): _____

_____

_____

_____

Other Efforts:

#_____ Number of Clients New to Salon

%_____ Client Retention Rate (90 days)

Retention Efforts: _____

_____

or % _____ Clients Re-booked at Appointment

$_____ Gift Certificate Sales

#_____ Contacts added to marketing / e-mail database

february
make over your marketing
from the inside, out

Even when it comes to a client's external makeover, true, lasting change only occurs when it comes from the inside, out.

How many times have you given a client a badly-needed long overdue makeover in the form of a more current, fashionable look only to bump into them a day or two later to find that they completely reverted to their old look? Have you ever wondered why people resist making even the simplest changes to their personal care and grooming routines so that they will not be stuck in unflattering and maybe even decades-old, stale styles?

The reason may be that no matter how much they need to make those changes on the outside, there is something on the inside that does not really believe in the need for those changes. Fear, self-doubt, low self-esteem—all of those inner factors can contribute to resistance demonstrated on the outside by some of your clients when it comes to change. Or perhaps it is simply the comfort of the routine, lack of creativity, lack of skills needed to maintain the look, or even a disdain for the reality that people do, in fact, judge one another by the outward appearance.

As human beings, we make judgments all the time about the "insides" of people based on what we see on the outside. Based on appearance, we often jump to conclusions about how intelligent, successful or popular someone is and we pre-determine whether we would want to be involved with them socially or even be personal friends with them—all based on appearance.

Even though many of the assumptions made based on the outward appearance are often wrong, we nevertheless repeatedly utilize the 'outside' of others as a legitimate determining factor relative to many of their 'inside' characteristics.

And this is my point: People use what they see on the 'outside' of you (or your staff, salon or spa facility, marketing materials, web site, etc.) to make the same pre-determinations about you. Like it or not—accurate or not!

And this is one of the reasons why it is so important to make sure that what is on the 'inside' of you is also continually updated; that you, personally, take the time needed to evaluate the state of your inner health—your mental, intellectual and emotional well-being. Because in many ways, what is truly on the 'inside' of you is being revealed on the outside.

> Like it or not, people use what the see on the **outside** to make decisions about what is on the **inside** of you, personally and professionally

If you are burned out, uninspired, worn out, frustrated, all of those things can and do manifest themselves on the outside in your eyes, face, attitude and conversations. Ambivalence and neglect are evident when someone truly just does not care about or believe in certain things.

In this year of the makeover, sure, you can try to limit yourself to making only cosmetic (external) changes to your business or your own life. But if you do, then no matter how badly even these superficial changes are needed, they probably won't last, won't generate participation and buy-in among staff, and will fail to make the maximum impact to your business they could make —unless they are accompanied by true, genuine belief in the necessity of these 'outside' changes *on the inside* (of you).

This kind of transformation is only possible when you have first taken an honest inventory of your inner self. No matter how necessary it is for you to perform all the tasks that continually take precedence over the time you need to care for your inner self, you are fighting a losing battle if you are not in the right place on the inside.

So how do you know what you need on the inside in order to create the lasting transformations that you want to make on the outside, in personal as well as professional areas of your life and in your business?

The way that you feel when you are burned out, unenthusiastic and uninspired is often an important indication that it's time to spend some energy renewing your inner self. Meeting with a counselor, a mentor, trusted friends, creating a support group, and reading up on topics designed to help us take stock of where we are mentally and emotionally and point us in the right direction for development, growth, renewal and affirmation; any or all of these could be a good place to start!

Many of the people who appear to be the most successful personally and professionally are also the most open to change; it's ironic, isn't it? The people who most seem to have their act together and who appear to be the most comfortable in their own skin are not the ones who think that have everything figured out. They know they don't, they know that no one does. What they do know is that the best way to move forward is to be open to honest self-exposure and evaluation, and even criticism, and to use what they learn to change.

Sometimes, just as with makeovers needed to update the outside, change is needed not because anything is necessarily wrong, but simply because times and conditions have changed. How many times have you heard someone putting down technology because they miss the days of personal interaction and hand written birthday cards, while not acknowledging that technology has also enabled us to interact personally with more people than ever before? Staying rooted in grief over something you cannot change may be keeping you from changing the way that you use new technology to enhance a core principle that you really believe in.

I love the phrase (most commonly associated with magic acts) where a really good magician seduces an audience to "suspend disbelief." The idea is that the audience becomes willing for the sake of the goal (to be entertained) to suspend their belief in the principles of reality. In other words, the audience agrees to cast aside all of the limitations that the physical world imposes in order to be open to the belief that the impossible is somehow possible. That an alternate reality exists where the laws of physics no longer apply.

As you set out to make over your marketing and change your business, suspend your disbelief. Set aside preconceived notions about what is possible and dare to believe that anything is possible. Set aside your prejudices and cynicism when it comes to promoting your own business and your own skills. Return to an attitude of absolute belief in what you have to offer as a professional, and in the unique benefits that your business provides to clients.

Take stock of your 'inside'—the principles, values and beliefs that make you who you are. Do your personal core guiding principles manifest themselves in the way that you do business?

Prepare yourself with the rest and renewal required to gain the endurance, determination and strength needed for this, the year of the makeover that you will embark on. Think about the things you would most like to be able to do, and what skills or training you would need to be able to do so.

> Suspend **disbelief.** Stop thinking that you know all that is possible.
>
> Dare to believe that **anything** is possible.

Think about your current clientele relative to your areas of technical expertise, skills and personal interests (as well as those of your staff).

Think about areas in which you would like to expand the types of clients you regularly serve, and what skills and talent you need to add to your salon or spa in order to attract and service those clients. Enroll in classes and create a plan for staff development that will add the skills needed to make those goals a reality.

Take an honest look at your actual appearance (and that of your staff). Would your clients look to you as an example? Do you and all of your staff show up to work with current styles and a sense of fashion? Regardless of your age (or that of the majority of your clients), you should choose to dress and style your hair, skin and makeup in ways that are both current as well as age appropriate. You cannot ask your clients to embrace the changes they need in order to look their best and be more successful personally and professionally if you are unwilling to do so yourself!

And what's more, if you want and need to grow your client base, remember that every single prospective client that you meet, in and outside of the salon or spa, is making a judgment about your talent, your education, your professionalism, your creativity and skills based, at least in part, on your personal appearance. Fair or not, unless they have seen a large sampling of your work or read a number of glowing customer testimonials, they have no other way to assess whether or not they want to 'try you out' when it comes to their salon and spa services.

And the same principle applies to your salon or spa itself. You have to periodically step back and view each operational aspect and every area of your salon or spa from the point of view of a potential new customer. From your advertising, to your web site, your directory listings, direct mail pieces, e-mail marketing, to how you answer the telephone as well as the appearance and environment of the salon or spa itself, and ultimately each customer's first experience; what words would a new customer use to describe all of those initial touch points of your business and contact with you and your staff?

It's often difficult for us to truly view our business from the standpoint of a new customer, for the simple reason that we are too close to it. There are many things that a new client may notice as either a glaring problem or a shining plus; but since we see the same things day in and day out, they may not stand out in the same way to our eyes or ears. An effective way to see your business through the eyes of a new customer is to enlist the help of a secret shopper; either by hiring a professional service to conduct a new customer shopping experience or by asking a trusted friend or business peer who is not known within your salon or spa to try out your business as a new customer and report back on various aspects of their first touch experience.

If you plan to build your own surveys, you can either ask several general questions to identify areas of concern or you can focus your questions on specific areas in order to address one service area at a time. You may have preconceived ideas or strong personal opinions about certain aspects of your business, but you should try to keep these ideas from influencing how you ask questions. Don't try to guide your 'mystery shopper' to support pre-drawn conclusions by creating questions that reveal your bias. This process will produce the most accurate information and lead you to the best solutions only if you approach both the process and the analysis of survey results with an open mind.

Here are some questions you might incorporate into your own customized 'mystery shopper' or general customer satisfaction questionnaire. If you are worried about overwhelming your secret shopper or about being overwhelmed by too much survey data yourself you can pick and choose only one or two questions from each area (booking, entry /greeting, appointment, retail, etc.) or focus on only one area in a given survey, and include an open ended question for additional information for each area.

Check the 'Resources' page of www.12monthsofmarketing.net for more resources and ideas for using surveys to improve business in the salon and spa.

The Appointment Booking Process:

- Was it easy to determine how and when to contact us to make an appointment:

    o by telephone

    o on the web site

    o with the information on our business card

    o from our yellow pages (or other directory) listing

    o with the information on our menu

    o with the information on our postcard (or other collateral, etc.)

- Was your phone call or web / e-mail request answered promptly?

- If you had to leave a message (or sent a request online), how long did it take for your call or e-mail to be returned?

- Was the stylist / esthetician / receptionist happy to receive your call? (Did you feel that your call was welcomed, or did you feel as though you were an interruption?)

- Did you feel as though you had the undivided attention of the stylist / esthetician / receptionist during the phone call? If not, please explain:

- Was it easy to make an appointment at a time that was convenient *for you*? And did you feel that *your* convenience was the priority?

- If you have an appointment reminder or confirmation process:

    o Was your appointment confirmed? or,

    o Did you receive an appointment reminder?

- Were you notified of the cancellation policy or told how to reschedule if needed?

- Please ask these questions in order to be able to compare to actual following the appointment:

    o what your service/s will cost

    o how much time the appointment will take

    o if not booking with a specific stylist / esthetician,
       ask who will be performing the service

- Optional: Call to reschedule your appointment. Was the stylist / esthetician / receptionist willing to reschedule, empathetic and accommodating? (If you have more than one individual doing secret shopping at your salon or spa, have only one individual call to reschedule.)

- Optional: Let the stylist / esthetician / receptionist know that another client referred you and give their name. (This will help you track how well your staff processes referral 'thank you's and/or referral rewards.)

The Appointment:

- Date / Time of visit, Services booked / received:

- Exterior—rate from 1 to 5, with 5 being the best:

    o Availability of parking

    o Visibility of business sign, condition of sign
    (clean; if lit, lights missing, etc.)

    o How far away is signage visible

        —from approaching streets

        —from the parking area

o Quality of exterior signage; if something is missing or could be improved, please describe:

o Condition of exterior as you approach:

— cleanliness of sidewalk, entry, building, etc.

— is the glass on windows/door clean?

— is the outside inviting or engaging? explain:

— what words would you use to describe the exterior as a whole (signage from street, on building, door, etc., and overall entry area)

- Upon entering:

    o Were you acknowledged upon entering? How?

    o Who greeted you and how would you characterize the greeting?

    o Was the overall atmosphere welcoming?

- Did your appointment begin on time?

    o If not, were you asked whether you could wait or notified how long your wait would be?

    o If the wait was significant, were you asked what time you needed to be able to leave?

- Was the waiting / interior entry area comfortable and welcoming? Describe:

- Was it obvious where you should wait?

- Were you offered a beverage or snack? Were you offered something to read, or a collection / book of salon styles to review?

- Were any "Try Me" stickered products available for you to sample? Did anyone tell you about its use or benefits or was signage present?

- If you had a jacket, did someone offer to take it, or were you directed where you could leave your things?

- Were you given a tour of the facility? Were you shown where the rest room was?

- Is our facility clean and attractive? (If not, describe:)

    o Waiting area

    o Rest room

    o Back bar / shampoo bowls

    o Stylist station or treatment area

    o Retail area/s

    o Register / check out

    o Do you have any areas of concern relative to the cleanliness of our salon or spa that we should know about?

- During your appointment, visit the rest room.

    o Was it clean?

    o Was it attractive? Why or why not?

    o Was it well-appointed? Adequate / attractive fixtures?

    o Were any retail product testers available for trial?

- During your appointment, find a time to examine our retail area/s:

    o Were you able to see and reach all merchandise available for sale?

    o Did you find our display areas attractive? If yes, what did you like about them?

    o Do display areas do anything to engage you or draw you in? Explain:

    o Are shelves and products clean and free of dust?

    o Are shelves well-stocked?

    o Are prices clearly marked?

    o Is it easy to choose products based on your needs (or, is it easy to understand what individual products are intended for?)

- Ask someone a question about a product or a line of products, and/or describe a particular condition of your hair, skin, nails, etc., for which you would like to purchase a product:

  o Are employees available to ask?

  o Are employees willing to speak about products?

  o Are employees knowledgeable about products?

  o Are employees knowledgeable about the condition you described?

  o Did you feel that your question was welcomed with enthusiasm, or that it was an interruption? Describe:

- During your service:

  o Did the service provider/s do a consultation with you to ascertain your desired outcomes?

  o How well did the provider listen to and interpret your wishes? Explain:

  o Did the provider/s tell you about the name / type and performance of the products that they used:

    —at the back bar

    —behind the chair (at massage table, pedicure, manicure, etc.)

    —for styling / finishing

  o Did the provider/s recommend additional products based on conditions they observed in your scalp, skin, hair, nails, etc.?

  o Did you receive the desired result (and/or another mutually agreed-upon result) during consultation?

  o Based on your result, how well would you rate the technical ability of this provider/s to understand, interpret and achieve specific results?

  o Did the service take about the amount of time that you expected; and/or the amount of time that was indicated during your booking call? If not, was it longer or shorter, and by how much?

  o Were all staff courteous to you? If not, describe:

    o Did staff interact with one another in front of you?

    o Would you describe staff-to-staff interactions as professional or unprofessional? Why?

    o If looking for a new salon or spa, would you be likely to return? Why or why not?

    o If you were looking for a new regular service provider/s, would you be likely to choose the individual/s who performed your service? Why or why not?

- After the service:

    o Was the checkout process fast enough?

    o Were you charged the amount that you expected to pay for the service? If not, were you charged more or less, and how much?

    o Did your charge correspond to our posted prices on the wall (or the printed menu), and the prices posted on our web site? If not, were you charged more or less, and how much?

    o Were you given a receipt, and was it correct?

    o Were you thanked for coming?

    o Were you asked to book your next appointment?

    o Were you told about our loyalty rewards program?

    o Were you told about our referral rewards program?

    o Were you given an incentive to return or a bounce-back offer?

    o Were you asked for your e-mail address and permission to add you to mailing list/s?

Collateral

- Review our menu (as posted on the wall/board at the salon or printed menu) sometime during your appointment:

    o Is the menu attractive, easy to read and easy to understand?

    o Is the menu up to date and accurate?

o Does the menu posted on our web site correspond to our printed menu and/or menu posted on the wall/sign at the salon or spa? If not, describe:

o Do you feel that our web site represents the same "feeling" that you receive about our business when visiting in person? Why or why not?

General Impressions

- What words would you use to describe the "feel" of our business, how you felt while you were in our business and/or after you left?

- What words would you use to describe the employees of our salon or spa (in general)?

- Please describe your overall experience with our salon or spa:

- Would you recommend our salon or spa to others? Why or why not?

- Please list any areas of concern for our salon or spa:

As you begin to evaluate the client experience, don't fall into the trap of thinking that making a few (or even several) small, surface changes will alter the client experience in a meaningful way. Result-producing, lasting change is rooted in fundamental, genuine internal transformation; if you espouse changes but don't truly believe fundamental changes are needed, or you have a cynical outlook on what improvements changing has the ability to produce for you, then any changes you make are likely to be non-impactful and short-lived. If you have a history of making changes that do not last and don't produce the results you say that you want, could this be one of the reasons?

In order to create real, lasting transformation that produces results, you first need to get in touch with the internal. In other words, what principles really drive the construction of and how you conduct the client experience from the first ad or referral to the appointment booking, through to the end of the appointment and follow up?

Identify commonalities at each touch point to help you identify the underlying philosophies, values or aspects of your employee culture that continually manifest themselves throughout the client experience. For instance, are your customer touch points more likely to be described as characterized by enthusiasm or ambivalence? Is the atmosphere relaxed (and relaxing for the client) or careless (and stressful for the client)? Can you see how it could be a fine line of distinction between those two descriptive terms?

Do you strive to create an atmosphere that would be described as relaxed, casual, 'folksy', etc., or do your touch points work together to create an aura of elegance, limited supply and exclusivity? Or are few intentional principles at play, resulting in haphazard, inconsistent and incohesive experiences for clients? Do the experiences of your customers vary widely by stylist or service area? Do the *real* characteristics of your customer's experiences contribute to the promotion of new services, professional products and retail sales? How are your personal values reflected in your customer's experiences?

What do you believe *should be* the driving principles when it comes to the client experience in your salon or spa? What words would you want your customers or your employees to use to describe your business to other people?

Identify what is at the heart of your personal philosophy when it comes to your work, the customer, retail sales, professional products, your staff, growing your business—and the list goes on. Because for better or for worse, what's really on the 'inside' is going to drive what shows up on the 'outside' of the customer experience no matter how much lip service is paid to cliché ideals, and no matter how well-intentioned you may be.

Let me put it like this. Imagine that you buy a new car and within a month, the car engine starts occasionally overheating. So you take the car back to the dealership, where during the course of the car buying experience (the "prospective client" phase of your relationship, if you will) you heard nothing but praise for the car, the manufacturer, and especially for the expertise and talent of the service staff of the dealership. With these assurances fresh in your mind, you rest assured that the dealership is committed to finding and fixing the problem. In fact, when you walk into the service area, right on the wall is a big poster proclaiming that the customer is king and quality is job #1.

A few days later you drive off with your (presumably) repaired vehicle, assured that the problem was identified and rectified. Two days later, you find yourself broken down on the side of the highway, thinking back to all of the promises made during the prospective-customer phase of the relationship, and to the sign on the wall in the service area. The customer is king and quality is a top priority? Really?

Does your salon or spa send the same kind of mixed messages? It could be, if the reality for your clients does not match up with the statements and promises you make about the values and principles that define the customer experience, the positive results you claim customers should expect to receive by doing business with you, the skills present in your staff's repertoire, and the performance of the products that you sell.

You might know "where you want to be" when it comes to your business, but in order to know how to get there, you need to know "where you really are" to begin with. This kind of honesty is important!

Let's say that you live in New York City, but that you don't really want to live in New York; you view yourself as a San Franciscan at heart. You want to travel to Seattle, and so you Google yourself up a map. You request directions to Seattle not from where you really are—New York City—but from where you would prefer to see yourself, San Francisco. Your directions come back, "drive north."

*What descriptive words are **common** to all (or most) areas of your business?*

*Are these the words you **want** to describe your client experience?*

If you are really in San Francisco and you want to get to Seattle, "drive north" is great instruction. However, if you are really in New York City, even though and no matter how much you don't want to be there, if you "drive north" you are going to end up in Canada!

Can you see why an honest evaluation of yourself and your business is important? You can't map out a destination to an end point without being honest about your starting point.

Ideas for February Promotions

February's promotional ideas are all about sharing the love you feel on the inside with customers on the outside.

Showing Love for the Makeover

Hair color and corresponding makeover services cannot be covered by one or two menu items anymore, and can be adapted for every age group. Expand your menu and create marketing initiatives to promote:

- Gray coverage hair color services plus age-minimizing skin care products and makeup palettes

- 'Going gray naturally' hair color services plus age-minimizing skin care products and makeup palettes

- Makeover hair color services that feature coordinating skin care and makeup palettes

- Seasonal hair color highlights, plus coordinating skin care and makeup palettes

- Women's Job Interview hair color services complete with skin care and makeup palettes

- Men's Job Interview hair color services complete with grooming products and grooming services

- 1st Job Total Makeover services for high school or college students, or for college graduates

- Homecoming, prom or graduation highlighting or hair color, plus coordinating makeup palettes and instruction in at-home application techniques

- Dance or music recital, competition and other student special event highlighting or hair color with coordinating makeup and skin care palettes

- Slumber party hair and makeup services (you might need to be willing to take these services 'on the road,' creating a traveling kit of supplies for out-of-salon services)

- Halloween, costume party/ball or similar special event radical color or highlighting services plus extreme makeup services and palettes

Even a short list like this should demonstrate to you that you can begin to cultivate a hair color service following among clients from a very young age!

February Month-Long Observances

February is American Heart Month

Cross market with a local health practitioner, fitness or nutrition professional. Give clients heart-health tips on signage, bag stuffers, your web site, in e-mail, Facebook or blog posts, etc.

Feature information about the stress-relieving benefits of aromatherapy in your e-mail newsletter and on your Facebook or blog posts highlighting the products that you sell which provide aromatherapy or other stress-relieving benefits.

February is Canned Food Month

Give a salon or spa-branded tchotchke, product or product sample, or create a special offer for clients who bring canned goods to appointments. Donate canned foods collected to a local charity and write a press release before and after the event to publicize the cause and your results. Feature the charity, its needs, and the benefits it provides in your community as well as the canned food drive promotion you are running in your e-mail newsletter and on your blog or Facebook posts.

February is Children's Dental Health Month

Cross market a youth offer with a local dental practice. Purchase salon or spa-branded toothbrushes for distribution in salon or gift to local day cares, youth services or other organizations.

For more ideas, see the promotions for "Tooth Fairy Day" on February 28 featured on page 49.

February—not June—is National Weddings Month

Partner with an event planner for cross marketing and begin promoting bride and/or groom styles and wedding party packages. For an extended set of Bridal and Wedding promotions including how to organize a Bridal Fair, see the February and May Chapters of Volume I of 12 Months of Marketing for Salon and Spa.

February Week-Long Observances

The First Week of February is Children's Authors and Illustrators Week

Hold a dual writing and illustration contest for local students or exclusively for the children of clients. Award products and/or services to one writer and to one illustrator. Extend a special offer to all entrants. Publicize and recognize entrants online and in press releases.

The Second Week of February is Dump Your Significant Jerk Week

Hold a "Best Break Up Story" contest and treat the winner to a makeover and a night out destination.

Or go big: "Dump Your Significant Jerk Week" is the perfect week to hold an "Insignificant Other" mixer. If this event proves popular with participants, plan to repeat this formula during June's wedding season as a "Best-Person–I-Never-Married" social event. Whatever you call it, this type of event will take some work, marketing partners, and some creativity to execute:

Partner with a local restaurant, wine shop or bar to host an "Insignificant Other" or "Best-Person-I-Never-Dated" mixer. Just what it sounds like, this is a chance for clients to bring a non-date but great guy or girl out to a mixer at a local destination so they can both meet other great singles in the area. Collect contact information from all attendees with an at-the-door entry form which will also serve as an entry form in a drawing for a prize package to be awarded at the end of the evening. Since you may have equal numbers of men or women in attendance, remember to create special bounce-back, service or product offers that are geared to either/both genders.

Before the mixer, collect entries from among all invited customers (yours and those of your event/marketing partners) and hold a drawing for one lucky guy and one lucky gal to receive a pre-mixer makeover. Remember—one of your primary goals for events is to gather more contacts among both clients and prospects for permission-based e-mail and direct mail marketing.

Create promotional offers for pre-event makeover bookings and a bounce-back offer. Take bookings at the event and make spa or salon-branded items (like shot glasses, event t-shirts, tumblers or mugs, etc.) or professional products available for sale.

After the event, send a bounce-back offer via mail or e-mail to all participants (you collected their contact information before the event for pre-mixer makeovers and at the event for all attendees, and hopefully you ensured that your marketing partners did the same).

The Third Week of February is International Flirting Week

Partner with a counselor or other expert on body language and social flirting etiquette and hold a client workshop on self-esteem, self-confidence and flirting.

February Holidays and Observances

February 1 is Spunky Old Broad's Day

With better health and expected life longevity than ever before, you can be sure that there are active seniors in your area who get together for meetings and outings. Holding a Spunky Old Broad's Day promotion is a great opportunity to reach out to the 55 and up crowd in your community. For long-term outreach, offer to sponsor a local chapter of the "Red Hat Society" or another local senior or senior women's social group.

Contact a local senior center or retirement living community and create an off-site seminar for seniors on age-specific skin, scalp, hair and nail care. Demonstrate age-minimizing skin care products and home nail and skin care for feet and hands.

Create an off-site service menu and take styling, manicure and pedicure services on the road for seniors who cannot get to your salon, or help to arrange transportation and set aside specific hours in the salon or spa to cater to these groups.

February 4 is Girls and Women in Sports Day

Create special offers for female members of local sports teams (schools, community parks and rec. leagues, amateur or minor league organizations, golf clubs, etc.)

Create a special gift certificate for clients to purchase as a gift for the coaches of their children's teams (and also suggest as a great gift for music teachers, educational tutors and other specialty instructors).

Support local parks and recreation women's sports as a booster, help to purchase uniforms, or place ads in catalogs, school programs and other publications including a special offer for local athletes and other team boosters.

Showing the Love from the Inside, Out

February 10th is White T-Shirt day. Create a clever, fun, beautiful, or hot! salon or spa-branded design and purchase t-shirts for contest prizes, client 'thank you' gifts, for employees to wear and/or for retail sale.

Hold a client contest for a white t-shirt design, with the winner to receive a special service/retail prize package. Post designs in your salon and on your web site and Facebook page or blog site and allow customers and the public to vote for their favorite designs.

Partner with a local restaurant or bar and hold a (wet) white t-shirt contest at a special client-appreciation event. Reward the winner with a gift card and a gift basket featuring some of your favorite products. Give complimentary makeup touch ups, smokey eye makeup application demonstrations, and mini-manicures. Be sure that everyone in attendance receives a bounce-back offer for your salon or spa and/or a copy of your service menu.

Or turn the tables and hold a (wet) white t-shirt contest for men at a local bar. Reward the male winner of this contest with grooming products, samples and a gift certificate or bounce-back offer for your salon or spa. Give complimentary grooming touch ups and demonstrations and be sure that everyone receives a bounce-back offer for your salon and spa and/or a copy of your service menu.

Valentine's Day

Marketing ideas for Valentine's Day, Dump your Significant Jerk Week and other cupid-inspired observances including Cheapskate Dates and a variety of "Twofer" type offers were featured extensively in the February Chapter of Volume I of 12 Months of Marketing for Salon and Spa (see below).

For a condensed suggestion: Take the pain out of this holiday for your clients by working with local restaurants, theaters, concert venues, bowling alleys and other date destinations to create Valentine's Day makeover and date packages.

Create your own packages by purchasing discounted gift cards for local restaurants online at sites like www.restaurant.com (where you can often purchase gift certificates at 50% or even 75% off). Create bigger event or engagement-night packages by partnering with local limo, formal rental, floral, jewelry and other similar partners.

Items that you can purchase in counter display-type quantities such as inexpensive jewelry, clutch bags, scented candles or oil burners would make great additions to your retail for Valentine's Day and year-round for clients to purchase as gifts.

Who needs money anyway? Create Cheapskate Dates!

Cheapskate Dates can be a great way to show the love to your clients! You can make a Cheapskate Date package into a thank you for your loyal clients or a gift package to be awarded in a drawing at the end of February. Partner with local restaurants, bowling alleys, concert halls, theatres or other date-destinations to create great date packages or offer multiple "date" prizes.

Cheapskate Offers

Create special "Cheapskate" promotions to run in conjunction with your drawings. Make sure to send all entrants (and everyone on your mailing list) the offers via mail or e-mail.

Create cooperative marketing offers with restaurant, bowling alley, theatre, chorale, symphony, or coffee shop partners; either purchasing gift certificates at half price or getting a buy-one, get-one offer donated. In this and in all joint efforts throughout the year, your strongest marketing partners should receive your strongest support when it comes to referring your clients to them via endorsements in your marketing collateral, distribution of marketing materials in your waiting area or at the point of purchase in your salon or spa, or verbally by you and your staff during the course of business. You will create even more incentive for businesses to partner with you, and to do so more generously, when they know that they are receiving a payoff in the form of new customers themselves.

Mix and match; if more than one organization will partner with you, create multiple or more valuable packages in order to share the love with even more of your clients. If a local symphony, choir or chorale is reluctant to donate tickets, consider purchasing an advertisement in their next program, offer to display their event posters in your salon or include their events in your newsletter or on your web site. Sponsor organizations like these both in order to attract the attention of their patrons and to incentivize them to donate tickets for your client drawing and gift packages.

Book the winning couple/s in for a glass of champagne (or sparkling cider), chocolates and a pre-date makeover. Make sure they walk out with a bounce back offer; chances are one of the guests enjoying this cheapskate date will be new to your business. This is your chance to impress them with the service, talent, fashion sense and the care with which they are treated by your staff. And it could be a chance to draw new male clientele into the salon or spa by showing them that your business caters equally well to them as you do to their girlfriends, wives and daughters.

Cross promote with your marketing partners to help them create "Cheapskate Date" packages to gift or award to their own customers. A pre-date makeover (or another offer) from you should be part of their prize packages. If you are partnering with a restaurant or bar, request that they display tent cards, salon-branded coasters or business cards throughout their establishment to promote your Valentine's Day offers. Extend your offers to employees who staff the businesses in proximity to your physical location, and to the employees of your marketing partners. They can be an invaluable source of referrals in addition to being prospective clients themselves.

"Two-fer" (two for the price of one)

One obvious variety of a Cheapskate Date is a simple buy-one, get-one (BOGO) service offering. Almost any service or product which you can afford to extend at this margin, and that customers actually want, will work; if you offer this for couples, one individual in the couple should be a new client to your salon or spa. If this is too extravagant, think about offering a buy-two, get-one free or half off product on a second service or product when one of higher value is purchased (putting your discount to the client somewhere under 25%). Or simply add-on another service or product so that the offer includes two things for the price of one.

Partner with a local bar for a two-fer drink and appetizer or with a local restaurant for a two-fer entree or dessert to pair with your own offer. Partner with a local coffee shop for a buy-one get-one donation, a bowling alley, local theatre or community music group—the possibilities are endless!

Updo, Dine and Dash

Ask a local restaurant to participate in creating an Updo, Dine and Dash Cheapskate Date. If they cannot donate a buy-one, get-one entree or meal gift certificate, ask them to sell you a gift certificate at half price. They will be getting a chance to impress prospective new diners during what can be slow winter months in order to create new repeat customers of their own.

If the offer is designed as a two-for-one for couples, two couples can even double date (and double your return when it comes to prospective new clients). Offer the gift certificates in a free drawing or as a reward or thank you for some of your best clients. You can even offer additional packages for sale.

My Heart Beats for You

Partner with a local physician or other qualified health professional to set up a blood pressure education or blood pressure check reception in-salon or at a local wine shop, including education on the health benefits of red wine and chocolate. If you prefer not to tout the benefits of red wine, choose a non-alcoholic juice or health drink that also provides anti-oxidants, stimulates release of endorphins, boosts energy or provides other benefits.

Love Yourself First

Why should couples have all the fun? Whether you celebrate Valentine's Day as a single or a couple, love yourself! Create special "Love Yourself" promotions around your most pampering services and retail products, or gift free, salon-branded chocolates or aromatherapy products with retail purchases to clients.

This is a great time for you to expand your retail offerings beyond professional products in order to create a true gift center. Purchase aromatherapy products like candles and room sprays. Purchase boutique-quality, unique gift and greeting cards and gift bags. Make it easy for customers to envision your products and gift certificates as "gifts" by pre-packaging gift baskets and displaying them along with gift certificates or gift cards for your salon or spa.

Hold a contest in February and have a drawing to award one aromatherapy gift basket and/or gift card to a winner. Utilize entries to help build your e-mail marketing contact database, and extend a special offer in March to all participants.

February 15 is National Call-In Single Day

Hold a special February 15th "Call-In Single" promotion and reward callers with exclusive offers like "love yourself" pampering retail products or free branded gift chocolates (in partnership with a local chocolatier) with appointments.

Hold a February 15th "Call-In Single" happy hour for the 'uncoupled' among your clientele, or hold a "Call-In Single" party in conjunction with a local bar or restaurant. Have a drawing and reward a winner with a makeover or another service. Create baskets for door prizes and have drawings or contests throughout the event. Collect contact information of attendees and follow up with a bounce-back offer following the event.

Working with a professional counselor or life coach, hold a workshop for singles on how to successfully navigate the dating scene to achieve relationship goals and how to prepare oneself for healthy, enduring relationships. Or hold a workshop on flirting, body language and attraction.

Show Love for Local Schools on February 17: P. T. A. Founder's Day

Local schools can be a great source of prospective clients. Extend special offers to leaders and parents of your local school's PTA (parent-teacher association). Create a special offer for the families of your child's school, local private schools, and other educational organizations. For an extended look at the back-to-school market including reaching out to students and teachers, read the section on the Back-to-School market beginning on page 166.

February 24 is Tortilla Chip Day

Partner with a local south-of-the-border style restaurant (or local gourmet market) and give clients a tasty tortilla chip and dip sample at their appointments. Create a display and special customer offers to cross market with these businesses.

February 28 is Tooth Fairy Day

Partner with a local dental and/or orthodontic practice to create cross-marketed offers to extend to all clients.

Give clients tips about dental hygiene or the benefits of orthodontics, including a list of suggested services and time frame (such as, how often they should be receiving preventive care, when a child should first visit a dentist, etc.)

Set up a display at the point of purchase including whitening and dental hygiene tips as well as lip balms, lip glosses, lip plumpers or lipsticks promoting "the perfect smile" to clients. Create a tip sheet for proper application of lip liner, plumpers, lipsticks and wrinkle-reducers (products that reduce fine lines around the mouth). Post tips and tricks in your e-mail newsletter and on your Facebook or blog sites.

February is National Bridal Month

Start marketing bridal packages now, especially if you want to attract large wedding parties. Partner with a wedding planner, wedding facilities, caterers, formal wear sales and rental, limo rental, etc. and create a bridal package offer, do cross marketing, or work cooperatively to hold a Bridal Fair.

February Planning and Tasks

Select from manufacturer's retail promotions plus salon-branded items like nail files, branded sunscreen, lip balm, brushes, combs, water bottles, flip-flops, robes, towels, t-shirts and tanks or other items that can boost point of purchase and event sales or be used as gift-with-purchase items or as client gifts.

Design and print (or order) postcards, flyers, and artwork needed for March and April promotions, charitable endeavors and events.

Finalize details for March and April events, promotions, contests and activities. Identify and capture needed marketing partners and delegate responsibilities. In March/April, remember to factor in spring break and other school holidays which provide another opportunity for family rates, kid's cuts or teacher's cuts promotions.

Planning should be well underway for April and May events, including identifying needed marketing partners and remembering that marketing and communications should begin no later than 6-8 weeks prior to events.

Communicate in February

Items to include in your e-mail or print newsletter, web site, Facebook and blog posts and in direct mail communications this month:

- Last chance for bi-monthly promotions that expire at the end of February
- Solicit contest entries due in February and announce January winners
- Promotions and events scheduled during the next 6-8 weeks (all the way into April)
- Alert clients to openings on the books for your clients whose locks are too long (and who forgot to pre-book) and for those who need help preparing for a special night out
- Send an e-mail or postcard to customers that you have not seen in a while
- Communicate loyalty and referral incentives to clients
- Create and pre-sell winter, spring, and/or summer break family haircut packages
  - A spotlight product, service and/or staff member of the month

February Calendar / Suggested Communications and Tasks Schedule

SUN	MON	TUE	WED	THU	FRI	SAT
1st week of Month						
1st of February—Merchandise for February						
1st of February—Begin collecting entries for February contests						
		Order signage, event supplies and promotional materials for March - April promotions			Send February Newsletter with coupons, announce contests and winners, new products and services, coming events, openings still on the books, events and promotions	
2nd week of Month						
		Order in gifts, salon-branded items, impulse buy and other items for March			Write press releases for any events/results reporting or future events / charitable focus	
3rd week of Month						
		Finalize, lay out and review plans for March - April - May events and promotions			Send February "last chance" promotions and openings on the books e-mail and/or direct mail	
4th week of Month						
Last day of February—Take down any February-only promotions						
Last day of February—Draw February contest winners						
Begin marketing spring and bridal packages and promotions	Order event supplies, postcards, gifts and salon-branded items needed for April promotions				Send March focus e-mail / direct mail	

February Worksheets

$_____ Retail Sales Goal

Promotions_____

_____

_____

_____

_____

$_____ Avg. Retail/Client

$_____ Retail Sales Results

$_____ Service Sales Goal

Promotions_____

_____

_____

_____

_____

$_____ Avg. Service/Client

$_____ Service Sales Results

$_____ Event Revenues Goal

Events _____

_____

_____

_____

_____

#_____ Attending Event/s

#_____ Apts/Booked at Event

$_____ Event/s Sales

$_____ Total Event/s Results

$_____ Charity/Fund Raising Goal

Charity Events _____

_____

_____

_____

_____

#_____ Attending Event/s

#_____ Apts/Booked at Event

$_____ Charity Event/s Sales

$_____ Total Charity Results

February Marketing Summary

Marketing Partners: _____

_____

_____

_____

Marketing Collateral Needed (or Used): _____

_____

_____

_____

Other Efforts:

#_____ Number of Clients New to Salon

%_____ Client Retention Rate (90 days)

Retention Efforts: _____

_____

or % _____ Clients Re-booked at Appointment

$_____ Gift Certificate Sales

#_____ Contacts added to marketing / e-mail database

march
make over your
employee culture

In a perfect world, when you came to your team with a great idea, every member of your team would instantly recognize its merit, would immediately "buy in" with enthusiasm and without question, would agree to immediate implementation and would agree wholeheartedly on all of the steps necessary to execute it. And they would all beg to be included and to be assigned responsibility.

If this sounds like the world you live in, rejoice and read no further; you work in the perfect company—I don't even get that kind of buy in when I present a great idea to myself! My guess is that in the world you live in, the scene plays out in a radically different manner. See if you recognize your team in any of these alternative scenarios:

- You introduce an idea to staff and the pessimist/s in the room instantly roll their eyes and tell you all the reasons why it won't work, is stupid, and otherwise a waste of their time.

- You introduce an idea and the seasoned (cynical) veteran on your team tells you that they tried something "just like that" before, and it didn't work (in other words, why are you wasting their time?)

- You introduce an idea, but having been frustrated in efforts to innovate by both the pessimist and the seasoned cynic on previous occasions, this time, you introduce it as policy. Something mandatory, not optional. You still get the eye rolling and the resigned shrug that means, "Ok, if you want us to waste time on that, I guess you're the boss!", but otherwise, no verbal opposition. For a day or even a week or two, the majority of your staff seem to be trying to do what you asked. But a few weeks later, no evidence of your idea remains and all staff have gone back to business as usual—except that the failed policy has now created more pessimists and cynics to deal with in the future.

- You don't bother introducing the next initiative. Instead, you model it for staff or implement, fund, and run it completely on your own, inviting other staff to participate. Despite the success you achieve among your own clientele, your co-workers continue to sit back and wait for business to come to them. Or, they invite you to go ahead and perform your magic on their behalf as well!

Sometimes it seems almost impossible to make even the smallest changes in your salon or spa when it necessitates the cooperation of your team. It can feel like your staff actually want new ideas to fail, even if it means less success for everyone.

As human beings, we all bring our own ideas, prejudices, experiences, likes and dislikes into the employee group. Just because someone joins your team, it does not necessarily mean that they all do so with the same level of commitment and enthusiasm that you desire or even demonstrate. And even if someone joins your team with a high level of enthusiasm and energy for business-building activities, it still doesn't ensure that they will agree with your ideas on how to build clientele or even who your "ideal clients" should be relative to marketing activities. And it does not mean they will agree with the environment and "feel" that you want all of your clients to experience in your salon and spa.

What does all of this have to do with employee culture?

Everything.

Your employee culture is a reflection of the sum total values, beliefs, attitudes, ideas, experiences, assumptions and behaviors shared by your staff. And this culture is reflected back to your clients in every area of your business.

If your employee culture is characterized by attitudes that are negative, lazy or careless, unmotivated or cynical, it is because those traits are present to some extent in one or more of your staff, and it is because these negative traits are allowed to dominate and influence daily operations.

Success depends on whether you can **harness** the **diversity** of everyone's strengths, passions and creativity to pull **toward the same goals**.

Does this mean that you should only hire people who think exactly like you? Not at all. It is the variety of experiences, talents, skills and interests—the differences within us as people, when shared—that leads to higher levels of creativity, imagination, resourcefulness, abilities and strengths. But your business will grow and thrive only to the extent that these strengths, passions and creativity can be harnessed to pull toward the same goals; and when this occurs in a spirit of positive energy and optimism rather than dominant negativity.

Have you ever seen a marching band in action on the field during the halftime period at a football game? You might see a hundred or more people, all working together to play the same song. By mutual agreement, all using their individual strengths, abilities and different instruments to deliver a performance for the audience. Every step they take is choreographed specifically to further engage and entertain the audience visually, even beyond the music. They create a visual, changing design that, like the music, is made up of completely individual routes and roles, purposefully designed and choreographed to create a visual whole made up of the sum of all its parts.

Each member has different skills and strengths, and many are skilled soloists in their own right as musicians and/or even as dancers. But as band members they come together with an understanding that the good of the whole is greater than the glory of any one individual. They agree to pool their strengths, skills and abilities in order to achieve a group goal—to perform the same song, to the same beat, as directed by the band leader, in order to please their clients—the audience.

School band members know that they will only be playing together for a short time, maybe even only for one year; yet they still come to this agreement and shared goal. In the case of your business, where some of you may work together for decades, isn't it *even more important* for you to agree to work together toward the shared goals of attracting and pleasing your clients? Of meeting your customer's needs and making them feel that they are, in fact, vitally important to your business?

I have worked in a few companies that harbored employees who were well-known to regularly thwart ideas, offend customers or co-workers, undermine initiatives and even overtly defy orders. Leaders within these companies knew they had these problem individuals, but they often chose not only to retain them for years, but even to promote them for a variety of reasons. They may have believed these employees had irreplaceable skills, knowledge or power, or may have thought they could "win them over." Sometimes they did so because they discounted the negative impact these employees had on their co-workers. Some were retained out of compassion or a sense of absolute loyalty to the employee, with the employer failing to realize or even knowing that they often lost other individuals who were potentially their best employees, and even lost customers out of this misplaced sense of loyalty.

Whatever the reason a leader chooses to retain individuals who kill creativity and initiatives, they are also choosing (whether they know it or not) to negatively influence the overall employee culture. These individuals will continue to demonstrate cynicism, lack of motivation, rude or bullying behavior, resistance to change—even outright defiance, and all the more so whenever these traits are rewarded with tolerance, increased power, and the knowledge that they have the ability to control corporate environment and initiatives through their behaviors.

Furthermore, they are teaching other individuals who may have some of the same tendencies that this behavior is effective. These people damage the morale and stifle the creativity of their more positively inclined, enthusiastic co-workers.

Employer loyalty is a highly-laudable quality, especially in today's economy where many companies have been forced to downsize. Not only do companies have to reduce payroll hours or let people go, but there is also a larger supply of qualified, talented individuals who are in the job-seeking market (so employers have the ability to pick and choose from among the cream of the crop to fill any open position or even to replace low-performers).

But employer loyalty is misplaced when it is the cause for retention of an individual that is damaging your company from the inside-out, or even actively damaging your client relationships and initiatives.

Am I advocating a no-tolerance, slash and burn policy where your employees are concerned? No; but I am suggesting that as an employer and a business owner, you have an obligation to think about the extent to which the actions of each employee contribute to, *or work against*, the team as a whole, the good of your customers and the goals of the entire organization.

Only you can determine the point at which the damage being done to employee morale, initiatives and client relations outweighs the value that you believe an individual contributes to your company. Only you can determine at what point you believe that an individual is not open to change or is un-teachable when it comes to modifying their behavior for the good of the whole organization.

But with those "only you" statements comes a great deal of responsibility, because only you have the power to protect your business and other employees from a destructive co-worker or an initiative-killing staff member.

Whether you are building a business from scratch or reshaping your business culture through education, accountability and normal employee turnover, determining which characteristics you want to define your employee culture will help you make better training and hiring decisions as you move forward.

What kind of employee culture do you want your salon or spa to have?

Some traits you might desire are:

creative	open minded	accepting
enthusiastic	growth minded	teamwork
community	trust	honesty
drama free	gossip free	customer centered
competitive	developing	technically skilled
happy	energetic	continuously improving
community	sharing	inspiring
strength	fair	problem solving
loving life	compassionate	career (vs. 'just a job')
accountable	peaceful	blame free
free of fear	constructive	encouraging
supportive	dynamic	flexible
visionary	empowered	mastery
freedom to grow and fail	commitment	personal responsibility
future oriented	long term focus	inclusive
courteous	productive	evolving
accomplished	open communication	goal oriented
intimate	respecting privacy	sales oriented
complimentary	responsive	customized services
engaged	skilled	educated
charitable	urban	organic
family friendly	sophisticated	traditional
celebratory	upbeat	people first

Your salon or spa's employee culture is impacted by a number of factors; not only by the experiences and personalities of the employees themselves, but also by your corporate mission, vision, goals, values, client and employee policies, etc. For the purposes of this makeover, focus on identifying and defining the components that most directly impact your marketing:

- What is your official corporate mission and vision? Is it communicated to employees? Is it played out in your day to day operations or is it just words in a pretty frame on the wall? Would your clients be able to guess what values and statements are part of your official mission and vision statements based on their experiences in your salon or spa?

- What policies do you have in place regarding employee standards of behavior, conversation, attitude, conduct, dress and appearance? How are they communicated to employees? Do employees follow them? Do you? Are there consequences for those who routinely violate policies, especially when it is clear what they are or when it clearly impacts client relations?

- Are you, as a leader, afraid to impose standards on others out of a reluctance to appear authoritative, a fear of losing friendships or a desire to maintain a "cool" or laid back working environment?

- How are decisions made and communicated? Do employees have a say in the process? Are there certain employees who dominate decision-making? How is negative feedback expressed, and how do you handle it in response? How are disputes between employees resolved? Do you have written standards relative to inter-staff communications in front of clients, or what is inappropriate to speak about with clients in public areas?

- Do you have a policy to protect your client's privacy? Does it cover employee gossip in or outside of the walls of the salon? (After all, clients do tell their stylists everything!)

- What do you want the atmosphere in your salon to feel like? More importantly, what do your clients want it to feel like? Reflecting the preferences of your regular clients as well as what your ideal prospective clients would want is necessary if you are to retain current customers as well as grow your client base. In fact, it is more important that the atmosphere in your salon reflect *their desires* than it is for the atmosphere to reflect your desires (or those of your employees) where those two things do not align from décor to music to policies, etc. Even the education that you and your staff take should reflect what would best serve your client base and help you attract more clients in desired demographic segments.

No matter how idealistic your intentions and no matter how obvious you feel it is that your salon or spa needs to grow, ultimately, to create the kind of culture you need to serve your clients and grow your business necessitates that you obtain employee buy-in, support, and engagement. In other words, your employees need to consciously agree to support the environment that you want to create through their attitudes, behaviors and actions.

The Gallup Organization has polled employees in multiple surveys over the last decade which indicate that the number of employees who feel they are truly engaged at their place of work hovers around 30% on average. That means that at any given company, 7 out of every 10 people do not feel personally connected to, or invested in, the good of the organization they work for. It is just a paycheck to these individuals; they save their passion, talent and energy for investment elsewhere.

As a small business, you might enjoy a greater degree of employee engagement for the simple reason that it's more difficult for disgruntled or disengaged employees to fall off your radar.

But just imagine how your business would grow and thrive if *all of your employees* were positively charged and engaged when it comes to shared ideas for client service, for growing your customer base, for increasing retail sales, introducing new services, growing your business and increasing profits?

Imagine how your business could grow and all of the good that it could do if your employees supported your community involvement and charity goals. Imagine not just the increase in revenues that might come your way but also gains in community spirit, in the reputation of your salon or spa and in the positive impacts that your business can have in the lives of your clients and within your community.

So how do you get maximum employee buy-in?

How do you overcome cynicism and negative behaviors, especially when they have become entrenched as an accepted part of your employee culture?

1. Determine, honestly, where you are, right now. You cannot map out a journey without pinpointing both your starting point and end goals.

2. Write down the words and phrases that would describe the employee culture that you would have or that you would create in a perfect world.

3. Write down what would have to happen and what—or even who—will have to change for you to get from the point where you are now to where you most want to be.

4. Write down all of the potential action steps you could take to make those changes happen.

5. Of the action steps that you noted, which could you take right away? Which steps could you take that would involve minimal resources, or encounter the least opposition? Sometimes taking 'baby steps' when it comes to change helps you to begin to convince employees to buy-in who might otherwise be afraid of change or be inclined to follow those who oppose change.

6. For those action steps which require more time or outside resources than you have available now, lay out a long-term plan, seek outside advice, and set a time line to work toward them.

The following strategies can help you to introduce change, marketing programs, customer initiatives and other improvements to your staff:

- Communicate thoroughly, effectively, and often. Don't assume that co-workers understand your motives or know what lies behind your desire to make changes, even if the reasons seem painfully obvious to you. Be sure that you explain to staff why changes are necessary. Periodically restate and discuss the changes you made, or changes you are pursuing for the long term to ensure that everyone stays on the same page. Do not be surprised if you have to talk about things more than once or that you have to remind some employees about their role in the change process more than once.

- Explain to staff not only why the desired changes are good for your business but also what the negative consequences will be to the organization overall as well as to individual employees of not implementing changes.

- Most importantly, relay to employees clearly and specifically how the changes will benefit them. Beyond improvements it can bring to stylists and to the business overall, this may mean that initiatives need to be accompanied with employee incentives on a regular basis. Salaries and performance reviews should be tied to corporate initiatives and goals both to incentivize participation and to give you the means to hold employees accountable.

- Reward behavior that you want more of. Rewards occur in many forms and may include monetary inducements but can also be encouraged through acknowledgement, recognition, and thank you notes and letters.

- Introduce your ideas to influential employees ahead of time to garner support or head-off opposition before it occurs. Having one or more of your staff already 'on board' with an idea before you introduce it to the rest of your staff can help ensure a warmer reception.

- Don't introduce new ideas in the form of general, vague suggestions. If you are serious about an initiative it should be accompanied by a system and schedule for implementation, scripts, staff training if needed, a method for tracking results, incentives, and the measures by which you will hold staff accountable (and consequences, if needed). Initiatives should be presented with your resolve for their implementation, a commitment to tracking results and holding staff accountable for participation.

If this will be the first time in a long time that you have made accountability part of a new initiative, a change in employee standards, a change in customer relations, etc., and if you have employees who regularly subvert or even openly oppose or ridicule change, then this is your moment. This is your chance to show that you are putting the business first, because that is what is best for the customers, best for all employees, and best for your business.

Finally, when you make hiring decisions, do so not only with creative talent and technical skills in mind, but be sure that you also allow your desired employee culture to play a major (or even deciding) role in the process.

Ideas for March Promotions

Even though most of your primary responsibilities probably fall under the category of enhancing the way your clients look or feel on the outside, so much of what you do affects them on the inside, and helps to bring what is on the inside, out. Take time to look beneath the surface of things during March and get down to what is most important to you and your clients.

March Month-Long Observances

March is Employee Spirit Month

Design and order spa or salon-branded t-shirts, aprons or other clothing suitable for employees to wear in the salon. Give salon-wear to employees and request (or require) it be worn on Fridays, to special events, or every day.

Give recognition awards to co-workers who exemplify the spirit you want in your salon. Partner with a masseuse to come and give mini-massages (and take bookings) as a surprise treat for staff and clients. Or go big! Choose a day to close an hour early to hold an in-salon party including an actual awards ceremony. Or invite staff to a dinner or cocktail party at a local wine shop, bar or restaurant and hold your awards ceremony there for staff or expanded to include significant others. An annual employee awards show can also be a great alternative to holding an annual holiday staff event. More venues will be available and it will not reduce the strain of the busy holiday season.

March is Music in our Schools Month

Donate a percentage of specified sales to the music department of your local school; donate salon or spa gift cards to your school's music staff. Extend a special offer to school music staff or to individuals who participate in community music groups such as city dinner theaters, chorales, orchestras or bands.

Extend a special offer to music teachers and students within their studios. Send music teachers and school music directors a copy of your menu for recital or performance hair and makeup services.

March Week-Long Observances

The Second Week of March is National Money Week

Partner with a financial planner, tax expert or retirement planner to hold a money management, banking, retirement or another financial workshop for clients. Create a special offer to cross market to their clients.

Working with your accountant, a financial planner or a representative from your local bank, hold a workshop for children to teach them about and help them set up their first bank and savings accounts, or hold a workshop for parents on saving for college. Add $5 of your own money to each account started at the event or reward those who set up accounts at your event with a gift card for your salon or spa.

See whether your bank offers rewards or commissions for referring new clients to them for accounts, savings plans, etc. Ask your banker for information about accounts they offer which offer cash back, high interest accrual or other rewards and work to move your personal and business accounts to those types which will most benefit your business. Begin a dialogue with your banker about retirement and succession planning.

The Third Week of March is Well-Elderly Week

Educate clients on the benefits your products and services provide specifically for seniors or about the skin or hair conditions common to seniors and which products seniors (and all of your clients) should use for healthy, beautiful aging.

Extend a special offer to seniors on relevant products or services.

Work with a local senior living facility to host a workshop on healthy skin, scalp and hair care for seniors and extend services to seniors who cannot get to your salon or spa in their homes or at a senior center. Many retirement living communities provide individual and group transportation for their residents. Work with a local senior community and set aside blocks of time each month for their appointments.

Provide manufacturer's samples or "Try Me" stickered product testers to a local senior center along with a stack of your business cards, service menu and a special offer for their patrons.

The Fourth Week of March is National Bubble (Blowers) Week

Educate clients about ingredients commonly found in hair and skin cleansers and how to choose the healthiest products, as well as why the products you choose to use in services and sell via retail are better for them.

Purchase salon or spa-branded bubbles to give away as a gift-with-purchase and include information about the healthy cleansers that you sell, or send branded bubbles home for the children of clients to play with.

March Holidays and Observances

March 1 is National Beer Day

On March 1st (or all month) offer clients a beer at their appointment (or root beer; check your local regulations regarding serving alcohol).

Hold a "beer appreciation" promotion or happy hour event and gift a beer or bar gift card when you pre-sell men's haircut or grooming packages.

Target your male clientele and/or prospective male customers with a special offer such as a buy 3, get 1 free or a pre-sold $3 off each of 4 haircuts (either to be used within 90 days).

Design and purchase a salon or spa-branded coaster that includes a special 'happy hour' salon or spa offer that can be placed on the tables of a local bar or restaurant as part of a cross-marketing effort, or use the coasters as bag stuffers or custom business cards.

Extend a special beer 'happy hour' offer to the staff and patrons of local businesses and feature demonstrations, touch ups, consultations or mini-services.

March 2 is Old Stuff Day

Your old stuff can be someone else's new stuff! Give clients a salon or spa-branded goodie, a complimentary add-on trial-sized product or break on the cost of a specific product or service when they provide a receipt indicating a recent donation to a local thrift store, a shelter, or another non-profit organization.

Hold a special swap event where clients exchange books, jewelry, shoes, jeans or some other type of item and enjoy mini-services like pedicures, manicures or massages, and receive makeup or hair color consultations. Charge a small cover fee to be donated to a local shelter or another charitable organization.

March 3 is Unique Names Day

Hold a contest for the "Most Unique Name" of clients provable by driver's license or birth certificate and reward the winner with a gift certificate and one or two of your most uniquely-named products. Extend a special offer to all entrants and add contacts to your database.

Collect entries, asking customers to help "rename" your salon or spa services with unique names or with names that rhyme, are slang, or some other means. Reward winner/s by treating them to one of the services for which they created a unique name.

March 4 is Employee Appreciation Day

Give recognition awards to staff who exemplify the spirit you want in your salon. Partner with a retailer, restaurant or night-out destination to reward your employees with gift cards. Surprise all employees with a small gift and a personal thank you note. Post client compliments and kudos for staff work and customer service.

National Dentist's Day is in March

See ideas for February's Children's Dental Health on page 43, Tooth Fairy Day on page 51 and National Smile Week on page 170.

March 15 is Incredible Kid Day

Allow clients (and/or the public) to nominate local "Incredible Kids" via entry form in the salon and/or online. Award one (or more) of the nominees with a product and/or service prize; extend a special offer to all entrants. Write a press release about the entrants and the winner (with permission).

Partner with a local photographer and hold a child I.D. card event.

Partner with school photographers to provide touch up services prior to school photos.

Partner with local photographers to create combination packages for students' senior pictures, or for prom or graduation pictures.

March 17 is St. Patrick's Day - Smile, it's Happy Hour!

When it comes to "Happy Hour" in the salon or spa, there are many ways to craft a new, repeating, regularly-scheduled event designed to make clients feel good about coming in, coming back, and bringing co-workers and friends with them from the moment they enter your business. Your happy hour should be crafted not only to make clients happier but also to make *you* happier; design them to help fill up the books during slow hours, promote new services and products, promote retail sales and add-on services, promote filling the books for new stylists, etc.

While the mind naturally goes to the idea of alcohol when you hear the term 'happy hour,' it doesn't mean that yours has to be intoxicating per se—so don't dismiss the idea out of hand. If you can serve alcohol but worry about clients driving afterward, develop a Sangria recipe unique to your salon; you will cut some of the alcohol content without losing a drop of taste or the spirit of the event.

If you would prefer to (or must, due to state or local regulations) go non-alcoholic, keep the spirit alive with "mocktails" for client consumption and "hairtinis" or "skintinis" (special product cocktails for the hair or skin). Partner with a nearby natural foods store, deli, restaurant or juice bar to help create beverage offerings; or create a co-sponsored happy hour for all clients (preferably at your salon, or experiment with a travel case and provide impromptu mini-makeovers for hair, skin, make-up or nails in your partner's establishment).

No matter where you celebrate, ensure that the collection of attendee's contact information and bounce back offers are part of the mix. If possible, hold a drawing each week during your set happy hours for one lucky attendee to win a service or product gift basket.

However you construct your happy hour, make it a special time in your salon (something that is in contrast to what occurs during regular hours in some way). Happy hour can be a chance to turn up the music and let your clients get a groove on. Include referral or bring a friend rewards, spot-prize drawings and contests, and even games, cards or entertainment.

Weekday-Relaxer or Weekend-Readier

Create a Friday 3-6 PM 'date prep' or 'de-stress' happy hour for clients to get ready for a night out with a special someone, or get ready to go out with the girls (or the boys) while they relax for an hour or so with a glass of something. This can be a great way to let go of the stress of the week and get in the right frame of mind to relax during the weekend. Even if they are not going out, it's a great way for clients unwind after a long stressful week.

Gift-Wrap your Clients

Create a happy hour package with free beverage that features services designed to "gift-wrap" clients for the evening such as a cut with color highlights or blowout and style plus mini-facial and cosmetics at a special package price (or just a blowout and style with cosmetic touch up for a quicker turn). Don't miss out on the opportunity to send styling products and cosmetics home with your clients—offer special Happy Hour pricing on retail products as well!

Building (happy) Books

Hold happy hours during what are normally slower times on your books during the week (such as weekday afternoons) to plump up bookings during those hours. Hours in between the lunch and dinner rushes may also be slower hours for restaurants as well; partner with a local restaurant to provide snacks or food or beverage coupons for distribution in the salon or spa in return for the opportunity to gain cross marketing referrals by extending their marketing collateral and special offers to your clients.

Happy Hour How-To, Must-Haves and Menus

A true happy hour event or offer will have social appeal. Give clients a reason to come to your salon or spa beyond their regular appointment (more frequently) and to bring friends with them. As you begin to plan, ask yourself, who do you want to attend? If the answer is "everyone," you aren't being realistic and are not likely to construct an attractive happy hour. Identify types of 'ideal' happy hour clients from larger subgroups within your clientele, or from your target market (the type of clients you *most want* to attract); such as:

Single or married working professionals for an end of day or end of week decompress or prep for night on the town

Stay-at-home or soccer moms and dads who are dying for and deserve a few minutes to themselves

Sports oriented, blue collar, or other general male-oriented groups

Senior citizens

Baby-Boomers

Male clients

College students and young adults, teenagers or 'tweens'

Girlfriend Groups

You can see why setting up a target group is important; what appeals to one generation or group vs. another will vary widely, from what they want done to their hair to what they want to drink to the music they want to listen to. It may be as simple as pleasing your staff and attracting individuals with some of the same demographic characteristics that they have, or by pleasing an employee group from a nearby business, etc.

The menu must include something yummy for the client; something that makes them—well, HAPPY! Find a restaurant or bar to partner with so that during happy hour at the restaurant or bar patrons receive a business card or coaster with an offer from your salon; and during your happy hour, clients receive a special incentive to go to your partnering bar or restaurant.

If other businesses near you are interested, create a bigger, combined happy hour for clients, sharing costs and contacts in a cooperative marketing effort.

Happy Hour (brand) Extensions

Order salon-branded coasters and gift them to local bars or restaurants that have happy hours. Their alcohol distributors sometimes provide them with free coasters; why not substitute those with coasters that draw attention to your business or to your services as a beauty industry professional? An average coaster is almost twice the size of a business card, so it should be no problem for your design to incorporate a referral reward or new client offer, upcoming special events, or a special, compelling offer for people who bring the coaster in to your salon or spa.

Extensions of your Brand, with a Twist!

Order salon-branded coasters with your contact information, happy hour details and/or offer to use as bag stuffers in the salon or for when you offer water, coffee and other beverages in the salon. You can even distribute coasters as business cards within your community and ask your marketing partners to use them or distribute them at the point of purchase to advertise your happy hour and services.

On the Flip Side

Your "coaster" (which can also be used as a business card, bag stuffer, or other advertising medium) has two sides and one of the first rules of marketing is: Do not waste the flip side of any marketing piece! The flip side of your coaster can do double duty and include an area for people to give you contact information; or, you can use the flip side to list other offers, a brief version of your menu, a client testimonial, or special features you offer in your business, such as special equipment, trendy popular services, TV with sports, news or other interests or Wi-Fi connectivity.

Your happy hour does not have to include alcohol, but if you do, have safeguards in place. First, make sure you know what the regulations are in your city / county / state for serving alcohol. There may be different regulations for serving alcohol at no cost than there is if you have a cover charge or charge per beverage.

If you are going to incorporate alcoholic beverages, remember that most clients will probably be driving from your location to their next destination, so do not over-serve and be sure to incorporate food as well. If a client arrives already intoxicated, appears impaired, or you believe that you have a guest who is experiencing a problem, have a plan in place and procedures for arranging transportation and safely delivering clients home, or for summoning medical or other attention if necessary. Finally, these are working hours for you and your staff; save your own happy hour drinking for when you are off the clock.

Luck of the Irish

Irish or not, give clients the opportunity to enter to win something this month. Depending on local regulations, create a gift basket with a pint or two of a favorite regional micro brew (or root beer) and 'a pint' (mini or full-sized) of retail products to support your Beer Buzz or St. Patrick's Day promotions. Or, partner with a local restaurant to provide a free cocktail to clients. Make sure all entrants receive a special offer from you.

March 21 is National Fragrance Day

Work with a private label manufacturer to create a custom fragrance, room freshener, candle or another product with a unique fragrance branded exclusively to your salon and spa for retail sale, client thank you gifts, gifts-with-purchase, contest awards, to create ambience, etc.

March 23 is Chip and Dip Day

Treat clients to a tasty chip and dip treat during appointments.

Hold a contest and have a chip and dip tasting happy hour at your salon or spa. Reward the winner with a special gift basket and extend a special offer to all entrants. Publish the dip recipes on Facebook, your e-mail newsletter, or even in a printed-book for client gift or retail sale.

March 29 is Take a Walk in the Park Day

Sponsor a 'Walk in the Park' event in your community to benefit a local charity. Inquire about opportunities to support community clean-up events or provide funding for park projects or plantings. Write a press release to publicize community needs and document your efforts. Post information and pictures on Facebook, your website, blog and other social media and encourage clients to get involved.

Support city parks and recreation by sponsoring a team for spring or summer sports. Host a get together for your sponsored team at a local park and provide mini-services and refreshments, or extend a special offer to team members and their families.

Check with city government about upcoming street fairs or park events where you can take a booth to perform mini-services, sell retail products or gift cards, and take bookings.

Create a 'mini-park' area near your salon or spa which can be enjoyed by employees at lunch or improve the outside appearance for your customers.

March Planning and Tasks

Select from manufacturer's March-April retail and back bar promotions in light of the events and promotions you will conduct in April, May and June.

Design and print (or order) gift certificates, postcards, flyers, and supplies still needed for April, Mother's Day, and for any other promotions or events coming in the next 6-8 weeks, all the way into June.

Identify businesses with which to cross promote for Mother's and Father's Day, establish partnerships and begin to identify and delegate responsibilities. Complete April planning, confirm partnerships and assigned responsibilities in terms of events, promotions and marketing.

Set target goals, create a way to track and show results, and be sure that staff are on board and incentivized to support retail and gift certificate sales for Mother's Day and Father's Day and other activities planned for April - May - June.

Communicate in March

Items to include in your e-mail or print newsletter, web site, Facebook and blog posts and in direct mail communications this month:

- March-April events, promotions, charitable activities and contests

- Special interest items such as sentimental or humorous 'behind the chair' anecdotes, special achievements and education of staff, photos from events or great styles, makeovers, etc.

- Let clients know which promotions expire in March and what products are coming new to the salon in April

- Begin marketing for Mother's and Father's Day gift certificate sales by the end of March

- Solicit contests or drawing entries due in March and announce February's contest winners

- Use e-mail to help fill openings on the books by letting clients know of open time slots or cancellations, following up with clients who did not re-book at their last appointment, soliciting bookings for clients who have a special date, interview or another occasion to prepare for, etc.

- A spotlight product, service, and/or staff member of the month

March Calendar / Suggested Communications and Tasks Schedule

SUN	MON	TUE	WED	THU	FRI	SAT
1st week of Month 1st of March—Merchandise for March 1st of March—Begin collecting entries for March contests						
		Order from manufacturers retail promotions for products to support April - May marketing plans; design related signage			Send March Newsletter with coupons, announce contests and winners, new products and services, coming events, openings still on the books, events and promotions	
2nd week of Month						
Begin promoting sales of Mother's Day gifts and gift certificates		Order in gifts, salon-branded items, impulse buy and other items for April and May			Write press releases for any events/results reporting or future events/charitable focus	
3rd week of Month						
		Finalize, review and lay out plans for April - May - June events and promotions			Send March "last chance" promotions and openings on the books e-mail and/or direct mail	
4th week of Month Last day of March—Take down any March-only promotions Last day of March—Draw March contest winners						
If you have not already, start marketing spring promotions and bridal packages		Order event supplies, postcards, collateral, gifts and salon-branded items for May contests			Send April focus e-mail / direct mail	

March Worksheets

$_____ Retail Sales Goal

Promotions_____

_____

_____

_____

_____

$_____ Avg. Retail/Client

$_____ Retail Sales Results

$_____ Service Sales Goal

Promotions_____

_____

_____

_____

_____

$_____ Avg. Service/Client

$_____ Service Sales Results

$_____ Event Revenues Goal

Events _____

_____

_____

_____

_____

#_____ Attending Event/s

#_____ Apts/Booked at Event

$_____ Event/s Sales

$_____ Total Event/s Results

$_____ Charity/Fund Raising Goal

Charity Events _____

_____

_____

_____

_____

#_____ Attending Event/s

#_____ Apts/Booked at Event

$_____ Charity Event/s Sales

$_____ Total Charity Results

March Marketing Summary

Marketing Partners: _____

_____

_____

_____

Marketing Collateral Needed (or Used): _____

_____

_____

_____

Other Efforts:

#_____ Number of Clients New to Salon

%_____ Client Retention Rate (90 days)

Retention Efforts: _____

_____

or % _____ Clients Re-booked at Appointment

$_____ Gift Certificate Sales

#_____ Contacts added to marketing / e-mail database

april
make over your
talent and skills

The last few chapters addressed making over internal and interpersonal aspects of your business. Understandably, these can be difficult areas to address; when it comes to dealing with the attitudes, motivation and behavior of others, it always is. But these areas are also the most critical to the real health, well-being, growth and sustainability of your business now and for the long haul.

The remaining chapters will discuss more operational, externally-oriented components of business and marketing where you can unleash your creativity to create exciting, effective and measurable plans for the future. First, let's talk about a makeover for you and your staff in terms of the expertise you currently have, the knowledge you need in order to serve your clients now and the skills you need to add in order to attract more clients and grow for the future. In order to maintain operations and effectively manage growth, you need a formal plan for, and dedication to, on-going training and education for yourself and for each member of your staff.

When it comes to making over your talent and skills base, you can develop goals based on one or several factors:

    a. expressed needs / wants of current clients

    b. new services you want to launch

    c. new products you want to launch or incorporate into services

    d. desired upgrades to technology or equipment

    e. skills to attract ideal / desired client base

    f. interests / needs of current general client base based on social trends

    g. changing demographic composition of your neighborhood or community

    h. background and education of your employees

    i. interests and raw talents of your employees

    j. desired skills for new hires

    k. knowledge needs in areas of business operations

    l. human resources / employee management

    m. leadership

    n. marketing, retailing, merchandising, sales

    o. promotions and events

    p. finance, bookkeeping, taxes

This may be the first time that someone has suggested you actually take classes in areas related to the 'business' side of your business since you left cosmetology school—classes you should take beyond the ones you actually want to take in order to advance your technical skills as a stylist, esthetician or massage therapist.

Acquiring new skills and techniques relative to practicing your artistry and craft likely interests you far more than does a social media marketing class; but the fact is, unless you can afford to outsource the non-craft areas of your business, you have an obligation to get smart about these business-related responsibilities.

Investing in training to launch a new service or product line will usually result in a direct return on investment. If you launch a new service, or improve services with a new product line, you can reap new revenues, right? But you may not realize that the same holds true in non-craft areas as well.

Let's say that you want to add manicure services to your salon. You can expect to receive new bookings for appointments or add-on manicures to existing services as time goes by simply by letting your current clientele know that you added these services to your menu. You will probably gain some new business from clients who may have been receiving manicures elsewhere, and you can attract the occasional new client by updating your menu, web site, advertising or directory listings.

What do you need to learn in order to do more than just get by?

But imagine how much more quickly you could reap a return on your investments in staff, training and products if you (and/or your staff) had training and expertise in holding events so that you could bring current clients together to a launch event and gain new service appointments immediately; not only with clients who previously received manicures elsewhere, but also among clients who have never had manicures before. Imagine having the know-how and tools to quickly educate and attract new clients through e-mail, Facebook and other social media site marketing efforts, and to turn your current clients into a buzzing word-of-mouth network in order to gain new clients in all service areas.

Knowing how to fill up seats at an event (and to do so with the right people), how to partner with other businesses to effectively cross market, and how to efficiently market to large groups of individuals within your community will lead to growth. This same growth will then necessitate that you also gain additional education in areas of human resource management and leadership, finance, financial planning, bookkeeping, succession and retirement planning and other areas of operation to ensure that, as you grow, new clients and new services can be accommodated on an on-going basis.

All too often, opportunity for growth is missed not because it's not there, but because we aren't ready. If you wanted to grow and grow quickly, would you be ready?

Have you laid a foundation with the skills and knowledge needed to accommodate rapid growth?

One of the popular marketing fads of 2010 was the dramatic upsurge in online sales of location-based discounts and new client offers sold on sites like groupon.com and livingsocial.com. Companies eager to grow their client base jumped on the trend, including a large number of salons and spas. It seemed like an almost risk-free, fast growth idea; however, in the rush to attract new clients, many businesses failed to anticipate some of the complications that could arise. One of the unanticipated problems encountered occurred for businesses that sold through a lot of deals only to find that they were not prepared in terms of time, service providers, space and other resources to accommodate everyone who purchased their deal. These business leaders were initially very excited about the prospect of the revenue, but did not adequately plan for how to deliver the customer experience needed to win over a new customer for the long term. It is reasonable to assume that some of these companies actually thwarted their own efforts to attract new clients by selling a product they couldn't deliver, and it's also reasonable to assume that they endangered or even lost relationships with their regular clients because of the run on products and services by deal seekers (and their consequent inability to properly serve existing customers).

It is easy to be content when you are getting by; almost anyone can do that. But to be successful in a way that will endure, you have to develop a growth mentality within yourself, cultivate it in your employees and make it an entrenched part of your employee culture. This growth mentality must include the ability to foresee the consequences to your business in terms of how it will impact your staffing levels, your finances, your facilities, and to identify what education, skills and training you need to develop in order to be prepared for growth and opportunity, before it comes.

Many times small business owners have to fulfill roles far outside of their own personal areas of interest and beyond their experience and training. You might not have realized that when you signed on to own your own business you were also signing on to do your own accounting, taxes, human resources, marketing, cleaning, and property management. As a small business owner and entrepreneur, I have found myself in the same situation.

It would be easy to believe that I need to become an expert in every area of my business in order to succeed; however, I learned a valuable truth prior to launching my own business as a result of watching Marcus Buckingham's short video series (6 videos that are each 10-15 minutes long) called *Trombone Players Wanted*. I highly recommend that you purchase the series to watch yourself, and to watch with co-workers as a staff development and team building exercise, regardless of what business you are in. There is a link to this video series on the bottom of my blog at www.savvystylist.net and on my website at www.12monthsfomarketing.net.

The main theme of this short but profound and transformative series suggests that you will be the most successful, happy and fulfilled when you work in your strengths and within your areas of personal passion most of the time. You may have the intellectual ability to do your own marketing, but no passion for it. Or like me, you might have the ability to do your own bookkeeping and taxes, but you might also dread and dislike those tasks.

> You will be the happiest *and* the **most profitable** when you work the most in the areas the that you love the most.

Marcus Buckingham makes the point that you will thrive, be most productive and most profitable working in those areas that you love. And that while for a time you may be forced to work in areas that are not your strengths and on tasks that you personally dislike, your goal should be to work yourself out of those tasks, either by becoming profitable enough to outsource them or by delegating or 'trading' tasks with other individuals who do enjoy those areas of responsibility.

One of the questions I have learned to ask myself when I am tempted to believe that I have to do something myself that is outside the areas of my own strengths and passions is whether I could make more money doing what I love than it would cost to hire out the task. In other words, if balancing my checkbook is going to take me six hours to complete, how much revenue could I generate doing something that I love and something that I am "good at" during those same six hours.

Generally, the answer is that I can *always* make more working from my strengths during those hours than I would pay to have an accounting expert do the same task (plus, they can do it in a fraction of the time that it takes me, and they actually do it correctly!) If your passion and strength lies in working behind the chair, work to partner with people in your business who have strengths that you lack when it comes to completing other tasks that have to be done, but which you personally dislike, in which you are not skilled or for other reasons (such as time constraints) you do not want to do yourself. Try to find professionals who would be willing to work in trade on some projects.

Buckingham makes another good point; there may already be individuals working with you who love to do what you dislike (and vice versa). And by hiring strategically to your weak areas, and giving staff a chance to grow, you are working to create an environment where you can spent most of your time working to your strengths, where staff have a path for growth and development and for developing their own careers by taking on new responsibilities. You will be creating the best atmosphere for employee development, employee morale, continuous learning and growth, and maximum productivity and profitability—not to mention, you will get to spend your time doing what you love!

Ideas for April Promotions

Being able to recognize our own strengths and weaknesses, and creating plans to make changes and improvements both personal and professional is exciting, because then we can truly focus on identifying and pursuing the specific results we desire to gain in the future. This kind of reflection also helps us to identify strengths and traits in others that we admire; focus your April promotions on celebrating the strengths, virtues and accomplishments of employees and clients.

April Month-Long Observances

April is National Humor Month

Hold a "Best Joke" or "Best Prank" contest. Reward the winner with a makeover and tickets to comedy club. Extend a special offer to all entrants.

Partner with a local comedy club for a combination offer to retail in your salon or spa, or purchase tickets from a local club at a reduced price and gift, award, or sell them to clients in the salon or spa.

Purchase reduced-price tickets in bulk from a local comedy club and hold a customer or employee-appreciation event at the club.

April is Guitar Month

Partner for cross marketing with music stores and music teachers.

Invite a local music teacher (or studio of teachers) to demonstrate for clients or to hold a workshop for clients who may be interested in lessons for themselves or their children. At the event, demonstrate performance and recital makeovers for student's hair and makeup. Create a recital or performance makeover service to add to your menu.

Extend a special offer to all music teachers in your community and/or to all employees of local music stores. Take nominations and reward one music teacher in your community and the person who nominated them with a makeover and product gift.

April is Lawn and Garden Month

Partner for cross marketing or a joint drawing or contest with a local nursery or landscaping business. Give them a gift card to give to one (or more) of their customers, and ask for an equivalent gift certificate for their business to give to one (or more) of your clients. Put spring gardening advice and tips in Facebook posts and your e-mail newsletter.

April is Stress Awareness Month

Fill April promotion and retail scripts with highlights about the stress-relieving benefits provided by your services and products. See the de-stressing marketing ideas beginning on page 92.

April Week-Long Observances

The Second Week of April is Personal Training Week

Partner with a gym or personal trainer for cooperative or cross marketing. Partner with a trainer to give a free workout demonstration or one-day fitness boot camp for your employees and/or clients.

Give some of your gift cards to local fitness trainers. Subsidize your employee's gym memberships or purchase gift cards for your employees. Check with your insurance provider to determine whether they may provide subsidies for gym memberships or discounts based on employee fitness.

Working with a local personal trainer, hold a month-long fitness challenge for staff and invite clients to participate. Post goals and results on Facebook, your blog site, your web site, and in your e-mail newsletter. Hold a kick off event and hold a celebration event at the end of the month featuring touch ups and makeover demonstrations.

The Third Week of April is Customer Awareness Week

Examine the customer experience at your business from beginning to end; identify and make changes needed to improve. Make a list of the characteristics you would find in your "ideal clients" and steps that you could take to attract them.

Customer Appreciation

You have heard it before, and it's true. Your clients will notice when you take the time to do something personal for them. A personal thank you note written to each client takes only minutes a day, and costs very little (e-mail thank you notes cost even less), but will go a long way toward reinforcing your role in the lives of your clients. It is a personal touch in an impersonal world. It conveys your gratitude for their patronage. It is an opportunity for you to remark on a topic of conversation or area of concern they shared with you, so that they know you truly cared and listened. It is a moment when you can ask, "Were you satisfied with your haircut (or massage, or manicure, etc.), do you have any questions about care or maintenance, and is there anything else that I can do for you?"

It is another opportunity for you to ask them to book their next appointment or to ask for a referral. It is a simple act, but very few people take the time to do it. If you make this activity part of your professional routine, it will get noticed, it will bring clients back. It will facilitate more referrals. It will provide you with more opportunities to communicate with your clients.

Order salon-branded thank you notes that you can personalize with a message and signature. Include a copy of your business card (every time) because it is the perfect way for your client to refer a friend or family member to you. If space allows, place a menu, client referral or special offer on the inside flap or back of the thank you note. If you have a points system, you can customize the note by including any points the client has accumulated as well as how many additional referrals, purchases, service visits, etc., that they need to move to the next rewards level.

Implement a (formal) thank you note program for all clients with the goal of thanking 100% of your clients. Try it for a month and see how easy and effective it is!

Customer Recognition

Recognition is... free! Have you considered a 'client of the week' (or month) feature in-salon and in your newsletter? Recognize clients for work in the community or other achievements. Draw attention to worthy causes they support. Herald (with permission and with respect to privacy) the arrival of new babies, new spouses, promotions, retirements, etc. Select a deserving 'client of the month' to receive a free service or makeover. Ask clients to nominate a deserving member of the community who deserves a makeover or free service (or series of services). Document recognition in your salon through press releases to your local newspaper and periodicals.

The Fourth Week of April is National Dance Week

Partner with a local dance studio/instructor for cross marketing. Promote the giving of salon or spa gift cards as dance teacher gifts. Create a special "Dance Teacher's Gift Basket" that includes a gift card, pampering products, and one or two of your favorite dance albums or musical movies.

Invite a local dance teacher or studio to hold a workshop for clients who may be interested in lessons for themselves or their children. At the event, demonstrate performance or recital makeovers for student's hair and makeup. Create a recital or performance makeover service to add to your menu.

Extend a special offer to all dance teachers in your community and/or to all students and families of local dance studios. Take nominations and reward one teacher and the student who nominated them with a makeover and product gift.

The Fourth Week of April is National Karaoke Week

Partner with a local restaurant or bar and hold a customer karaoke night or rent a machine and close the salon early for an employee karaoke party (along with family and friends).

April Holidays and Observances

April 2 is Children's Book Day

Children's causes are easy to build momentum around. In April, solicit new book or cash donations to donate to libraries of local schools, day cares, children's services organizations or similar charities. Give participating clients a break on service or retail pricing and/or a free spa or salon-branded or boutique quality bookmark to thank them for participating in support of their community. Beautiful, one-of-a-kind boutique quality bookmarks would also be a unique impulse-gift item to add to regular retail year round.

April 5 is Look Alike Day

We all want to look like movie stars! Create or update your celebrity look book and create signage and station talkers with celebrities sporting a variety of current styles and fashions to help make visual suggestions to clients who would enjoy (or who desperately need!) a new, trendier look.

Hold a contest for staff and clients for the best celebrity look-alike makeover; take before-and-after pictures and let clients vote in the winning stylist/client pair. Or hold a celebrity look-alike contest, soliciting entries in the salon and via e-mail, your web site, etc., rewarding the winner/s with a prize basket and sending a special offer to all entrants.

April 7 is No Housework Day

Partner with local housekeeping businesses for cooperative offers or cross marketing.

Take nominations from clients and the public via Facebook, your web site and in the salon and reward a local housekeeping professional with a day of pampering.

Partner with a housekeeping service and reward a deserving or contest-winning client with pampering in their home in the form of 2 hours of housekeeping and in the salon or spa with 2 hours of services.

April 10 is Golfer's Day

Spring is here (or just around the corner) and golf course business should be heating up. Partner with local golf courses, driving ranges, golf clubs and related organizations for cross or cooperative marketing.

Extend special male-oriented offers (such as a 3+1 free or $3 off 4 haircuts) along with a grooming, hair or skin care product package to male clients and men's organizations. Work with a men's club to hold a drawing to award one member with a complimentary service and product package; use the entries to help build your communications database and extend special offers.

April 20 is Volunteer Recognition Day

Ask local area non-profits or local schools to nominate extraordinary volunteers within their organizations. Reward winner/s with a day of pampering. Create bigger rewards by partnering with other businesses to create a larger prize package, or multiple packages. Honor volunteers with recognition in your salon newsletter, on your web site and in Facebook posts, and submit a press release to local newspapers and radio stations.

Administrative Professional's Day is in April

Check online for the exact date of Administrative Professional's Day in April (it changes year to year) and promote sales of gift cards for administrative staff of clients and local businesses beginning in March. Solicit entries from local businesses for outstanding administrative pros and reward a winner with a gift card and aromatherapy-based products or even with a full a day of pampering.

Send manufacturer's samples or a "Try Me" stickered product and a gift card or bounce-back offer to the administrative staff of businesses near yours or to the administrative staff of your business park or mall office.

April 22 is National Jelly Bean Day

Treat clients to jelly beans and/or hold a contest where entrants guess the number of jelly beans in a container in the salon or spa. Take entries in the salon or spa and also post a picture on your web site and Facebook page and solicit entries (and new contacts) online.

April 30 is Hairstylist's Appreciation Day

Solicit feedback about your business from clients on an on-going basis. Use kudos to create special Hairstylist's Appreciation Day displays with comments posted at stations or written into thank you notes as part of an employee appreciation gift for stylists from you and/or from your partnering businesses. Use customer comments on a regular basis to provide reviews and build your reputation online. Include customer raves on your blog and web site and in Facebook posts.

Since the holiday season can be so busy, consider holding your annual employee party during March (employee spirit month) or in April on National Hairstylist's Day. Celebrate employee milestones, contributions and share client kudos. Create a family-friendly event and include the family and friends of staff.

National Stress Awareness Day is in April

April is Stress Awareness Month—the perfect opportunity to focus client attention on the stress-relieving benefits your services and products provide. From massage to skin and hair health to aromatherapy, stress-relieving services and products play a major role in nearly every area of the salon and spa.

de-stress (1) In moderation, dark chocolate and red wine can have beneficial effects including endorphin release, anti-oxidants and improved attitude through indulgence. In the spirit of health, create a one-time or on-going Wine and Chocolate Wednesday reception or happy hour as a client (or employee) thank you event. Reward a drawing-winning client with wine and chocolates to take home.

de-stress (2) Aromatherapy benefits can be found in most of the products you use at back bar, during the client experience in the chair, and in your retail offering. Educate clients on specific benefits that your products provide with shelf and station talkers at point of sale and in retail displays. Thank your most valuable clients with miniature or sample sizes of aromatherapy-based products.

Enhance retail sales by offering aromatherapy gifts for moms, teachers, coaches, friends and others; or use them as client thank you gifts.

Incentivize retail sales with aromatherapy gifts-with-purchase (such as a small sachet, mini salon-branded personal fragrance, room fragrance or candle).

de-stress (3) Add mini hand or neck massages to your service menu or as a free add-on with certain services. This extra 5-10 minutes can help create a client experience that could never be replicated in another salon or spa.

de-stress (4) Hold a 'de-stress the client' contest or drawing where clients enter themselves and a friend and winners receive (for instance) $25 gift certificates for use in May. Or tailor this as a perfect gift for Mother's Day with the winning entry receiving a gift certificate for themselves and their mom or daughter for use in May. Follow up! All entrants should receive a special related offer from you via e-mail or mail.

Market all of your de-stressing promotions and products to caregivers, public servants, health care professionals, day care providers, stay-at-home moms, teachers—anyone who really deserves, and really needs extra-special pampering and stress relief. Hold a stress-awareness and stress-relieving workshop or happy hour featuring wine and dark chocolate, sample and demonstrate stress-relieving products and services.

April Planning and Tasks

Select from manufacturer's bi-monthly promotional offerings in light of what you have planned for May and June promotions and events.

Purchase any last minute items needed for Mother's Day, design and print (or order) special gift certificates and products for Father's Day, summer skin care and summer impulse-buy products (sunscreen, hand sanitizer, lip balm, etc.,) and items needed for wedding, anniversary, bridal or graduation packages. Identify and order any special gift certificates, postcards, flyers, and supplies still needed for events or promotions coming within the next 6-8 weeks (all the way into July).

Set aside and take the time to plan ahead. You should be completely finished with preparations to support Mother's Day and May events early in April. Complete planning for Father's Day, wedding and graduation promotions, and plan events to celebrate the end of school year and beginning of summer.

Communicate in April

Items to include in your e-mail or print newsletter, web site, Facebook and blog posts and in direct mail communications this month:

- April-May events, promotions, charitable activities and contests
- Prom, graduation and other end-of-school year events
- Aromatherapy benefits of products you sell
- Highlight stress-relieving services or products
- Mother's Day (and even begin talking about Father's Day)
- Promote your bridal hair, skin and makeup packages
- Last chance for retail or service promotions expiring in April
- Last minute openings on the books
- March winners, April contests, drawings and opportunities
- A spotlight product, service or staff member of the month

April Calendar / Suggested Communications and Tasks Schedule

SUN	MON	TUE	WED	THU	FRI	SAT
1st week of Month						
1st of April—Merchandise for April 1st of April—Begin collecting entries for April contests						
		Order signage, event supplies and promotional materials for May - June promotions			Send April Newsletter with coupons, announce contests and winners, new products and services, coming events, openings still on the books, events and promotions	
2nd week of Month						
		Order in gifts, salon-branded items, impulse buy and other items for May			Write press releases for any events/results reporting or future events / charitable focus	
3rd week of Month						
		Finalize, review and lay out plans for May - June - July promotions			Send April "last chance" promotions and openings on the books e-mail and/or direct mail	
4th week of Month						
Last day of April—Take down any April-only promotions Last day of April—Draw April contest winners						
Begin marketing Father's Day and June promotions		Order event supplies, postcards, gifts and salon-branded items needed for June promotions			Send May focus e-mail / direct mail	

April Worksheets

$_____ Retail Sales Goal

Promotions_____

_____

_____

_____

_____

$_____ Avg. Retail/Client

$_____ Retail Sales Results

$_____ Service Sales Goal

Promotions_____

_____

_____

_____

_____

$_____ Avg. Service/Client

$_____ Service Sales Results

$_____ Event Revenues Goal

Events _____

_____

_____

_____

_____

#_____ Attending Event/s

#_____ Apts/Booked at Event

$_____ Event/s Sales

$_____ Total Event/s Results

$_____ Charity/Fund Raising Goal

Charity Events _____

_____

_____

_____

_____

#_____ Attending Event/s

#_____ Apts/Booked at Event

$_____ Charity Event/s Sales

$_____ Total Charity Results

April Marketing Summary

Marketing Partners: _____

_____

_____

_____

Marketing Collateral Needed (or Used): _____

_____

_____

_____

Other Efforts:

#_____ Number of Clients New to Salon

%_____ Client Retention Rate (90 days)

Retention Efforts: _____

_____

or % _____ Clients Re-booked at Appointment

$_____ Gift Certificate Sales

#_____ Contacts added to marketing / e-mail database

may
make over
the client experience

The editors of television reality shows condense what they feel are the most compelling, provocative, exciting and important conversations, activities and events that occur over the course of a week or even longer, into a one or two hour-long show. That might mean distilling one hundred and sixty eight hours (more than ten thousand minutes) into just 35 or 40 minutes of actual show time, minus commercials and "coming up next" teasers. They try to produce the most intriguing, engaging and provocative episode possible in order to entice viewers to watch the show, to follow contestants, to visit their web sites and, in some cases, even to decide the outcome of the series via public vote.

To make over the client experience, view each client visit as a condensed, exaggerated reality show. Your client only gets to see, hear, smell and experience the elements that *you* decide to edit down into the block of time they are present within your salon or spa for their appointment. As the producer and real time editor of the customer experience within your salon or spa, how can you orchestrate each one to be intriguing, engaging and provocative to the client?

Intrigue: (verb) meaning to fascinate, arouse the curiosity of, or amuse.

To be intriguing is to be at the same time both enticing and mysterious. If you are intrigued by an organization, you know something about it, but not everything, and you want to know more. Your interest level is heightened. You are willing to be drawn deeper into experience with them. Intrigue also implies mystery. In the case of your clients, if they are intrigued by your salon or spa, they consciously or subconsciously feel that they do not already know all that you can do for them, but they do know that you have more to offer. If they are intrigued, it is because based on their preliminary experiences with your salon or spa, they want to find out what else you can do for them. They believe that you have something more to offer them.

intrigue: (v.)
meaning

to fascinate

to arouse the curiosity of

or to amuse.

In order to be fascinating to your clients you must create experiences that cause them to be motivated enough to act on this intrigue in the form of trying more products and receiving new services.

You have to create compelling programs (such as V.I.P. exclusive rewards, referral or graduated purchasing rewards, or other loyalty programs) that both draw and motivate them to act.

You must construct events from the customer-interest perspective which not only entice clients to attend, but which also interest their friends, family, co-workers, neighbors, etc., in order to generate new contacts and referrals.

If your business is intriguing, it means that the sum total of all that you have going on in your salon or spa interests clients as well as prospective customers enough that not only are they willing to subscribe to your communications, they also actually open your e-mails, read your direct mail pieces, and visit your web site and Facebook or blog pages.

And if you think creating intrigue sounds nice, just wait until you know what stimulating full-on client-engagement can do for you! When your client experience is powerfully-positive enough to actually engage a client, you can expect them not only to read your communications and try new products and services; they will do even more.

Engaged clients will begin to view themselves as insiders, part of your 'club' if you will. They will attend and enjoy your events and bring people with them. They will participate in two-way dialogue with you, provide you with constructive feedback, and even help you generate new ideas. They will respond to your questions on Facebook and leave reviews for you. The engaged customer will vote for you in online "best of" polls. They will be an active source of referrals and they will work to earn rewards and participate in your programs.

Engaged clients believe that they are part of something. They believe that they are important to you and to your business. Apart from having a family or social connection to your business, the only way a client will become engaged will be because you deliberately engineer a series of consistent experiences and touch points which demonstrate to them, over the passage of time, clearly and unmistakably, that they are a unique, valued and vitally important person in your life and in your business.

Here is a fact that many businesses just do not seem to understand: A client is never going to put more into your relationship than you are. Imagine a still pool of water that provides a reflection. The reflection on the water may be a fair image of the original, but the original is still by far the strongest, clearest side. Like it or not, the engagement (or lack of engagement) demonstrated toward your business by your clients is a direct reflection of your engagement with, and interest in, them. Your engagement with and interest in the client is the original, their response is the reflection. Just as with the clear pool of water, the reflection is never going to be stronger than the original!

That reality should motivate you to thoroughly examine the experience you provide to each client during their 30 minute 'reality show' of an appointment in your salon or spa. It should make you uncomfortable enough to challenge your own preconceived ideas and those of your staff about the quality of services provided in your salon or spa, the employee culture, your physical environment, your marketing and communications, your promotions, etc. It should be an incentive for you to move beyond your own apprehensions relative to confronting or even removing staff who are in the wrong positions, who need more education, who need to update their skills, who need to change the way they present themselves, or who simply need to move on.

You are never going to get more from the relationship you have with a client than you are willing to invest. Rarely, if ever, is a client going to waltz into your salon or spa and intuitively understand the amount of money, time and energy that you have invested in your salon environment, staff, equipment, technology, communications (i.e., the value that you provide to them); you are going to have to show it to them in your interactions, you are going to have to tell them about it in your communications. And you are going to have to do this over and over again, and you are going to have to do it in such a way that they understand how much it benefits them (not you).

Once clients feel that you are engaging with them more for your benefit than for theirs, their level of engagement will decrease, and so will the trust that they have in you. In this age of social media and the power of instant communication, online reviews and referrals, it is more important than ever that you work to develop this engagement, based on trust, with your clients. Their reviews, rants and raves will play an integral part in how effectively your internet (web site, blog, Facebook, e-newsletter) efforts will be in drawing new clients from within your community; they will even play a direct part in influencing the first hand referrals that your most engaged clients will generate.

> You will never **get more** from the client relationship
>
> than you are wiling to **invest**.

Intrigue motivates clients to find out more or even to try more and engaged clients will be interacting with your salon or spa in even more meaningful ways. But to be its most powerful, the client experience must be provocative.

Beyond engagement, being provocative to your clients means something even more. An involvement of the emotions and the senses, this word often embodies the idea of desire that is a reflection of both love and lust, both need and want.

Provocative is a word that implies both accompanying action and intent. When used in a romantic connotation, the word 'provocative' implies that one party is purposefully and intentionally acting in order to stimulate an emotional response in another that will be demonstrated by acts of passion, affection and love. To provoke someone means that you are intelligently, intentionally doing certain things that are specifically designed to illicit desired responses and actions on the part of someone else.

To be provocative is a powerful thing!

If you are not intelligently and intentionally designing each customer experience from beginning-to-end, then you are leaving some of the details up to chance. You are missing opportunities to stimulate engagement and loyalty. And some of the details that you are missing or leaving to chance may actually be working against the experience that you want to create. This may be why some of the customer reactions and responses that you are provoking are not what you expected or desired.

What kind of emotional reactions do you want to produce in your clients? If at any point of their overall experience with your salon or spa they have a negative impression from your web site, social media, direct mail, the phone call to book the appointment, their greeting when they arrive, their experience in the chair, in the retail area or at check out, or even the way they are dismissed from your salon or spa—if any one of these moments is characterized by disinterest, disregard or even disrespect, then the emotional and intellectual response they have toward your business will reflect that.

While some deficiencies in the customer experience may be evident or even glaring and long-known, others can be difficult to discover or may not even be discoverable by you. For instance, employees who refrain from gossip or inappropriate behavior when you are in the building may reveal another side of themselves only when you are well clear of the salon or spa.

Am I saying you have to take up a 24-hour a day, 7-day a week residence in your business to ensure the quality of each client experience? Not a chance. Even if it were possible, which it's not, it would not be healthy for you. Nor would a micro-managerial, suspicious and controlling approach to management be likely to enhance your employee culture.

But there are other things you can do in order to obtain a more comprehensive and unfiltered picture of what constitutes the "real" client experience in every area and with each team member of your salon or spa.

Going back to the mystery / secret shopper idea presented in February, hire a professional firm or draw on a trusted individual from within your family or social circle who is not known in your salon or spa to conduct a secret shopper experiment, booking appointment/s at times when you are not there. Even if you cannot afford to hire professionals, you can still compensate these individuals by reimbursing them for the services and products purchased, or by giving them gift certificates for use in your salon (or the salon they usually frequent).

If you can afford to hire a consultant or company that specializes in this service, you may receive not only results and survey information, but they may also be able to provide you with specific recommendations, retraining or education for staff, assistance in implementing new policies and procedures, guidance in the redesign of touch point collateral such as your web site, menu or marketing pieces, or even with assistance in re-crafting the overall client experience in your business.

Another way to garner a wider perspective is to create a focus group, or even multiple small groups made up of current clients. Give each group a questionnaire designed to give you feedback about specific aspects or service areas of your business. Solicit honest, no-holds-barred feedback, and provide anonymity of individual surveys to encourage greater freedom of expression. No matter how positive or negative the results, thank participants for their honest feedback with a gift certificate and goodie bag. At some point following the group's work, send every participant a summary report noting specific changes that you made based on feedback.

If any customer touch point is characterized by **disinterest, disregard,** or **disrespect,** the emotional response your clients will have toward your business (and toward you) will reflect that.

You also can (and should, regularly!) brainstorm, solicit feedback and ideas, and involve your staff in the analysis and redesign of the client experience. They have firsthand, practical knowledge and may have effective, creative improvement ideas that they have never shared, simply because they were never asked. They may have suggestions that would truly differentiate the customer experience within your salon or spa. And involve your staff, because ultimately they must 'buy in' to the concept of making over the customer experience for the makeover to be effective and lasting. They will only be able to effectively implement needed changes if they truly understand the deficiencies and thoroughly understand, trust and believe in the solutions.

You probably know your employees well enough that you could spot a half-hearted, disingenuous attempt on their part to go along with your improvements from a mile off. More importantly, so can your customers, and it flavors the way they perceive your business and the potential that you have to intrigue, engage and provoke them to a long-term, love-and-lust-filled relationship with your business!

Remember the analogy about viewing the customer experience as though it were a condensed, one-hour version of a week-long reality TV show? Think about the emotional and intellectual response you have as a viewer of one of these shows when a disingenuous, dishonest, little-bit-crazy or otherwise unlikable cast member is exposed. Think about how much stronger your negative response to this character becomes as the series progresses and your impression of that 'villain' is reinforced over and over again. This is exactly how it is for customers in your salon or spa when they are repeatedly exposed to negative actions or behaviors of any of your employee 'cast members' or to deficiencies at any point of their experience with your salon or spa.

The client experience lasts a couple of hours at most. It is a compressed, exaggerated, condensed version of all of the points of contact that any one individual customer has with your business. They don't have the opportunity to see all that goes on behind the scenes. They don't have the ability to know whether a negative moment they experienced is a rare or common occurrence, whether they just caught a staff member on a bad day, or even just a rare bad moment.

Each customer only has their recurring time slot to experience your business and you only have a very small amount of time with any one individual to win their repeat business, loyalty or referrals. The question is, how will you, as the editor and producer of their reality show, work to edit each 'episode' down to its most intriguing, engaging and provocative best in order to keep each client watching?

Ideas for May Promotions

Your promotions in May should be designed to showcase your business so that it creates intrigue, generates active customer engagement and compels your clients to action in order to build a bigger role for your business in the lives of your clients. Make it your goal to meet more clients' needs, be the connector for them with community leaders and charitable causes and become a facilitator of their social lives.

May Month-Long Observances

May is National Blood Pressure Month

Invite a local practitioner to do a seminar in-salon or obtain a cuff and set up a station with aromatherapy stress-relieving "Try Me" stickered products so that clients can do their own blood pressure checks in the salon. This might also be a very interesting and enlightening way to measure the before-and-after results of some of your most stress-relieving services!

May is National Photograph Month

Partner with a photographer for a photo shoot or to do a series of before-and-after shots (such as for celebrity look alike makeovers).

Cross market services with photographers, focusing on offers for graduation and weddings.

May is National Smile Month

Partner with a local dental practice for cooperative or cross marketing and/or include a consultation as part of pre-photography makeover package. For more smile-related promotions, see page 43 'Children's Dental Health Month' and page 49 'Tooth Fairy Day' ideas.

May Week-Long Observances

The First Week of May is Teacher Appreciation Week, and National Teacher's Day is in May

Every community in the U.S. has hundreds (if not thousands) of teachers (schools, music, dance, tutors, para-educators, etc.) living within its bounds. Create a "Teacher's Bonus" package loaded with pampering, stress-relieving, or make-my-life-easier extras for teachers (or even all employees) of your child's school or for all local public and private schools and other teaching professionals.

Seek nominations for a "Favorite Teacher" in your city. Reward the winner with a post-school-year or summer makeover and day of pampering. Send runners up prizes in the form of products or samples and extend a special offer to all entrants.

Send samples or a stickered 'Try Me' product tester to be placed in the break rooms of local schools along with a copy of your menu and a special offer or a discount code teachers can use in your salon to receive special pricing, add-on services or a salon or spa-branded tchotchke.

Use signage, your e-mail newsletter, scripting, etc., to let clients know that a gift card from your salon or spa would be a great way to thank their children's teachers, and don't forget to include music teachers, dance teachers, etc. in your suggestions; many studios will be in the final stages of preparing for spring recitals.

The Second Week of May is National Nurse's Week

Extend a special offer to nurses and/or to all of the employees of local hospitals, senior assisted living and nursing homes, and local medical practices.

Send samples or a stickered 'Try Me' product tester for placement in the Nurse's Lounge of local hospitals or care centers along with 'de-stressing' and pampering offers and a copy of your menu.

The Second Week of May is National Police Week

Extend a special offer or create an on-going program for members of the police force and their families.

The Third Week of May is Work-at-Home-Mom's Week

Extend a special offer or free gift-with-purchase to stay-at-home working moms (or any mom). Reach out to local chapters of M.O.P.S. (Mothers Of PreSchoolers) with a special offer or even to host meetings in your salon or spa. Send gift cards, product samples, special offers or branded tchotchkes to M.O.P.S. leaders and/or group members.

May Holidays and Observances

May 2, Melanoma Awareness Day / May 27, Sunscreen Day

Summer is almost here; educate employees and clients on the harmful and premature aging effects of the sun and how best to protect hair and skin. Design and purchase salon-branded, clever, cute or hot-messaged cover-ups, t-shirts or tank tops with messages about protecting the hair and skin. Purchase salon or spa-branded sunscreens for retail or sample sizes for gift-with-purchase, client thank you gifts and employee use.

May 5 is Cinco de Mayo

In honor of the 'Cinco' extend a $5 promotion to clients (such as $5 off every $50 spent in May on retail and/or services, or $5 off a specific service or product). Cinco de Mayo is also another great opportunity to partner with a local restaurant or bar for a special happy hour complete with cooperative or cross-marketed offers.

May 6 is Tourist Appreciation Day

Reach out to your city's tourism council to find out how to place an ad in local tourist guides. Create a marketing piece and special offer to place in local hotels, motels, restaurants, tourist stops and other points of interest. With wedding season coming up, out-of-town wedding guests might appreciate a special offer to help them freshen up from the road before the wedding.

The Second Sunday in May is Mother's Day

Promoting sales of gift cards and retail products suitable for Mother's Day gifts should be a priority for you and your staff beginning by the middle of March, since you may only see clients once between then and Mother's Day.

Mom and Me on Mother's Day: Partner with a local brunch spot (or hold an event in-salon via catering partner) and create "Mom and Me" gift packages which clients can purchase for themselves and a guest. Breakfast, lunch, or tea—create a bigger package by partnering with wine shops, tea shops, florists, gift boutiques, etc.

Partner with a retail boutique to create a Mom and Me fashion show event. Themes might include Mom and Me at vacation destinations with summer fashions, baby-themed Mom and Me parties with independent sellers or baby clothing and furniture stores, or Mom and Me fashions with styles for school-aged children. Bring out the "inner diva" in those that attend with free mini-makeovers or touch ups. Offer clients 10% off products used if purchased at the event. If you do not normally carry cosmetics, purchase a nail lacquer, lipstick, eyeshadow and/or other cosmetics displays for the event and for sale leading up to Mother's Day.

Moms as Queen for a Day: Have clients enter contact information for themselves plus a special woman in their lives and hold a drawing where winner/s will receive a "Queen for a Day" salon or spa package.

Turn this into an opportunity to provide a "Queen for a Day" experience to one or more needy members of your community. Draw public attention to your event and your cause through a press release and publication in your newsletter and on your salon web site, your Facebook page, your blog, etc.

Create Mother's Day gift packages that can be sold in pairs, one for the client and one for their mom, daughter, sister, aunt, or best friend as a buy-one, get-one prepaid, pre-booked service in May with the stipulation that the 2nd participant will be a guest who would be a new customer of your salon so that it gives you an opportunity to win a new client.

For more promotion and marketing ideas for Mother's Day, see the May Chapter of Volume I of 12 Months of Marketing for Salon and Spa .

May 17 is Pack Rat Day

Partner with a professional organizer to provide de-cluttering tips to clients or extend cross or cooperative marketing offers. Hold an in-salon seminar for clients on the reasons to, and simple, effective ways to simplify and de-clutter their lives.

Happy Employees are Engaged Employees!
May 18 is Pizza Party Day

Host a pizza party for employees, or partner with a local restaurant or caterer and gift pizza samples to clients all day long.

Sponsor a pizza party for the class of your winning teacher (for National Teacher's Day) or send pizzas over to the break room of a local school for teachers to enjoy, along with copies of your menu and a special bounce-back offer.

Or turn the tables and send a set of gift cards to your favorite local independently-owned pizza place for their employees and/or employee families' use.

May 20 is Employee Health and Fitness Day

Partner with a local gym to extend a special membership offer to your employees (and extend a special salon or spa offer to theirs). Invite a local fitness expert to attend your staff meeting and provide your employees with education and advice on health and fitness.

Throw in the Towel: May 25 is Towel Day

Summer is coming and with it, trips to the beach and the pool. Purchase salon-branded towels for retail, client gifts, gift-with-purchase, etc., and begin to send your brand out of the salon and into the community. Salon-branded towels can do double duty when used in the salon to help reinforce your brand at the back bar or in the chair. Purchase enough so that they can be included in client gift or contest prize baskets throughout the year.

Expand your retail by purchasing specialty hair drying, extra-absorbent, spa or boutique-quality towels for resale.

May Planning and Tasks

Select from manufacturer's bimonthly promotions to support June, July, and August retail and service promotions, contests and events. Purchase any items needed for bridal and graduation packages or Father's Day. With summer starting, consider adding summer skin care and impulse buy products like personalized or salon-branded sunscreen mini's and lip balms to your retail offerings. Remember to plan now for items and marketing materials needed for events and promotions going out for 6-8 weeks (all the way into August).

Plans for Mother's Day, Graduation and Bridal should be in the bag by now, and Father's Day planning should be finished by the beginning of May. Plan for June, July and August including events to prevent a summer slowdown. Begin planning for Back-to-School events and promotional packages.

Communicate in May

Items to include in your e-mail or print newsletter, web site, Facebook and blog posts and in direct mail communications this month:

- May-June Events and Promotions

- Mother's Day, Prom, Graduation, Father's Day, and Bridal packages, events and marketing partners

- Last chance for promotions expiring in May

- April winners, May contests

- Last minute openings on the books

- A spotlight product, service or staff member of the month

May Calendar / Suggested Communications and Tasks Schedule

SUN	MON	TUE	WED	THU	FRI	SAT
1st week of Month 1st of May—Merchandise for May 1st of May—Begin collecting entries for May contests						
		Order from manufacturers retail promotions for products to support June - July marketing plans; design related signage			Send May Newsletter with coupons, announce contests and winners, new products and services coming events, openings still on the books, events and promotions	
2nd week of Month						
		Order event supplies, postcards, collateral, gifts and salon-branded items for July–August contests			Write press releases for any events/results reporting or future events / charitable focus	
3rd week of Month						
If you have not yet begun, start promoting Father's Day gifts and gift certificates		Finalize, review and lay out plans for June - July - August promotions			Send May "last chance" promotions and openings on the books e-mail and/or direct mail	
4th week of Month Last day of May—Take down any May-only promotions Last day of May—Draw May contest winners						
		Order event supplies, postcards, collateral, gifts and salon-branded items for June-July contests			Send June focus e-mail / direct mail	

May Worksheets

$_____ Retail Sales Goal

Promotions_____

_____

_____

_____

_____

$_____ Avg. Retail/Client

$_____ Retail Sales Results

$_____ Service Sales Goal

Promotions_____

_____

_____

_____

_____

$_____ Avg. Service/Client

$_____ Service Sales Results

$_____ Event Revenues Goal

Events _____

_____

_____

_____

#_____ Attending Event/s

#_____ Apts/Booked at Event

$_____ Event/s Sales

$_____ Total Event/s Results

$_____ Charity/Fund Raising Goal

Charity Events _____

_____

_____

_____

_____

#_____ Attending Event/s

#_____ Apts/Booked at Event

$_____ Charity Event/s Sales

$_____ Total Charity Results

May Marketing Summary

Marketing Partners: _____

_____

_____

_____

Marketing Collateral Needed (or Used): _____

_____

_____

_____

Other Efforts:

#_____ Number of Clients New to Salon

%_____ Client Retention Rate (90 days)

Retention Efforts: _____

_____

or % _____ Clients Re-booked at Appointment

$_____ Gift Certificate Sales

#_____ Contacts added to marketing / e-mail database

june
make over
your retail

To be truly prepared to re-think your retail—prepared enough to consider making radical changes in order to become more profitable and become a resource for more clients and prospects—you may also need to be ready to let go of old ways of doing and thinking.

You may need to be willing to change the way that you select products, the way that you allow (or don't allow) people to stock their own retail at their individual stations and how much staff input to take into consideration or you may need to completely alter your approach to retail. And you need to be open to expanding your retail offerings beyond hair, skin and makeup products. It is up to you to redefine the way that you 'do' retail so that you can create a truly unique product offering that clients will not find at their local grocery, drug or big box store, or at any online outlet.

Why?

Because like it or not, your clients can get nearly any professional salon or spa product that you sell from online and mass retail outlets. And because when it comes to hair, nail, skin care, makeup or other products, you have to accept the fact there is little, if any, differentiation any more in the minds of clients relative to the superiority of products purchased in the salon.

In part, this is because your clients can now purchase products that used to be found exclusively in professional settings at their corner drugstore, grocery store, in the mall, and on the internet. While the salon or spa used to be the sole resource for so-called 'professional products,' this is no longer the case. Even so, many distributors and manufacturers are continuing to focus a significant amount of energy and resources telling salon and spa professionals that they will sell more retail by educating customers on the superiority of their product lines, while at the same time some of these same manufacturers are selling the very same lines in mass retail outlets.

As a salon or spa professional, you may be educating customers who then actually do turn around and purchase the very products you counseled them to buy—but do so in mass retail outlets, not in your salon or spa. As more and more professional products become available online and on the shelves of mass retailers, the strategy of educating clients as to the superiority of any manufacturer's professional products may result in sales of those products, but it will not necessarily mean that those retail dollars will be spent in the salon or spa.

As more products have found their way onto drugstore and grocery shelves, many within the industry who desire to fight diversion simplistically chalk it up to manufacturer's greed. While it's true that manufacturers can make additional profits by selling in retail outlets as well as in salons, it is not entirely accurate to assume that greed is the main reason or even the driving force behind this blurring of the lines. Yet many people within the industry hold this view and also still believe that diversion can be reversed through an outcry of protest by industry professionals to manufacturers, or even by cautioning customers that the products may be contaminated.

More is at play than greed; a revolution has already occurred that makes 'diversion' an inevitable and established fact. One of the consequences of steadily advancing technology and the ever-expanding resources available on the internet has been that consumers have access to nearly everything, nearly all of the time. And that is just what they—the consumers—demand, and expect. If they want to buy their favorite professional brand strengthening color-care shampoo and conditioner at 1:00 AM on a Sunday morning, rather than wait until 10 o'clock on Tuesday morning when your salon or spa is next open, then that is what they are going to do, and it is what they should be able to do. As consumers, they have the power of the dollar, and it should give them some say in how and when they make their purchases.

Does that mean that as salon and spa professionals, as true hair and skin care experts, that all of your retail product knowledge training and education was wasted and that you no longer have an obligation to educate clients about products? Absolutely not. Does it mean that educating clients about retail products won't bring some return in sales? No. This will still help to sell retail products. What it will not do is keep customers from buying more and more professional products from an ever-widening number of outlets.

What would your retail need to look like if it were going to actually capture the interest of customers?

Educating clients about products, and specifically about the products on your shelves, will continue to result in retail sales. And as your client's advocate (notice that I said you are the client's advocate, not the manufacturer's spokesperson) it is still one of your primary responsibilities to educate clients about the problems, conditions and needs of their hair, scalp, nails and skin. It is still your responsibility to caution clients against inferior products or products that would not be appropriate to meet their unique needs.

But you also need to be aware that your client will have access to the same products that you sell and to other products of equal quality from a variety of other stores, both local brick-and-mortar and virtual, or online stores. You need to be aware that your clients also have access to an unprecedented amount of information. They can and do research and fact-check the information that you share with them. They also have networks of friends and family spanning not just your community, but around the globe, who will also have a role to play in influencing their ultimate purchasing decisions—other people who may recommend a competing product over your own. Your clients may already be internet junkies who so love a product they first purchased from you that they want to order them 6 at a time, at a discount, with free 2-day shipping from a big-box online retailer.

Consumers have 24 hour a day, 7 day a week access to shopping outlets, product and industry information and the ability to enjoy instant buying gratification. Why shouldn't they? And countless retailers, both brick-and-mortar and on the internet, are competing to meet the demands and desires of these consumers.

Do companies (including product manufacturers) want to make a profit? Absolutely they do, don't you? But it is also true that the blurring of the lines—the availability of formerly professionally-sold products form an ever-increasing number of retail outlets—was an inevitability anyway, given the changing, growing demands of the educated consumer.

The question is *not* how to combat diversion.

The question is: How will you change *your* mind set when it comes to your retail? How can you make over your retail to restore it to the place of prominence it deserves to be, and the level of profit that you need it to be?

If you have thousands of dollars and a significant amount of floor space tied up in retail that isn't moving, should you be carrying the retail that you are carrying? Should you be carrying retail at all, or would that space become more profitable by being converted to service? Are you ready to completely re-think your retail?

Providing superior, exclusive, professional products can no longer be your sole approach to retail. I believe that salons and spas can still do a significant amount of business selling retail products, but with the reality of diversion, I believe that the salons and spas that will be successful selling retail products in the future will approach retail sales with an entirely new mind set.

First, some good news: If the lines are blurred in one direction, they are also blurred back the other way. What I mean is that it's time to re-think and transform your retail, expanding it to include more than just the professional products traditionally sold in salons and spas.

Instead of thinking that your retail center should be composed of one or more manufacturer's product lines, begin to think about what your retail would need to offer in order to actively engage your customer's minds and emotions. Imagine having a retail center that actively drew your customers to itself and took them on an intellectually and emotionally provocative visual journey; a retail gift center filled with products, tools, and other items that truly scream, "Give me!" when it comes to choosing gifts for clients friends, co-workers, or family. Because, let's be honest, does shampoo really scream "Give me!" as a gift-giving option all on its own? Imagine a retail center that brought new customers in to your business all on its own, giving you the opportunity to win a new service client.

One of the basic rules for success in business is this: Make it easy—almost *painfully-obviously easy*—for a shopper to buy from you. A line up of products, floor to ceiling, with nothing more to differentiate them from one another than a few shelf talkers, is not designed to spur sales, to engage the customer, or to be suggestive of gift ideas. If this essentially describes your current retail center, then plan on doing a lot of dusting.

If you are ready to re-think your retail, you must stop thinking of it as a professional products collection, and you must start thinking about it from the standpoint of a truly unique, boutique gift shop. Consider the following scenarios:

Scene 1: After receiving a haircut at your salon, your client walks through your retail area to the reception desk where there is a small counter display with pink nail polish and lip gloss. While paying the customer is asked, "Is there anything else that you need?" to which they reply, "No, thanks," and leave.

Scene 2: The same client arrives for their haircut and while walking past the retail area to reception, they come within arms' reach of a small round table covered by a pink cloth with a beautiful display built up on it that features mesh-bagged gift sets that each hold pink nail polish, lip gloss, branded over-sized custom nail file, a gift certificate and a glam pink or black bag with a small notebook and pink pen. A large sign at eye-level height proclaims, "Your Daughter's Top 10 Pink Picks for Prom" or "Pre-Teen Sleepover Package" or "Pretty in Pink, Perfect for any Princess!" Client number 2 suddenly remembers that her daughter is hosting 6 girls for a sleep over and will need goodie bags, or that her niece's birthday is coming up on the weekend or that her daughter and her daughter's two best friends are going to be getting ready for prom together—or a similarly appropriate upcoming event.

All the client has to do in the second scenario is pick up one (or several) of these pre-packaged gift sets. Not only have you just increased your retail sales, you've increased the overall dollar amount of your retail sales potential by expanding your retail to include the items needed to turn "products" into "gifts." Not only have you just solved a problem for your client and saved them time and effort they would have needed to shop elsewhere, you have also expanded your role in their minds.

If you don't see your retail as a gift shop, why should your customers?

So the next time they need a great gift for a girl, your salon or spa may be one of the *first* places they stop for a suitable solution. And you can use this concept to help support any type of promotion or reach any market you want to reach:

Do you want to sell more men's grooming products?

- Studies show that (in general) men shop differently than women. In general, men like to shop with purpose and brevity. The more simple and direct you can be in creating displays and messaging, the better.

- Tell them exactly which products they should buy depending on their hair, skin or grooming needs; and go a step further in pre-packing products into grooming sets for them.

- Incentivize purchases of individual or bundled men's product/tool packages with promotional items like nail care kits, golf balls (why not salon-branded golf balls, or golf balls with a design or a clever 'manly' message?) golf tees, money clips, bottle openers, salon-branded tape measures, t-shirts—there are so many possibilities!

- Expand your retail and make sure that your "must have" men's shopping list and displays include the small electric tools men need for a great shave or beard trimming.

- Research shows that women are still buying most of men's grooming and care products on their behalf; gear messaging to appeal to this decision-maker.

Do you want to sell more makeup?

- Purchase a glittery clutch, purse or tote and load it with the products clients will need for a night out, like a smoldering lipstick, shimmering metallic eye shadows needed to create the perfect smoky eye, mascara, branded travel toothbrush and floss, branded brush or comb and a gift certificate to a local restaurant, comedy club or other destination. (For the gift certificate, partner with a local restaurant, club, etc., for a joint package or purchase gift cards from them at a reduced rate to resell or package for your clients.)

- Set up a skin bar in your salon or spa or hold a Skin Bar happy hour so that clients can really experiment with products and learn from you how to apply them, so that they can recreate that "just out of the salon look" at home.

Do you want to cater to large groups of employees, like teachers or students?

- Create a specially-priced school year makeover haircut and color that delivers low-maintenance and easy styling and a scheduled re-booking package at the same rate for the school year. Generously incentivize referrals.

- Create a special reward program for teachers (or all school employees). Create exclusive add-ons, events, offers and promotions for educators.

- Incentivize patronage with salon or spa-branded gifts or branded practical items like sewing kits, nail kits, red pens, highlighters, dry erase markers or sharpies, post-it note pads, teacher-saying notebooks, pens, etc.; and fashionable tote bags so they can take supplies to the classroom in style.

Every promotion you purchase from a manufacturer, every holiday, and every market that you want to target provides you with an opportunity to expand your retail beyond traditional salon and spa products so that you can turn your business into a true gift center, become a better resource, and create a bigger role for your business in the lives of your clients.

Add non-product retail items to your inventory; in particular, add items that can help turn your products and gift certificates into *true* gifts, with items like greeting cards, gift bags, gift baskets and other presentation ware. Add items that are branded to your salon and spa in order to extend your brand beyond your walls and out into the community with your customers.

Don't try to compete with drug stores and mass retailers! This is an opportunity for you to stand out, not blend in. Add items that are boutique-quality, one-of-a-kind, zany, très chic—you get it!

Do your clients even know that you have gift cards?

You know that your gift cards make great gifts, but how do you make sure that your clients share this realization? You can communicate and reinforce the message visually (and here is that basic tenet of marketing again!), making it *painfully obvious* to your clients by staging gift certificates or gift cards on displays right along with greeting cards (thank you cards, birthday cards, congratulations cards, secretary's day cards—you get the idea).

- Put gift certificates or gift cards on display, right in front of that gift set display featuring your night-out makeup kit, evening clutch, spa basket, or book tote.

- Put gift cards on display with your men's grooming products and travel or gym bag. Pair with gloves and lotion to soothe dry skin during the winter.

- Display gift cards along with gloves and polish for gardeners to preserve that manicure!

- Pair it with polishes and salon-branded flip flops, towel and beach tote for a summer manicure, pedicure or waxing package.

- Use gift cards to incentivize your clients to refer friends to your salon or to bring them along to your events like evening makeup and hair demos, skin bars, fashion shows, bridal or holiday fairs.

While you are re-thinking your retail with fresh eyes and an open mind, in order to create the perception in the minds of your clients that your salon or spa is a true gift center, you have to view your retail as an actual gift shop and not just a place to maybe sell a few hair, makeup or skin care products at the end of an appointment.

The last thing you want is for your clients to stand in front of your shelves with a feeling of indifferent déjà vu (or just walk right past them) because there is no difference in their minds between what you have to sell and what they can purchase at their corner drug store. Yet all too often, this is the perception of your customer.

As industry professionals, you know that what you offer is *different* and *better* than what is available to your clients at the drug or grocery store. You have spent thousands of dollars on introductory product packages, you have purchased seasonal and bi-monthly promotions, you have a stack of gift certificates gathering dust behind the counter—all ready and waiting for your clients to realize just how much better your products are, and how much better the services are that they receive in your salon or spa. Meanwhile, your clients have walked in and back out, sometimes pausing to see what you have on the shelf (more often, not) and with even less frequency, occasionally buying themselves one of their favorite, familiar products.

You are only one small degree of separation away from the daughters, moms, sisters, dads, sons, brothers, friends, neighbors and co-workers of your clients. Just think about how many hundreds, no, thousands of prospective clients are represented by this one small degree of separation! Yet only rarely do your clients —who have a full calendar of birthdays, anniversaries, weddings, promotions, recitals, graduations, dinner parties, and a myriad of other events for which to purchase gifts—do so from your salon or spa. Rarely, if ever, has it occurred to your clients that a gift set and certificate from your salon or spa would be a perfect and convenient gift choice. And in fact, I will go even further and suggest that even when your clients do choose spa gift baskets for gift giving, they are probably purchasing them from the local mall or drug store.

Why?
I'm so glad you asked!

They do so because those retailers have made it painfully, obviously easy for them to do so. They have a larger mind-share when it comes to gift-giving in the minds of your clients. They have created the impression that they are the best resource for gift selection. They have out-marketed, out-displayed, out-merchandised and out-messaged you. Unlike these stores, which clients only visit out of choice, you are practically guaranteed to see your regular clients once every six to eight weeks (or even more frequently); so why are *you* letting this happen?

Whether it's the mall or the drugstore, spa basket gift options are all under one roof from the baskets to the products to the greeting cards, tissue paper and the bows, aromatherapy products, candles, spa robes and slippers, chocolates, polishes and more; these other retailers have made it *easy* and *efficient* for people to buy from them.

Get the point? Why would clients view the hair or skin products on your retail shelves and gift certificates you have hidden behind the counter as a legitimate gift option in light of the competition for gift mind-share? Why would they view your line up of hair, skin or makeup products as anything other than an occasional personal self-indulgence?

What have you done to show them, to make it painfully obvious to them, that you have so much more to offer?

And back to my original point, what are you doing to make sure that you actually do have more to offer? If you are losing ground in retail profits to diversion as well as to the competition of other retailers, then maybe it's time to re-think what your product *is*.

Ideas for June Promotions

June's marketing messages and promotions need to be focused on showing your clients how much more you have to offer, and how much more the products that you carry do for them than products they can purchase anywhere else. Demonstrate and then communicate to them that you have the ability to create a unique retail and gift center.

June Month-Long Observances

Sweeten Up Your Retail: June is National Candy Month

Partner with a local candy shop or chocolatier for cross and cooperative marketing to clients; purchase salon-branded candies or chocolates for client gifts or retail.

Send salon-branded candies along with business cards, copies of your menu of services and a 'sweet offer' to the teachers of local schools, residents of local senior living centers, or to be distributed to new home buyers by local realtors.

Treat clients to candy goodie bags at appointments or send them home for kids.

June is Adopt a Shelter Cat Month

Hold a benefit event or donate a portion of sales to a local animal shelter; partner with your local shelter to facilitate pet adoptions. Retail cat "bling" collars, bowls, toys or other items. For several more ideas on adding retail products for pet lovers and promotions designed to attract them, read the September Chapter of the first volume of 12 Months of Marketing for Salon and Spa.

June Week-Long Observances

The First Week of June is National Sun Safety Week

Sell spa or salon-branded sunscreen, lip balm with SPF, sunglasses, cover-ups, or design a message t-shirt or tank top to promote client education about products that contain sunscreen and protective properties for hair and skin. Promote safe-tanning alternatives and retail products.

The Second Week of June is Auto Service Professional's Week

Extend a special offer to staff (and their family members) of local auto repair and car sales organizations. Or cross market with local automobile sales businesses. This industry is predominantly represented by males; extend your Father's Day offers to this group as well.

The Third Week of June is 'Meet a Mate' Week

Remember the 'Insignificant Other' events and promotions you ran in February? This is the perfect week to hold a 2nd event titled "The Best Guy (or Girl) I Never Married" mixer. Partner with a local restaurant or bar for this event, include ice-breakers and pre-event makeover appointments.

Invite a local counselor to hold a workshop or series of group events for single clients who want to hone up their dating skills to improve their social lives.

Send a special offer to members of local "Events and Adventures" types of adult social groups. Send gift cards to the organization's staff. Hold a drawing for a pre-event or pre-adventure makeover. Gift spa or salon-branded tchotchkes or product samples to club members or staff members.

June Holidays and Observances

June 1 is National Go Barefoot Day

What a perfect day to promote pedicure, manicure and waxing services! Create a series package to offer at the beginning of the summer season to carry clients through until fall with healthy, silky, smooth and beautifully adorned nails, hands, feet and skin.

Host a beginning-of-summer fashion show with a boutique clothing or gift store or with an independent jewelry seller featuring bracelets, rings and anklets. Invite both sets of clients and promote and demonstrate summer manicure / pedicure / waxing series services. Set up a display and sell bracelets, rings and anklets on an on-going basis, with changing displays for the seasons.

Hold a seminar at a local senior living community and share information on proper hand and foot care; this demographic needs specialty care in this area. Ask your manufacturer or distributor for samples that can be gifted at the event, or used for demonstrating services. Take bookings at the event, or if appropriate, work with the senior living center to provide mobile manicure/pedicure services at the retirement community on set days.

Make summertime easier for at least one of your clients by holding a drawing for free manicure, pedicure and/or waxing services.

Extend a buy one, get one (percentage or dollars off) or reward customers with a free bracelet or anklet when a client brings a friend (new to salon) at the same time for a manicure or pedicure appointment.

Purchase spa or salon-branded flip-flops for clients to buy or give away as a gift-with-purchase incentive for clients to wear at the beach, the pool, or in their neighborhood this summer to extend your brand beyond the walls of your business.

June 6 is National Yo-Yo Day

Purchase salon or spa-branded Yo-Yos for retail or gift-with-purchase for clients. Gift branded Yo-Yos to the team you are sponsoring through parks and recreation or as an end-of-year gift to the students in your child's school or class, or to the students of local teachers or music or dance teachers you have honored in the past.

June 8 is Best Friend's Day

Create a special offer for clients to buy-one, get-one (service, gift certificate, etc.) at a percentage or dollars off when they book an appointment for themselves and their best friend (when their best friend is someone new to your salon).

Create a special best friend's ice cream social or happy hour to demo summer hair, nails or makeup how-to plus summer care and/or color consultations while giving mini-manicures and pedicures to best friend duos.

June 15 is Smile Power Day

Continue building cross and cooperative marketing relationships with local dental practices and promote Smile Power Day.

Purchase salon or spa-branded toothbrushes, floss, lip balms or private label lip glosses for distribution at the dental practice in support of a beautiful smile, along with a bounce-back offer from your salon or spa.

See page 43 "Children's Dental Health Month" and page 49 "Tooth Fairy Day" for more smile-powered promotion ideas.

June 16 is Fresh Veggies Day

Chances are there is a Farmer's Market or another city street type of market that meets in your community. Extend your influence into the community by taking a booth and demonstrating easy summer hair, makeup styles, manicures, pedicures, skin care or massages and book appointments for your salon or spa. Hold a drawing for passers-by (so that you can collect contact information) and award prizes including gift cards, one or two of your best-selling retail products plus any of the salon or spa-branded goodies you have been purchasing during the year. Extend a bounce-back offer to all entrants and be sure that contacts are added to your communications database.

The Third Sunday in June is Father's Day

Purchase special items to add to your retail offerings specifically for men during the month prior to Father's Day (and plan to sell those that do well again during the holidays).

If your regular and/or 'ideal' client base is primarily female, create Father's Day promotions designed to market to women the products they should purchase for their special men. If your salon caters to a significant male base, or men are one of your primary target markets, utilize gifts-with-purchase and buy one, get one type of promotions to encourage clients to refer more men to your spa or salon. Create special Father's Day gift baskets with men's favorite products, gift cards, and other gift goodies.

Create Father's Day gift packages that will be meaningful to your bottom line as well as to recipients. Pre-sell a package of 8 haircuts at a discount of $3 each to be used by December 31st (or 4 haircuts to be used by October 15th). You will be creating a pattern of frequent re-booking, keeping your books full and giving a practical gift that practical men will appreciate. Increase the value of the package by adding a men's retail product duo in gift bag (which you should also have for sale at point of purchase and stylists stations). Even if you have mainly female clientele, you can still create retail gift baskets including products for men such as shaving, scalp, and skin care products and gift certificates. While sales of men's grooming and other personal care products have increased exponentially over the last decade, the vast majority of male grooming products are still being purchased on their behalf by women.

Gather male client contacts (female clients can enter their dads, husbands, brothers, sons, etc.) and at the end of June, draw a winner for a free daddy-daughter or father-son haircut in July. Send a men's grooming package offer (such as buy 3, get 1 free, or take $3 off haircuts re-booked in 3 weeks) to all entries.

Partner with a local sports bar or sports activities facility and create gift certificate duos that include service at your salon and a round of golf, game of bowling, bucket of balls at the driving range or batting cage, etc. Partner with a local sportsman's club or retailer and create a package with hunting or sporting goods (or gift certificate) as well as men's skin care products and gift certificates.

June 24 is Swim a Lap Day

Send a list of tips to your community pool that they can post on bulletin boards or include on their web sites or newsletters to tell their patrons how to care for their hair or skin during the summer in light of extra time spent outdoors, at the beach, or at the pool. Provide samples of hair and skin moisture-restorative retail products for distribution in their locker rooms along with a bounce-back offer for your salon.

Don't forget that many hotels have pools too, and pass summer, swimming and travel hair and skin care tips on for their guests as well as product samples and service offers.

June 27 is Sunglasses Day

Sunglasses could be a natural, stylish and fun product to add to your retail gift and product mix in the summer and year-round. Work with a promotional products or other wholesale provider to obtain a countertop or stand-alone sunglasses retail display. Purchase spa or salon-branded sunglasses for client (or employee) appreciation gifts, to gift-with-purchase, for retail sale, and to include with client prize packages.

Extend the brand of your salon beyond your walls and promote your services everywhere your clients go. Purchase branded impulse buy items for summer like sunscreen minis, lip balm, tank tops, hats, water bottles, flip-flops, towels, cover-ups, sun umbrellas, nail files and more for client purchase, gift-with-purchase, add-ons or client thank you gifts.

Make sure that you and your staff are wearing branded t-shirts and tank tops this summer. Salon-branded apparel can also be great thank-you gifts for your best clients!

June Planning and Tasks

Select from manufacturer's promotions for items to enhance your marketing plans for July, August, and September including July 4th, Summer, Back-to-School, and other promotions going out for the next 6-8 weeks (all the way into August).

Double check supplies and purchase any final items needed for Father's Day, Graduation or Bridal/Wedding Party promotions.

Set aside time and lay out your marketing plan for the remainder of summer, including Back-to-School promotions. With the economy in its current state, parents among your clientele may value family packages for multiple cuts and family-sized products in advance of summer vacations and the Back-to-School season in August.

Remember that the Back-to-School student market is made up both of local students in need of cuts, styles, makeovers and retail products and with students who will be going away for college (who might appreciate liter sizes of their favorite products to take along, or care packages during the year).

For an extensive review of the Back-to-School Market and ideas on how to market to teachers, parents and students of local schools, read the 'Back-to-School Market' segment in the August chapter beginning on page 166.

Communicate in June

Items to include in your e-mail or print newsletter, web site, Facebook and blog posts and in direct mail communications this month:

- June-July events and promotions
- Father's Day gift certificates, packages and products, Graduation and Bridal services, family vacation or reunion makeovers
- Summer hair color trends and conditioning products—those locks are going to get dry, lightened, brightened and damaged, so tell clients how to keep hair healthy all summer long
- New products, last chance for promotions expiring in June
- A spotlight product, service or staff member of the month

June Calendar / Suggested Communications and Tasks Schedule

SUN	MON	TUE	WED	THU	FRI	SAT
1st week of Month 1st of June—Merchandise for June 1st of June—Begin collecting entries for June contests						
		Order signage, event supplies and promotional materials for July - August promotions			Send June Newsletter with coupons, announce contests and winners, new products and services coming events, openings still on the books, events and promotions	
2nd week of Month						
		Order in gifts, salon-branded items, impulse buy and other items for July-August			Write press releases for any events/results reporting or future events / charitable focus	
3rd week of Month						
		Finalize, review and lay out plans for July - August - September promotions, including Back-to-School			Send June "last chance" promotions and openings on the books e-mail and/or direct mail	
4th week of Month Last day of June—Take down any June-only promotions Last day of June—Draw June contest winners						
		Order event supplies, postcards, gifts and salon-branded items needed for August promotions			Send July focus e-mail / direct mail	

June Worksheets

$_____ Retail Sales Goal

Promotions_____

_____

_____

_____

_____

$_____ Avg. Retail/Client

$_____ Retail Sales Results

$_____ Service Sales Goal

Promotions_____

_____

_____

_____

_____

$_____ Avg. Service/Client

$_____ Service Sales Results

$_____ Event Revenues Goal

Events _____

_____

_____

_____

_____

#_____ Attending Event/s

#_____ Apts/Booked at Event

$_____ Event/s Sales

$_____ Total Event/s Results

$_____ Charity/Fund Raising Goal

Charity Events _____

_____

_____

_____

_____

#_____ Attending Event/s

#_____ Apts/Booked at Event

$_____ Charity Event/s Sales

$_____ Total Charity Results

June Marketing Summary

Marketing Partners: _____

_____

_____

_____

Marketing Collateral Needed (or Used): _____

_____

_____

_____

Other Efforts:

#_____ Number of Clients New to Salon

%_____ Client Retention Rate (90 days)

 Retention Efforts: _____

_____

or % _____ Clients Re-booked at Appointment

$_____ Gift Certificate Sales

#_____ Contacts added to marketing / e-mail database

july
make over
your merchandising

Although closely related to the subject of retail as discussed in the previous chapter, the subject of merchandising deserves attention of its own. Now that you have begun to think about your retail in terms of what it takes to change the perception and truly capture the interest of your clients, you also need to make over your approach to how and where you can put your business—as well as your retail products—on display.

"Try me!"

If you are the primary grocery buyer for your household, you may have experienced a certain phenomenon; normally, no one will go along to keep you company when you shop, but weekends? Of course!

If you have frequented a big box retailer on a weekend you have observed (and probably enjoyed) sampling in action. How many times have you gone home with something you would not otherwise have purchased because of sampling?

There is a reason that big box retailers and product sponsors spend a small fortune on additional personnel costs as well as product costs in nationwide sampling promotions: It sells stuff. And what's more, it works as a means of gaining new customers for the short and in the long term.

If sampling did not result in profits for the manufacturer and the retailer, it would have been discontinued long ago. Instead, on any given weekend in a big box store, hardly an aisle remains free of an end-cap with a staffed sampling station. A tiny little bite size snack has the power to draw people into the store, and it has the power to generate product sales.

And don't miss the part where sponsors are willing to spend a lot of extra money in manpower; they don't just set out samples at the end of the aisle, nor do they just hand them out silently as you pass by. Nope. They spend the extra money, take up valuable space and sometimes even create irritating traffic jams in their own aisles in order to set up a personal, interactive experience—for you.

The individuals who staff these stations are trained and verbally armed with enough information about the product to sound like a product expert and an advocate, seemingly a regular user-purchaser-consumer, themselves. The attendant can tell you what the benefits are, about the ingredients, sometimes even about the manufacturing company. They tell you how good they think it is or why their husband loves it or how great it tastes or how it cleans or why you need the vitamins that are in it—in other words, they make not only a sales pitch but also a personal recommendation and endorsement.

They are doing exactly what beauty industry experts, magazines, manufacturers, distributors, educators and platform artists tell *you* to do all the time. They are doing exactly what you have probably encouraged your staff to do and what you may have even scripted and rehearsed in role-play scenarios during your staff meetings.

They are giving you a chance to try a product while they talk to you in a natural way about the product. They are "selling" to you.

This is something that you have multiple opportunities to do with your clients organically during every given appointment; but are you?

Even apart from setting out "Try Me" stickered testers and samples, are you actually talking about the products that you are—literally—sampling onto each client during their appointment? Do you tell clients what you love about a given product? What your spouse or kids or parents love about a given product? What your best friend thinks about it? What the last customer loved about it?

Why are you so afraid to talk about something you are willing to spend a fortune on?

Why are you so reluctant to tell clients about the good that the products you invest thousands of dollars in, reserve valuable floor space for and choose, prescriptively, to use on them is doing for them?

Can you imagine your doctor giving you a sample medicine or lotion but not telling you why they chose and administered that product to you, not giving you instructions for use, and not telling you what it would do for you? What problem it would solve? What condition it would relieve or improve? That is exactly what you are doing when you use professional products on your client's hair or skin without telling them what you are using, why you chose it, how it should be used and what they can expect when they use it at home.

"But wait!" I can just hear you saying,
"I thought you were going to talk about merchandising!"

How you present your merchandise verbally (whether referring to products, your skills, your experience—anything that you want the client to accept or 'buy') is one of the most powerful forms of merchandising that you have.

After all, what other form of merchandising is more important than the words of someone who is an expert at handling and using a product, who understands the benefits it provides, the quality of its ingredients, secondary benefits like SPF protection, vitamins and anti-oxidants or aroma-therapeutic traits—what piece of literature or signage, what counter top display or shelf talker is more powerful than your words? Nothing!

Verbalizing about the products you are using at the back bar or behind the chair (or on the massage table, etc.,) can, and should be, a very natural part of the way in which you provide services to customers. The last thing you want is to sound like a sales person; in fact, it's the fear of sounding like a stereotypical salesman that keeps many stylists and estheticians from talking about the very products that they know, beyond the shadow of a doubt, would be the most beneficial for their clients.

It's like you are trying to teach a cooking class and you also happen to carry all of the ingredients needed for each recipe for sale in your business. But because you are afraid to sound like a salesman, you don't tell your students what you are putting into the mix. As crazy as that sounds, isn't that what you are doing when you create a look that the client loves, but you don't tell them exactly which products and tools they need to 'make it' at home themselves?

Maybe you are not afraid to dialogue with your clients about products, but you really believe (and justifiably so) that your clients are in your care to escape and relax for a moment of personal indulgence, and that talking about products disrupts the experience.

Whatever is holding you back, you have to realize that until your customers hear and truly believe the depth of your convictions when it comes to the products you choose for them, based on your education and experience, they will not believe in them, either. And if you withhold product endorsements, you can appear ambivalent and neutral about the products you use. When the transfer of product knowledge is omitted from the customer experience, you leave the impression that products are actually an unimportant component of their overall experience.

Yes, they know you used shampoo and conditioner at the back bar. And they know that you emulsified something in your hands and then applied it to their hair prior to blow drying. And then you used something else when you pieced out their fringe, just before you sprayed some sort of finishing shine or holding product that had a great fragrance compared to what they are using at home. Your customers might have noticed fragrances and bottle colors...

        ...and when they are standing at the drug store trying to find similar products to use to recreate their look at home, they will try really hard to do a good job picking out replacements.

Why are they at the drug store? Because you did not tell them what was special about the products that you used—you remember, those products you spent thousands of dollars to obtain and invested hundreds of hours to learn how, when and why to use them.

They are at the drug store because they don't know.

They don't know, because no part of their customer experience was specially-designed to make them consciously interact with your products. They loved the way they looked when they walked out of the salon, but they did not know the importance of the products that you used, *because you did not tell them.*

In Volume I of 12 Months of Marketing for Salon and Spa, I said that relying on a passive, unintentional marketing strategy (like waiting and hoping that the phone will ring or that products will sell themselves) is an "accidental marketing" strategy. Doing nothing, yet hoping, inexplicably, that good results will nonetheless occur.

Do you know what makes **your** products better?

Your customers don't, because **you** aren't telling them!

Hoping that customers will intuitively understand how passionate you are about the professional products and tools that you use, in the absence of intentional activities and words on your part, is "accidental merchandising" at best. Non-existent merchandising might be a more accurate term.

It's like being a die-hard sports fan but never wearing your team colors, never cheering for your team or defending their honor with your words when rivals are around. If you never talk about your favorite team, can you really say that you are a fan?

And let's carry this analogy further. Within sports teams, players all have different roles to play and possess different strengths, specialties and skills. It's the same with the professional products and tools you use during the course of services and sell in your salon or spa.

It is your job to tell the story of your 'team' of products in your merchandising. Not all players are high-profile stars, but they all have a role to play. Some of them work behind the scenes to set things up for other players. Some take a leading role. Some help to defend and protect. Some add glitz and glamour, some sparkle and shine.

Now that you are convinced and ready to start showing off your products, remember that your merchandising, too, must be done from a client-centric point of view. This means more than telling a client what you used, it means communicating specifically how a product benefits the client, how it fulfills a need of the client, how it meets a desire of the client. Any messaging that does not speak to the wants, needs, and good *of the client* is a wasted message.

Even when you are promoting your staff or your own business, you should do so in a way that relates to the client. For instance, rather than making a you-centered statement like: "our stylists receive continuous education to keep their skills current," you might say, "you (the client) wanted textured, weightless cuts (or color to die for, younger looking skin, the perfect smoky eye, etc.) and so we learned <x, y, or z> and now we have just what you need right now! Book today for..."

In other words, your client spoke, and you listened. And not only did you listen, but you spent your own money and time to make it happen, for them. You made an investment in order to have something more valuable to provide to them.

In general, clients probably do not care that your stylists just took an advanced red hair color class; many of them don't want red hair, and they would be terrified of the idea. What they do want to know is that your stylists received advanced training in how to make *their* hair color—whatever that is—look better and last longer.

Most of them do not care that a manufacturer blends technology with natural products; they want to know what that marriage does for them. They want to know that a product will make *their* skin, hair, or nails healthier. They want to know what a given product does *for them*, *specifically*, not how it benefits people in general. And they certainly don't care how it benefits your business or that of the manufacturer!

Take a look at the manufacturer and distributor literature you received this month. How much of the language speaks about the specific benefits products bring to the client? This is the language that should be transferred to your verbal and visual merchandising.

Benefits speak louder than discounts; plus, discounts are boring. Discounting is old—it's been done to death! Since the onset of the recession, all we have heard from retailers is how much they are discounting the regular pricing of products.

While price can be a key determinant in a purchase, it is not the healthiest determinant with which you can create promotions. Why? Because they dilute your profits, lessening your ability to serve your clients and grow your business. And because deep discounts may spur occasional sales but they do nothing to drive the loyalty of the customer to your products or to your business.

Benefits do.

Instead of saying, "Back-to-School Savings" on liters purchased during the summer, say that products are high-performing and concentrated, and tell them what the value of the liters represent to them in terms of lasting longer and working better. Tell customers how it combats damage done by summer sun. That it lets them go an extra day without shampooing, that it helps their color last days or even weeks longer. That it washes out fast, goes on fast, holds all day—that the value of the product is greater than its cost in the long run and compared to other products. That these products will take extra-special care of the customer when they are too busy to take good care of themselves. That these products that will give college students a touch of home to combat homesickness (or that may even remind them to call home!) every time they use it.

The driving philosophy behind your merchandising should be to make it painfully obvious to your clients what they should buy, why they should buy it, how they should use it, and to make it incredibly easy for them to do so. Take all of the guess work out of your merchandising!

Don't tell clients that something would make a great gift, tell them who the product would make a great gift for, and what else they should include in the gift and then add, "oh, by the way, isn't it great that we have it all right here, ready to go, along with the gift card (gift wrap, greeting card, etc.)."

Merchandising is not signage and merchandising is not shelf talkers. Merchandising is not even a beautiful display. Merchandising is the art of creating an irresistible desire for something in the mind of the customer, and doing so in a way that makes it as easy as possible for the customer to obtain it. Take a look around your salon or spa; does any of your merchandising work to do this?

It is not about lining up products on a shelf; it's about displaying products in such a way that the customer is irresistibly drawn to them and provoked to pick them up and take them home. Like seeing puppies in a store window, good merchandising goes beyond the simple shelf talker that speaks about a product; good merchandising has the power to draw a customer all the way across the room, because it screams out a message that is important *to the client*.

In addition to clear, customer-centric messaging, effective merchandising is also characterized by repetition and consistency across channels. In this era of constant marketing bombardment, your client may need to see or hear a message ten times or more in order to remember it. This is why it is imperative for you to develop a system for and the habit of using all of your marketing channels to help reinforce your marketing messages, and you need to use this system consistently across all of your channels of communication.

Although we have not talked about branding, this is one of its most powerful strategies: Telling clients "who you are" in all of your marketing channels in a way that seems genuine when the customer compares what you say with their experiences at any and all touch points of your business.

Cohesion and **consistency** is power.

In the context of merchandising, this means that you will use the same imagery and fonts on your postcards, in your e-mail newsletter and on your in-house displays and shelf talkers—everywhere you are communicating a message to your clients. The more they are reminded of a message you are trying to send through repetitive, consistent direct and indirect visual and auditory cues, the more that your message will resonate with them and become part of their conscious mind and active memory.

The oft-cited logo imagery of the Coca Cola Company is an obvious example of a company that has stuck with certain iconic components with the result that you can pick out a Coke or any Coca Cola ad anywhere in the world. Their curvy bottles and old fashioned script in its unmistakable red is recognizable in any language.

This should be your goal when it comes to the advertising, marketing and merchandising you do; that customers and members of your community should be able to instantly recognize that they are receiving a marketing message *from you* whenever they see one. And when your messages are consistent across channels (print, electronic, logo, signage, etc.) then you will be more likely to break through the barrage of advertising messages you compete with every day.

This brings me to the subject of your brand, itself. 'Free' collateral provided by your manufacturer or distributor is unlikely to do anything to merchandise you as a professional and your salon or spa to your customers since it will be strictly representative of the product lines that you sell. While it's true that you want your customers to know you are the source for their favorite products, if that is where your value exists to the customer, what happens when a line changes, or when you want to bring in a new retail line? Your goal should be to establish your business and your services as the valuable resource for your clients, regardless of which manufacturer's product lines you carry.

I know that seems contradictory to earlier in this same chapter when you were encouraged to talk about your products specifically and prescriptively, but the two are not mutually exclusive. Discussing professional product benefits, usage directions, and the results clients can expect through use helps to build *your role* as their expert. Using manufacturer's signage to help promote product knowledge can be helpful, but any collateral that primarily promotes *the manufacturer's company* (rather than yours) is not helping to build the power that your brand has in the minds of your clients. It's building mind share for the manufacturer, *not you*.

While free collateral is—well, free, you should spend the additional time and money needed to create your own signage for retail areas, your point of purchase, station talkers, and especially for any communication piece that goes outside of your salon or spa (like postcards, flyers, business cards, rewards cards, appointment cards, etc.) All of your collateral should look, sound, and "feel" like you want your brand to feel. When a client sees something from your salon, they should connect it with your business first and foremost, rather than any product line that you carry.

The reason why is obvious; you want your clients to view *you* as their primary hair (or skin, nail, massage, makeup, etc.) resource, not the manufacturer. You want your client to be aligned with you and remain loyal to you in the event of a product change, not follow the product line to another retail outlet. Plus, if your client views you as the expert, they are more likely to buy their products from you even when the product lines you carry are available to them from other retail and online stores. It is your expertise that they need, not the manufacturer's product.

All of your merchandising should include your company name and logo, even those used inside the salon or spa. You can further extend the mind share that you have with clients (mind share is the conscious or subconscious awareness of you and your brand in the minds of your clients) by purchasing branded tools, equipment and supplies (such as your back bar towels, your capes or aprons, tool belts, counter tool holders and stands, chairs, pillows, table coverings, etc.)

Before you dismiss this idea as overkill, go into your local McDonalds (a company that already has huge mind share) or Starbucks, Ben & Jerry's, or another chain. See how many items, signs, retail merchandise and other "stuff" you can find with the company name or logo on it. How about the colors? If all the words were removed, you would still be able to guess whether you were in any one of those businesses because the colors themselves would be a giveaway. All of these companies are competing for mind share despite the fact that they already have incredible brand awareness. You probably have only one location; how much more important is it for you to establish your logo and brand in the minds of clients in order to gain brand awareness?

If it is important for your name and logo to be part of your internal merchandising, there can be no question that it is absolutely vital that any and all of the communications that occur outside of your salon or spa should be branded. Plus, any piece of collateral that will be distributed outside of your salon or spa (or distributed inside the salon or spa with the likelihood of leaving with a client or prospective customer) must include your business name, phone number, web address and physical address (and e-mail address, if applicable).

Make it as easy as possible for clients and prospective clients to contact you, find you online, make an appointment or come to your salon or spa. This is true whether you are merchandising to clients or to the general public in order to help build brand awareness and to make it as easy as possible for clients to refer their friends and family to you.

The Retailer's Advantage (www.theretailersadvantage.com) published this list by Rick Segel in January 2009 of the Top 12 Visual Merchandising Tips (adapted):

1. Take it outside. It might be more accurate to say, Work from the outside, in. The point is to use what is visible from outside of your business (sidewalk or traffic areas, doorway, windows, etc.) to draw people in to your business. Create excitement, buzz, intrigue; spark a sense of curiosity about what is inside.

2. Set the mood from the outside, in. How do you want your customers to feel when they are inside your salon or spa? Begin to create ambiance, set the mood and create customer's expectations as to what will happen once they come inside.

By the way, this does not only mean from the outside of the physical location of your salon or spa; you should begin to set the mood and create expectations with your web site, e-mail and direct marketing pieces.

3. Identify everything. Customers are in a hurry. What's more, they are bombarded with hundreds if not thousands of marketing messages every day. Every retail environment they enter is packed with items; some of which are relevant to their lives and some which are not—but most go unnoticed because customers cannot see through the clutter to what is important. So identify everything.

Use signage, color and displays to point out what is what. Tell people what they need to solve specific problems, and suggest additional items after you have their attention.

4. Embrace all of the senses. Setting the mood, stimulating curiosity and fully engaging customers in each client experience involves appealing to more than just the eyes when it comes to merchandising. Sounds, scents, how your products feel, sensations at the back bar and in the chair, the overall "atmosphere" created by your décor, the energy and attitude created by your staff—all of these beyond-visual components contribute to your overall client experience.

What messages are you sending with the music, scents and other environmental factors in your salon or spa?

5. Show customers how products will look in their home. Help customers to imagine exactly how products would look in their home, how a makeover would transform them, how to envision your products or gift cards as part of gifts for their friends and family. Helping clients to subconsciously visualize ownership or to visualize gift-giving helps them take the next step toward purchasing.

6. Group like with like. Are your products all lined up neatly on the shelves? Instead of rows of shampoos lined up by size, your displays should include areas where products that would/should normally be purchased together are grouped together. If your client needs a dry scalp shampoo, then they probably also need a moisturizing conditioner and soothing styling products.

Rows of products on your shelves are not conducive to intuitive selection; creating logical groupings of products helps your clients identify what they need to purchase. Group products that you want the client to purchase together to solve hair, skin or nail problems or to create looks with skin and makeup palettes, or to improve hand, foot, skin and nail health at home.

7. Group by lifestyle. Sun worshipers? Pet owners? Foot fetishes? Group products together on displays that cater to the hobbies, activities and obsessions of your clients.

8. Use the spotlight. Light attracts the eye. This is why we use up lights and spotlights in homes, hotels, museums and other settings—to draw the eye to those things we most want people to focus on. Those things which deserve extra attention and a moment in the spotlight. Use light strategically to draw the customer's eye to special promotions, new products, and gift displays.

9. Change. Displays. Often. People get bored easily and we stop looking at things when we feel we have seen it before. Our minds tell us that it's not new information and we do not need to pay close attention.

Conversely, when we enter a familiar place that has been rearranged, renovated or significantly redecorated, we stop and look again, pausing to see items set apart with color and light, those things which surprise and delight us. Also, by changing your layout and displays, you can help the 'same old products' to look new or stand out in ways that they were not before.

10. Don't be afraid of color. Just as with the use of light, you can use color to draw the eye to what is most important. And just as in the last tip, color groupings also need to change so that people don't stop looking at them.

Seasonal events, holidays and promotions can help to inspire palettes or you can use background colors which make your products and gifts 'pop' in contrast to get attention.

11. Integrate motion. Do you know that feeling when without even thinking about it, you immediately jerk your head around because you were attracted by motion out of the corner of your eye? Motion attracts the eye and can demands immediate attention.

When it comes to drawing attention to displays, you can use items that have integrated motion or you can even use items that move due to airflow from your HVAC, the opening of doors, even simple foot traffic like feathers, bubbles, sun catchers, etc.

12. Remember the rule of 3. Working in sets of 3's can help you to create displays that take the eye on a visual journey. Work at 3 heights (tall, taller, tallest) or widths (wide, wider, widest) in order to keep the eyes moving along a trajectory, along a set of messages, or a grouping of products.

Or use (at least) 3 items of the same color to create a strong focal point; use of color to help unify your displays can be especially important if you have a lot of small-scale merchandise.

Ideas for July Promotions

Make a special effort to ensure that all of your promotions focus on what is most important to the client; namely, the benefit to the client. Be sure your promotions are crafted in such a way that they are, in fact, appealing enough to compel your clients to action by offering additional value and incentives for the services and products that they most want to purchase (not just on the "dogs"—the products and services that you have been unable to sell).

July Month-Long Observances

Marketing from the Outside, In:
National Parks and Recreation Month

Chances are your city will be having a street fair or another summer event where you can take your brand and parts of your business out on the streets or to the park—to where tomorrow's clients are!

Take a booth; if you cannot afford do it on your own, partner with other stylists or a non-competing salon, spa or other business. Bring products, tools and equipment so that you can perform or demonstrate mini-versions of your most popular, trendiest and pleasurable services.

Demonstrate summer hair and makeup quick tricks and bring some of the retail products you are using in the demonstrations to sell. Distribute coupons or business cards featuring bounce-back offers. This can also be a great place to sell or give away spa and salon-branded goodies like sun screen, lip balm, glosses, sunglasses, water bottles, shirts, cover-ups, etc. Or show off the unique gift center that you have created in your salon or spa with a sampling of the boutique, beautiful, one-of-a-kind non-product retail items you have added.

July is Air Conditioning Appreciation Month

Partner with local HVAC repair/sales companies for cross marketing. Invite customers who might be suffering from summer heat in for a cool-off happy hour.

July is National Grilling Month

Hold a client or employee appreciation grill-out event. Grill out in a local park and have staff on hand to demonstrate quick hair styling, makeup, mini-massages, manicures or pedicures. Distribute salon or spa-branded goodies like water bottles, lip balms, sunglasses, etc.

July is Sandwich Generation Month

Partner with a local caterer, dinner preparation business, deli or sandwich shop to provide sample-size sandwiches for clients in a cross-marketed effort; create a special offer for their patrons, such as an offer that 'sandwiches' a complimentary add-on service between two others, or a product 'sandwich,' etc.

Partner with a deli or caterer to serve mini-sandwiches in your salon. Invite a party planner and create a workshop to teach clients how to create beautiful and delicious sandwich-based parties, luncheons or showers. Feature shower and party hair and makeup demonstrations as part of your event.

July Week-Long Observances

The First Week of July is Parks and Recreation Week

Sponsor a city league team (or your child's team) and give away branded products to players and parents. Hold a social event at the park or in the salon for coaches, parents and players with demonstrations, mini-services, ice cream, etc.

Create a special offer for city Parks and Recreation department employees and their families, and for players and families of Parks and Rec. teams. Give players or parents a special offer or salon or spa-branded tchotchke when they come in to your salon or spa wearing their team gear (or employee uniform).

The Third Week of July
is National Independent Retailer's Week: That's You!

Hold a special open house event to help sell through aging promotions or products; partner with other independent sellers or businesses located near yours and create your own independent retailer's summer fair.

The Fourth Week of July is World Hacky Sack Week

Remember hacky sacks? Purchase spa or salon-branded hacky sacks for retail sale, for client gift-with-purchase, as a gift for your sponsored summer league or child's sports team, or as a summer/street fair tchotchke give away.

July Holidays and Observances

July 1 is Second Half of the Year Day

Take time to sketch out your plan for the coming months; believe it or not, you need to start marketing now to have a strong back-to-school season.

Create "Second Half" offers: Sell 6 month pre-sold, pre-booked appointment packages to your regular clients. Or renew January's 'take $6 off 6' services for women or 'take $3 off 3' services for men's cuts; or some form of BOGO (buy one, get one at a percent or dollar off) offer. Even at a discount, with series of services pre-sold you will be more profitable and ensure that your books remain more constantly full over the coming months.

July 5 is Workaholics Day

We workaholics need your help! Create a service package for us that includes quick in-and-out times, a pre-set, pre-sold appointment block, and de-stressing mini added-on services (such as a hand or scalp massage).

Workaholics want to work, and we don't just work when we are at work, we will work any time, any place. And sometimes we will not go out and take care of ourselves because we just want to work! Add wi-fi to your business and let clients know that they are welcome to bring their electronic devices and stay connected during their service appointments. Because for us, the only thing that is better than working, is getting something else done at the same time we are working!

Start a "workaholics anonymous" happy hour or support group. Invite a counselor or life coach to come and speak to us (this will help us to feel like we are actually 'working' during our happy hour) about how to carve out a healthy work-life balance for ourselves and how to make the time we need to make for ourselves, for our families—and for our stylists!

Take Your Webmaster to Lunch Day

You should already be meeting with your webmaster at least once a month to ensure that events, promotions, and other news will be updated to the internet. (If you aren't, start now!)

Create special coupons or offers that are exclusive to your web site via special code, etc. Creating codes and other ways to track your offers will help you to know what's working, where, and when in terms of your promotional offers.

Once each month or quarter, hold a contest on Facebook, your blog or other social web site and reward one winner with a gift certificate or free product. Extend a special offer to members of your social networks redeemable by a special code. Hold a special mixer or happy hour for your Facebook, blog or web site followers. Collect contact information to add to your e-mail database.

Create an online "happy hour" by inviting your marketing partners to participate with you in extended Facebook, blog or other social network site-exclusive offers, hold online drawings, and distribute product knowledge in "Did you know?" style questions.

July 7 is Chocolate Day

My favorite celebration of the year! Partner with a local chocolatier for cross or cooperative marketing. Purchase salon or spa-branded chocolates for treats in the salon, for client thank you gifts, gifts-with-purchase, retail sale, inclusion in your prize baskets, employee appreciation, etc.

Get in the (Video) Game

July 8 is Video Game Day; a video game event could be a great way to celebrate with employees or reach out to male, tween or teenage clientele. Partner with a local game shop and/or local bar and hold a video game event or tournament.

Partner with an equipment rental or games shop and hold a Wii bowling tournament (something that has been very popular over the last couple of years, especially with seniors who may not be up for real bowling anymore). Be sure your event includes data collection and a door prize complete with gift cards and relevant product samples, as well as some branded goodies. Extend a special offer to everyone who registers and follow up with a bounce-back offer for everyone who attends.

July 12 is Different Colored Eyes Day

Create promotional collateral for "different colored summer eyes" including printed eye makeup application steps, specific color combinations, color palettes and product recommendations.

Hold an eye makeup workshop for clients.

Create a service item for your menu for attending women's events, providing makeup touch-ups and demonstrating application techniques.

Create a party services menu for teens and 'tweens' birthdays or sleepovers to demonstrate skin care and makeup.

Get to Know Your Customers (Day)

Getting to know your customers should be a priority year-round, but is mentioned here because July 16 is 'Get to Know Your Customers' Day. Be sure that you are keeping customer records including records of retail purchases, client referrals, event attendance and promotion redemption.

Make sure customers are getting to know you and your staff through regular e-mail communications, Facebook updates, your web site, and in-salon signage as appropriate.

Create a focus group from your client base including a representative from every stylist's or esthetician's regular clients to gain insight into salon operations, desired services, products, skills or deficiencies in your business which you can address.

July 23 is Gorgeous Grandma Day

Create a special open house event and/or appointment blocks for Gorgeous Grandmas in your community. Extend a special offer and invitations to local retirement communities, housing, senior centers and other senior services organizations.

Create Gorgeous Grandma gift baskets, bags or totes that include a gift card, moisturizing lotion, smoothing hair products, beautiful nail lacquers and coordinating moisturizing lipstick.

Funny is as Funny Does

In honor of Tell an Old Joke Day on July 26, hold a contest for clients to enter their oldest jokes and let customers vote for a winner. Create a prize basket complete with a new joke book as well a gift card, product samples and branded items.

July Planning and Tasks

Select from manufacturer promotions for products to support your marketing plans for August, September, and October. Obtain any additional supplies or products needed for your Back-to-School campaign. Set time aside and lay out your marketing plan and collateral needs for events going out 6-8 weeks, all the way into September. Begin thinking about holiday!

Your Back-to-School campaigns and promotions should begin in July. Multi-kid-cut discounts will be a big help for mom, but don't forget to reach out to teachers and your local PTAs—they need great hair, too! Begin planning the promotions you will run in early fall and start thinking through the initiatives and events you want to hold to meet your holiday sales goals. Plan now in order to hold a large-scale holiday retail event in early to mid-November with marketing partners in order to capture holiday spending before the mall and online retailers get all the attention.

Communicate in July

Items to include in your e-mail or print newsletter, web site, Facebook and blog posts and in direct mail communications this month:

- July and August events and promotions

- Educate clients on summer hair care and skin care

- Last minute openings on the books

- Last chance for promotions expiring in July

- A spotlight product, service or staff member of the month

July Calendar / Suggested Communications and Tasks Schedule

SUN	MON	TUE	WED	THU	FRI	SAT
1st week of Month						
1st of July—Merchandise for July						
1st of July—Begin collecting entries for July contests						
Focus marketing messages on summer hair and skin care and repair products and preventing sun, wind and swimming damage to skin, hair and scalp.	Order from manufacturers retail promotions for products to support August - September marketing plans; design related signage				Send July Newsletter with coupons, announce contests and winners, new products and services coming events, openings still on the books, events and promotions	
2nd week of Month						
Begin marketing Back to School promotions and packages.	Order event supplies, postcards, collateral, gifts and salon-branded items for August-September contests.				Write press releases for any events/results reporting or future events / charitable focus	
3rd week of Month						
		Finalize, review and lay out plans for August - September - October promotions and begin to think about Holiday			Send July "last chance" promotions and openings on the books e-mail and/or direct mail	
4th week of Month						
Last day of July—Take down any July-only promotions						
Last day of July—Draw July contest winners						
		Order event supplies, postcards, gifts and salon-branded items needed for September promotions			Send August focus e-mail / direct mail	

July Worksheets

$_____ Retail Sales Goal

Promotions_____

_____

_____

_____

_____

$_____ Avg. Retail/Client

$_____ Retail Sales Results

$_____ Service Sales Goal

Promotions_____

_____

_____

_____

_____

$_____ Avg. Service/Client

$_____ Service Sales Results

$_____ Event Revenues Goal

Events _____

_____

_____

_____

_____

#_____ Attending Event/s

#_____ Apts/Booked at Event

$_____ Event/s Sales

$_____ Total Event/s Results

$_____ Charity/Fund Raising Goal

Charity Events _____

_____

_____

_____

_____

#_____ Attending Event/s

#_____ Apts/Booked at Event

$_____ Charity Event/s Sales

$_____ Total Charity Results

July Marketing Summary

Marketing Partners: _____

_____

_____

_____

Marketing Collateral Needed (or Used): _____

_____

_____

_____

Other Efforts:

#_____ Number of Clients New to Salon

%_____ Client Retention Rate (90 days)

Retention Efforts: _____

_____

or % _____ Clients Re-booked at Appointment

$_____ Gift Certificate Sales

#_____ Contacts added to marketing / e-mail database

august

make over
the customer perception

If you needed to rent a car and were on a tight budget, you would not call a limo company for a chauffeur-driven rental; you would call a discount car rental and ask for the cheapest model, and you would turn down all the extras. It would never even cross your mind to call for a limousine, because you would know that kind of car would come at a premium cost. They charge a much higher premium; not just because these cars cost more to purchase and operate but also because of something more, and that something more is your perception in your mind that the experience of riding in the limo is *worth* more. Both vehicles can get you from Point A to Point B in the same amount of time. But since we believe that the limo experience is worth more, we are willing to pay more in order to partake of the experience.

Here's another example. In the grocery store you are often presented with two or three brand options for the same products. It's natural for us to perceive that the highest priced option is superior in taste, ingredients and processing. Provided the product is important enough to us and finances allow, we often choose a higher-priced option because we believe it to be better than the lower-priced or store brand, even though we may have no evidence that what we perceive to be true, is in fact, true.

There are some items we purchase that have ridiculously inflated values attached to them in our minds based on nothing more than a brand name. Jeans come to mind. Or imagine two leather purses coming off the manufacturing line sitting side by side—roughly the same size, with the same input costs; but stitch a designer label to one of them and it can be sold for hundreds or even thousands more.

While some logic applies in the case of the limo ride vs. the economy car (because input and operational costs are different), it does not necessarily apply in the case of the purses or similar items, yet some people are still motivated to pay significantly more for the additional intangible 'prestige' value they attach to designer products.

When it comes to pricing your products and services, there are many input costs that factor into play; not just your rent or mortgage and payroll costs, but also the costs of equipment, tools, products, insurance, advertising, supplies, utilities, education, and a myriad of other operating costs. To be able to charge more for your services than enough to simply cover basic costs, your clients must attach additional value to the services you provide and the products you sell. This additional value that clients attach to your services (due to your talent, creativity, the luxury of the experience you create for them, etc.) can also then be reflected in your pricing. And the prices you set in and of themselves can also influence the perceived value that your customers place on your products and services; and therefore, the price that they are willing to pay for them.

As if it were not enough to have to take all of those factors into consideration (not to mention figuring out how to set prices in light of that last somewhat circular statement) your pricing also has to be set in light of what the market will bear based on where your business is located, the economy, your target market, the competition and other factors.

No matter how talented you are, if your main client base is comprised of working and stay-at-home rural and suburban women, you will not be able to charge the same hourly premium that you could working from a downtown city salon or spa. True or not, people perceive that "downtown" salons are staffed with artists who have more education, are more skilled or more cutting edge; when in fact, an extraordinary stylist may be found anywhere. But people *expect* to pay more in the city, because as with the limo, they both know that the input costs are higher and they perceive that the experience is (somehow) worth more.

So then, if you are truly talented but not located in a major metropolitan district that allows you to charge a premium price right out of the gate, how do you increase the value that clients attribute to your business in order to grow and become more profitable so that you can plan for expansion, save for retirement, contribute to college funds, travel, and the hundred-and-one other things that you could think of to do if only the money were there?

First, do not adopt the pricing mentality that you will sell more than others, or more than you did before, if your prices are lower than those of everyone else. This might work for generic staples like gasoline, but even then, companies that sell lower-priced gas are often perceived as sellers of a 'cheap,' dirty or even possibly diluted product—all of which diminish the value that people assign to the product and influence how they talk about those products to others.

How do you increase the perceived value clients assign to your products and services?

Your pricing must reflect (at least in part) the value that you believe it has. If you do not believe in the worth of your products or services, why should your clients? And this same principle applies when it comes to your sale, promotional, discount or clearance pricing. You know the general discounting practices of your manufacturers and distributors; you know that you want to stock up when you are offered great liter pricing or buy 1 get 1 type of offers vs. the motivation you have to purchase at the regular price. Are your vendors sending you unspoken messages with their bi-annual sales, blowout, friends and family or other clearance sales; either that they are overstocked and need to reduce inventories, or that they could really afford to sell the same products at that price all year?

This is a serious argument against discounting overall, because discounting can have the effect of reducing the value that the customer mentally assigns to your services or products. However, there are other ways to craft offers and promotions that give clients more value for their money, without undermining the unique value that they ascribe to specific products or services.

So how do you sell more and increase the perceived value of your products or services? There are strategic ways to stimulate sales without reducing the price of any one product, and that is where add-ons, bundling and pre-sold series come in.

Just what they sound like, add-ons are either free or reduced rate services or products that are added on to another service or product to enhance the overall value of a promotion. An example of this would be adding on a free travel-sized conditioner with full size retail shampoo or conditioner purchase, or assigning it a "BOGO" (buy 1, get 1 or buy 2, get 1, etc., or two for the price of one, etc.) While there is no real difference between add-ons and discounts assuming the same products would be purchased, there is a big difference in the language used that affects consumer perception.

There is a difference in the client's mind when they purchase two retail products and receive a third as a free gift (to them, from you) than when they purchase one product at a 33% discount. In both cases, the client receives a one third price cut; however, in the first scenario the client is *rewarded* for purchasing two products while in the second case they are buying one cheaper (read, *less valuable*) product. Plus, in the first case, you moved three products while extending a discount to the client that was in actuality probably *less than* 33%, because in this promotion scenario you would be giving away the least expensive of the three products for "free."

> What **message** are you sending clients with your **"anything**-for-**$5"** bargain basket?
>
> That the products are **worth** $5!

While the practice of discounting a single product can lead to negative conjectures about the value of that product, add-on promotions preclude the client questioning why you are discounting any one single product. Think about it, when you see a distributor offering a deep discount, don't you wonder whether a product is being phased out, whether it's a slow mover, a poor performer, nearing some kind of expiration date or is undesirable for some other reason?

Instead of selling a bottle of shampoo that normally costs $16.00 at $12.00 (at $4.00 off, a 25% discount); you can sell a shampoo with a gift for the client of a travel-sized conditioner valued at $4.00. It's the difference between saying "save 25%" and saying "our free gift to you." Wouldn't you rather gift something to your client than dilute the perceived value of a product? Plus, add-ons can be a great way to introduce new products and services to your clients in order to begin generating a following and creating some buzz.

A close cousin to the add-on, bundling involves special pricing for products and/ or services that are sold as a package deal. Communications companies do this all the time, offering consumers a break on overall pricing when their home phone, internet and cable TV services are leased together. Insurance companies also often offer a discount on bundles of policies purchased (such as purchasing auto, home and life insurance from the same company).

You might bundle haircut and color services along with retail home care products. or create a makeover service of bundled packages including cut, blow out and styling, makeup and manicure. Or a complete men's grooming suite of haircut, styling and shave products for home use. Or pair curl-enhancing retail products with a professional curling iron. Straightening and thermal-protective products with a professional straightening flat iron. The concept of bundling lends itself well to the inclusion of strategically-chosen retail products; in other words, products chosen because they are directly relevant to the services with which they are bundled. It is also a way to build real value in for the client while also helping to stimulate retail sales—all without undermining your regular price points or the perceived value of any individual product.

Pre-sold series of services are wonderful because they help to keep your books full with less effort. While it might seem that you are working for less, if your client is coming in more often, you will make more money over time than if they extended the time between their regular services by even a week. At a time when some clients are delaying returning for services by two weeks or even longer, offering a special price for pre-sold, pre-booked series of services to keep clients on track means more money in your pocket and more frequent client visits. Series of pre-booked services also help to establish a habit of frequency for clients. And not only are they coming in for services more frequently, they are also coming in to your business more frequently, which gives you more opportunities to promote sales of retail products and gift items to them.

You can also reinforce perceived client value in your products or services by offering guarantees. Guarantees tell clients that you have so much confidence in your services and products that you put not only your revenues but also your reputation behind them.

And while we are on the subject of communicating with clients, you increase the perceived value that customers attach to your products and services by telling your clients about the benefits they provide. You cannot expect your clients to value a product when they don't know all of the 'good' it can do for them, when they don't know all of the good things that went into the product itself, or the manufacturing process. They do not know why the curl-enhancing cream you use behind the chair and offer for retail sale is better or how it is different than the curl-enhancing cream sold in the similarly-colored tube, but for less, at the grocery store. They do not know how much value that they should ascribe to the products that you sell, because you are not telling them. You are holding on to product knowledge like it's a trade secret—as though national security depended on it!

If you want to build perceived value in the minds of your clients around your products, tell them about what differentiates those particular products; what makes them better and what benefits they provide, including benefits beyond performance (like aromatherapy, vitamin enrichment, anti-oxidants, thermal and environmental protection, organic and natural ingredients, etc.)

Customer reviews and celebrity endorsements can also be used to stimulate desire in the minds of clients. Using celebrity endorsements in your signage and communications works because even though a given celebrity may have no actual expertise or authority relative to a product, as human beings, we still give their opinions more weight. We assume that since they have enough money to buy anything that if they like a product, it must be among the best. Celebrity endorsements also speak to the basic human desire for inclusion—the desire that many people have to be part of the "in crowd."

Copies of celebrity endorsement press sheets and "as seen in" articles are often available from manufacturers and distributors, and you can create your own by being on the lookout for celebrity product use highlighted in your waiting room magazines and trade publications in print or online. You can use them to create display sheets, station talkers, to include links on your web site or Facebook page, or to feature in your e-mail newsletters.

You can obtain customer raves and reviews by implementing a comment card program or soliciting comments about specific products either in-salon or online. If you have clients who regularly purchase certain products, ask them why they like the product so much, and feature that comment on an 8.5 x 11 display sheet at the point of purchase (with some of the products nearby) or create a smaller version to be attached to the mirror at each station. Create a display with a stickered "Try Me" tester of the product in the waiting area, or even in the rest room!

People are much more likely—and quicker—to express their opinion about your business when they are dissatisfied than when they are satisfied, or even delighted. Even if you have robust channels of communication with clients, raves can be slow to come in.

Be brave enough to ask your clients which products they love, and why. Ask them about their experiences with your products and which ones they can't live without.

Create a formal customer satisfaction survey about your products that includes open-ended comment fields.

To get feedback about specific stylists, products or services, reach out and contact individuals who have personal experience with them.

Create a focus group made up of clientele representative of multiple stylists or areas of service to participate in a group survey, discussion or question and answer feedback session. Reward them for their participation with a gift card and product samples.

Sampling itself can be a great way to solicit endorsements and comments while also building momentum around a product or service, and can be especially helpful in introducing new products to clients. Samples send the message that you are so confident that once your customers try a product they will want to buy it, that you can afford to give some away. Provide customers with a sample and ask them for their reaction to the product; how it performs, how easy it is to use, how it affects the senses, etc. Even services can be 'sampled' to clients in the form of mini-services or free introductory trials, giving you the opportunity to solicit feedback on the experience and the results to help promote it to other clients and prospects as well as to generate demand among those who sampled them.

Perceived value rises steeply when what you have is (1) strongly desired, (2) in short supply or available for a limited-time only, and (3) for which there are few comparable substitutes. Obviously, there are many options within any given community for common, basic salon or spa services, and hundreds of options for consumers when it comes to professional products, so it can be difficult to stimulate an increase in the value that customers perceive relative to these three conditions based on supply.

However, if you can bring an *uncommon* service or product in to your salon or spa, create entirely new ways to provide services or create unique combinations of what is available in your salon or spa, you can create scarcity in the form of uniqueness; and thus, increased perceived value.

One way to create scarcity is to establish celebrity status around yourself or one of the other professionals in your business. If you can attain celebrity status in your field by becoming renowned for skills behind the chair, awards, being published, or by becoming known for contributions to the community, then you can also increase interest in and desire for your services.

> Add something **uncommon** or **entirely new**; perceived value rises steeply for things with few comparable substitutes.

Many salons and spas make the mistake of over-generalization. Trying to be everything to everyone in order to serve as broad a market as possible. This approach can lead to a tasteless experience for the client. It might satisfy their basic service need, but without unique characteristics of its own, their appointment is unlikely to leave a lasting impression on them. Without a lasting impression, customer loyalty and referrals are unlikely to occur. Since there are so many places that people can go for most of the same services that your business provides, it is critical that you put real intention into creating a customer experience that is so uncommon, so unique, and so special that clients (literally) could not get it anywhere else, and would not dream of looking anywhere else for it!

Ultimately, to build perceived value and loyalty among your clientele, you are going to have to provide them with a truly extraordinary experience from beginning to end—from the first point of contact and throughout their service experience, to how you say thank you and what you do to follow up.

Think about the verbal and non-verbal messages you are sending that contribute to (or detract from) how special the client experience is. When a client phones to make an appointment, do they feel like they are an interruption or do they feel as though you were waiting for them to call? We all want to feel wanted; when a client feels as though they are truly important to you based on your interactions with them, then what you and your business have to offer will be more valuable, more important and more irreplaceable to them.

And the opposite is also true.

Clients who do not feel as though they are important to your business can easily replace your services with those of another salon or spa, and probably will.

If your clients feel as though they are interchangeable and insignificant to you, why would you be surprised if they feel the same way about you?

Have you ever been in an office or retail environment where employees were talking to one another rather than acknowledging you or addressing your needs—a situation where even if they may have helped you to complete a purchase, they didn't really take any interest in you? Their behavior screamed louder than words that they were far more interested in their own personal entertainment and in one another personally than in you, at all.

Even though most of us have experienced some version of that at one time or another (and so should be completely aware of how negative it is for the customer) it's still not uncommon to experience this in some salons or spas. Even though stylists and estheticians may work in one big, shared space, it is important for you to set and enforce policy when it comes to how employees communicate with one another in front of clients. If they gossip or discuss their social lives, clients are going to feel uncomfortable, for more than one reason.

If your clients feel like you think they are replaceable, don't be surprised if they feel the same way about you.

Clients may want to feel as though they can tell their stylists anything, but they definitely don't want to feel as though their stylists are passing that information on to others. And listening to stylists talking with one another about their own personal lives can make the client feel like the third wheel. The client needs to feel as though they are the single most important person in the world during the 30 minutes of their service appointment.

Remembering that your clients will never ascribe more value to your business or services than you build into their experience, it's vital that you create an employee culture where employees know and exhibit client-centric behaviors when they are in client-accessible areas (which may even include break and lunch rooms if they have proximity to the color mixing area, back bar, rest rooms—any area where clients can overhear conversations).

Attending to each and every aspect of the client experience is so important! The more value clients ascribe to your business, the more likely they are to

- be loyal
- refer others to you
- gift your services and products to others
- attend your events
- support your initiatives
- buy the products you recommend
- view you as an expert advisor
- visit your business more often

August Promotion Ideas

Spend time thinking about whether your regular promotions and messaging might actually be damaging the level of value that your clients assign to your products and services. Craft promotions that stress value, provide add-on services and products, highlight the education and expertise of your staff, and focus on how all of the ways that doing business with you enhances the lives of your clients.

August Month-Long Observances

August is Back-to-School Month / Family Fun Month

Hold a back-to-school open house complete with prize packages, special offers, fall makeup and hair demonstrations for students, etc. Attract attendees by holding a drawing for a complete set of free school supplies (or a school-year's worth of haircuts) at your event. Be sure all attendees receive a special offer for school-year haircuts or other services.

The Back-to-School Market

Parents and teachers have so much to do to get kids back to school, so make their back-to-school haircut appointments easy and special. Use youth-celebrity photos to help make suggestions for cuts and styles and extend special multi-booking appointment times so parents can bring all their kids in at the same time at a family rate. Offer to re-book the whole family 6 weeks later, together, at the same rate.

Tell parents about their children's scalp, hair or skin issues and write 'prescriptions' for recommended reparative products as well as how to use them. Create signage for products you carry that help to address skin, hair or scalp problems (such as flaking) that are common to school-age children. Include FAQ (Frequently Asked Questions) about common childhood problems such as exposure to lice at school on your website and in your e-mail newsletter, your Facebook posts, etc.

There are probably thousands of teachers in your community. Give teachers a calendar, school year book of offers or a set of coupons redeemable by month with a special offer or standing discount as well as a refer-a-teacher incentive.

Catering to teachers makes sense. Teachers appreciate value and convenience and they appreciate having style that is easy to maintain and replicate. They respond to special offers created for them. Their time is at a premium because most of their days start early and end late, so you might consider setting aside certain time blocks for teacher's appointments, or even set up a weekly teacher's happy hour. Teachers also represent much larger communities (of other teachers, parents, etc.) Many have large circles of acquaintances with the potential to be a source of referrals for you to a wide network of individuals throughout your community.

Ask your local school, local school district, or PTA to place a stack of flyers with your contact information and a service menu or postcard-sized offers in break rooms. Contact local schools to ask about advertising special offers to teachers, students and parents in school newsletters. Support local athletic, music, art, theater, and other programs. Attend school events, get involved in auctions and fund raisers. If the school will allow you to, provide them with copies of a flyer or large postcard that can be inserted into student folders.

The back-to-school season presents a time and opportunity-concentrated market; most students get their hair cut just before the beginning of the school year. Even kids who wear their hair long get everything freshly 'mussed' (and mussed with the right products), before they head back to class to face their peers. Chances are you have clients who come to you for their services but take their kids to what they perceive is a less expensive walk-in salon. They are not saving time and they may not be saving money doing this, but their perception is that they are.

While clients are in the chair this summer chatting about their kids and a new school year, ask some questions to help you build your family and school markets:

"how many kids do you have, how old are they?"

When your client is checking out, book their next appointment and offer them an opportunity to book their children's appointments at the same time with some type of "family rate" discount or with a free add-on service. When you book multiple clients and perform multiple services during the same block of time, you make more efficient (and more profitable) use of your time. Pass some of this back to the client in the form of special rates to incentivize them to bring more of their family members to you for services.

The onset of the school year is especially important to junior and high school students where peer pressure is tough. Having a custom cut and style from you, someone personally interested in the client and the well being of their families, will ensure that at least their hair is something they will not have to be nervous about.

This is a great opportunity to create some type of BOGO offer (buy-one, get-one) where the client pays full price for their cut and color and style, but saves on their child's haircut. For instance, if a client has 3 kids, they might receive a special offer were they would pay full price for the (most expensive) two services, and receive two services at half off, or buy-three, get-one free. At this time of year, a BOGO-style offer can make a big difference to the budget of working families with school-age children and can mean years of repeat client services for you.

"where do your kids go to school?"

Target local schools, PTAs, and school districts with offers for teachers, administrative and other staff, as well as parents and school patrons. Public schools may have regulations or policies which prohibit you from extending offers to their employees or students, but private schools are also an option. While private schools may in some cases represent smaller student bodies; more of their parents are probably *more likely* to be part of your prime client demographic targets in terms of home ownership, income, professional work status etc.

Back-to-School Buzz

The bottom line for teachers and parents is that they talk to one another in the parking lot, the classroom, at meetings, sporting events, the coffee shop, and even in the grocery store aisles. They share referrals. If it's good, they ask each other, "who does your hair?" It's a market well-worth courting and the effort of extending special offers and events.

Plan a Back-to-School Reception. Invite teachers from local schools to your salon for a relaxing mini manicure, massage or makeover. Partnering with a local caterer, provide light snacks and beverages such as sangria or champagne to celebrate the arrival of a new academic year (and remember to celebrate with them again at the end of the year!) Be sure that you collect contact information and that each attendee leaves with a bounce-back offer and collateral featuring your referral and loyalty rewards.

August is National Eye Exam Month

Partner with the practice of local optometrists for cross or cooperative marketing.

August is National Golf Month

Renew the offers you extended to local golf clubs, men's clubs and sports facilities in March. Extend a fall offer for men (or women) to local golf courses men's and women's clubs.

Invite a golf pro to hold a workshop for clients who might be interested in getting into the sport. Create an offer to extend to their students for cross marketing.

Create a special offer for the employees of local golf clubs, sports and recreational facilities and sporting goods stores.

Purchase salon or spa-branded golf towels, polo shirts, t-shirts, tanks, visors, hats, water bottles, tees, balls, towels and other paraphernalia to create special promotional kits, gifts with purchase, contest prizes or to add to your retail offerings.

August Week-Long Observances

National Night Out is in August

Create a date night for teens, young adults or grown ups in your clientele. Renew your cooperative marketing partnership with local restaurants, bowling alleys, movie theaters or other date night destinations and create a summer makeover and night out date package. If there is a drive-in movie theater near you, this could be a really fun summer outing to include. If your client base trends toward the sporty, consider a destination point such as a batting cage, paint ball, laser tag, miniature golf, go-cart course or similar venue. Award one or more winners with freebies and sell the specially-priced date package to clients of all participating businesses.

Partner with local bars, wine shops or restaurants and make "surprise" visits to their establishments on Friday nights. Hold a drawing at each "surprise" event and award one person a gift certificate and product. Use contest entries to help build your contact databases and extend a special bounce-back offer to all at the event, and afterward by follow up e-mail.

The Second Week of August is National Smile Week

The 2nd week of August is National Smile Week. Partner with a dental, orthodontic, cosmetic surgeon or dermatologist practice for cross marketing; display one another's business cards, promotional offers, gift certificates and service menus.

Purchase spa or salon-branded toothbrushes and give away to local day cares, schools and at your front desk.

Create a cooperative offer with a local dentist, orthodontist, dermatologist or cosmetic surgeon; hold a contest via your web site, Facebook blog, etc., for the 'best smile' with before-and-after makeover photographs that demonstrate the power of a great smile.

Or hold a "Best Smile Contest" event at a local bar or restaurant and reward the winner/s with a gift card and products. Extend a special offer to all in attendance and plan to collect contact information at the event. Demonstrate lip gloss, lipstick, and wrinkle reducing serums during your event. Gift salon or spa-branded lip balms to those in attendance plus a postcard or business card-sized bounce-back offer for your salon or spa. You might even take along a counter top lipstick or lip gloss display and sell products at the event.

Create a promotional product kit for the "perfect smile" including lipstick, lip gloss or branded lip balm, wrinkle reducing serum or cream for the area around the lips, teeth whitening products, salon or spa-branded floss or flossers, etc.

Or repeat some of the events you held in February for "Children's Dental Health Month" and "Tooth Fairy Day."

The Third Week of August is Weird Contest Week

The 3rd week of August is your chance to be creative; just how weird can you be? And remember, weird contests deserve weird prizes. Or turn the tables, hold a contest for clients to suggest the 'weirdest' contests, reward the winner and hold the winning contest in September.

August Holidays and Observances

August 5 is Work Like a Dog Day

Working hard is tough in the summer when so many other people are on vacation and taking long weekends! Hold a happy hour in-salon (or at a local bar or restaurant) for hard-working clients, or hold an employee appreciation night out.

If you hold a 'Work Like a Dog Day' happy hour or other event, donate a portion of proceeds or cover charge to your local animal shelter.

Partner with a mobile animal groomer and hold an event at a local dog park, demonstrating people and doggie makeovers and giving away doggie treats, branded tchotchkes and/or product samples along with bounce-back offers for your salon or spa.

August 6 is Wiggle Your Toes Day

Tout the health, well-being and cosmetic benefits of pedicures and post "did you know" bits of information in your e-mail newsletter, on your web site, Facebook page and your blog. Tell customers about the products that you sell that can improve the health, condition and appearance of their toes.

Create a special offer for pedicures in August to help repair damage caused by going barefoot during the summer. Cross-market with a local orthopedist.

Purchase branded flip-flops for regular client use that clients can take with them; incorporate it into your service cost if needed. Extending your brand beyond your walls is a great way to establish and grow your influence.

If you have access to local lake or ocean beach areas, take your show—and some of your employees—on the road for a day at the beach. Take along the tools and products needed to demonstrate to beach-goers how to achieve great beach wave hair, or how to quickly transition from beach hair to night-out hair and makeup, etc. Include bounce-back offers and product samples along with spa or salon-branded lip balms, flip flops, hacky sacks or other fun items.

August 9 is Book Lover's Day

To celebrate Book Lover's Day on August 9th, hold a Back-to-School event to benefit a local library (school, private school, day care, etc.,) or donate books to a local social services agency for waiting room use or distribution. Give clients a branded item or a free mini add-on service or product when they bring a new book to donate with them to their appointment.

Create a book swap or lending library in your waiting room where clients can bring books they have enjoyed to share with others on a bring-one, take-one basis.

Create a "Recommended Reading" bulletin board in your salon or online and ask clients to make literary recommendations.

Hold a contest and give one of your favorite books away to the winner/s along with a bounce-back offer or gift card for your salon.

Create a special offer for the employees and/or patrons of local libraries and for the teachers and library staff of local schools.

Create and host a book club at your salon or spa that meets once or twice each month during slower hours. Feature complimentary makeup touch ups, consultations, and other demonstrations at each meeting. Sell (or give away) branded tchotchkes such as book totes and boutique quality bookmarks and product samples.

Create a special book mark as a gift for clients (with your business information and a special offer or 'punch card' on the back) or purchase beautiful, one-of-a-kind boutique quality bookmarks for sale in the salon.

August 11 is Kiss and Make Up Day

Play up these words and create special "Kiss and Makeup" promotions featuring lipsticks and lip glosses bundled with coordinating makeup or skin care products.

Purchase salon or spa-branded lip balms or glosses for client gifts, for gift-with-purchase, or retail sale. Purchase a special lipstick or lip gloss display from your distributor for the point of purchase.

Hold a makeup application class for junior high school, high school and/or college students to help them develop more confidence in their appearance before going back to school.

August 15 is Relaxation Day

Extend a special offer to local teachers for free massages with their August appointments so they can relax before facing all those kids going back to school.

Create special offers to relax the budget for school employees when they book appointments for themselves and family members at the same time. Or repeat some of the "de-stress" stress-relieving offers you extended in April.

Focus marketing messages in your signage, Facebook and blog posts, and in your e-mail newsletter on the stress-relieving benefits provided by specific products and/or services that you offer. Post ideas, tips and tricks on quick ways to relax during the work day on bag stuffers, Facebook posts, etc.

Offer free scalp, hand or foot massages during clients appointments or as a new add-on service in your menu. Treat at least one client each day to a complimentary 5-minute scalp massage at the shampoo bowl.

Hold a Relaxation happy hour and invite a massage therapist to attend and give mini-massages to clients and/or to employees. Partner with a massage therapist to trade services for you or a staff member, or for one staff member each month.

August 20 is National Radio Day

Reach out to local radio stations and extend a special offer to all station employees. Partner with a local radio station to hold a special night out auction or event in September to benefit a local animal shelter.

Create an on-going relationship with local radio stations and submit press releases to them throughout the year; they may be willing to help to publicize your contests, especially those where you are asking for public nominations or benefitting local charities.

August 25 is Second Hand Wardrobe Day

Hold a closet sale of gently used but still fashionable clothing, shoes, sunglasses, jewelry, etc. If space permits, invite some of your more fashionable clients to donate items from their closets in addition to those donated by you and your staff. Designate proceeds to a special cause such as a needy individual in your community, a women's or children's shelter, to purchase school supplies for local children or for a specific upgrade or furnishing for the salon.

Invite clients to donate outgrown clothing of school-aged children for a swap or to a local charity. Gift those that donate with a free mini add-on service, a gift card, a retail product, a salon or spa-branded tchotchke, or with a special offer for their next appointment.

Utilize either event to also help move aging inventory, sell branded tchotchkes, collect participant/attendee information for your contact database, do mini-services, demonstrate fall hair and makeup and give hair color consultations, etc. Make contact collection an organic part of the event by holding a drawing for a gift card and prize basket. Invite a local clothing retailer to participate and include a fashion show as part of your event either in-salon or at a partnering bar or restaurant.

August 27 is Just Because Day

Hold a special "Just Because" event and invite clients in for a fall fashion style, hair and makeup demonstration open house complete with special event-only appointment prices and product promotions.

On August 27 (or on random days throughout the year) stock a fishbowl with a number of random, exceptional "just because" offers and let attendees "fish" an offer out of the bowl; include a couple of coupons for free products, services, buy one-get one offers, motivational quotes, product knowledge, tips and tricks, weird and fun facts about your salon or your city, etc. Have fun... just because! If clients enjoy this, consider doing this once a month or once a quarter.

August Planning and Tasks

Choose from manufacturer's retail promotions to support your September-October promotions and events. Purchase supplies needed for events.

Design and print (or purchase) the marketing and promotional materials you need for events and promotions occurring in the coming 6-8 weeks (all the way into October).

Purchase salon-branded and other pet products for retail or giveaways for September's pet-focused events.

While it may still feel like summer, it is already time to get a handle on planning holiday promotions and retail events with cross-marketing partners and multiple vendors in November. In some salons, holiday retail accounts for up to 25% of their annual sales; but you have to plan ahead and begin communicating with clients early in order to capture a healthy share of the money they plan to purchase on gifts.

Finish planning promotions and events for September and October. Plan now to hold a Holiday Shop event in November and invite independent sellers, boutiques, pet stores, wine or gift shops and other local businesses in your area to participate in a Holiday Shop in-salon or at another location so that you can capture a share of your customer's holiday shopping budgets. Partner with a caterer and wine shop for food for the event and hold by mid-November in advance of the serious holiday retail season.

Communicate in August

Items to include in your e-mail or print newsletter, web site, Facebook and blog posts and in direct mail communications this month:

- August and September events and promotions

- July winners and August contests

- Report on charitable endeavors

- Save the date for October and November events

- Sneak peek at your November holiday event or sale

- Teacher and student special offers

- Suggest which retail products are 'must-haves' as well as great values for outbound college students

- Last chance for promotions expiring in August

- A sneak peek at what clients can expect for the fall

- End-of-summer hair and skin care recommendations

- Last minute openings on the books

- A spotlight product, service or staff member of the month

August Calendar / Suggested Communications and Tasks Schedule

SUN	MON	TUE	WED	THU	FRI	SAT
1st week of Month 1st of August—Merchandise for August 1st of August—Begin collecting entries for August contests						
Time for Back-to-School! Focus extra marketing efforts on schools, family cut packages, PTAs, teachers, etc.		Order signage, event supplies and promotional materials for September - October promotions			Send August Newsletter with coupons, announce contests and winners, new products and services coming events, openings still on the books, events and promotions	
2nd week of Month						
		Order in gifts, salon-branded items, impulse buy and other items for September - October			Write press releases for any events/results reporting or future events or charitable focus	
3rd week of Month						
		Finalize, review and lay out plans for September - October - November promotions and events. Begin planning for Holiday sales and events			Send August "last chance" promotions and openings on the books e-mail and/or direct mail	
4th week of Month Last day of August—Take down any August-only promotions Last day of August—Draw August contest winners						
		Order event supplies, postcards, gifts and salon-branded items needed for October promotions			Send September focus e-mail / direct mail	

August Worksheets

$_____ Retail Sales Goal

Promotions_____

_____

_____

_____

_____

$_____ Avg. Retail/Client

$_____ Retail Sales Results

$_____ Service Sales Goal

Promotions_____

_____

_____

_____

_____

$_____ Avg. Service/Client

$_____ Service Sales Results

$_____ Event Revenues Goal

Events _____

_____

_____

_____

_____

#_____ Attending Event/s

#_____ Apts/Booked at Event

$_____ Event/s Sales

$_____ Total Event/s Results

$_____ Charity/Fund Raising Goal

Charity Events _____

_____

_____

_____

_____

#_____ Attending Event/s

#_____ Apts/Booked at Event

$_____ Charity Event/s Sales

$_____ Total Charity Results

August Marketing Summary

Marketing Partners: _____

_____

_____

_____

Marketing Collateral Needed (or Used): _____

_____

_____

_____

Other Efforts:

#_____ Number of Clients New to Salon

%_____ Client Retention Rate (90 days)

Retention Efforts: _____

_____

or % _____ Clients Re-booked at Appointment

$_____ Gift Certificate Sales

#_____ Contacts added to marketing / e-mail database

september
make over
your communications

It is not enough to ensure client-centric experiences in the chair; you have to view *every* client touch point through the eyes of clients and prospects, including your communications. While some salons and spas have multiple channels of communication open to and from customers, some have yet to build channels out beyond use of the telephone and in-salon signage.

Whether you need to simply tweak existing communications or make them over completely, it should be comforting and exciting to know that it has never been easier, faster, or less expensive to communicate with your clients and prospects—anywhere in the world they might be!

For instance, a web site that costs as little as just a few dollars a month (compare that with the hundreds of dollars you have spent on local yellow page listings!) gives you the ability to communicate anything you want to say to customers 24 hours a day, 7 days a week and can extend your influence throughout your neighborhood, the larger community, and beyond—to anywhere in the world that someone possesses any type of device capable of accessing the internet.

And it's not just about what you put on your official company web site; imagine for a moment that you submit a press release to a local radio station for a charity event that you are hosting, and you receive a donation from someone in another state, or even another country. All made possible by the internet, which facilitates not only web site content, but streaming media. While it means more work for you, the great news is that technology has gone a long way to leveling the playing field for small businesses (vs. large corporations with the resources to reach out worldwide on their own).

Does that mean that decades and even centuries-old tools like the telephone, handbills, flyers, business cards and mailers are out of vogue? No, they are more important than ever, in part because you have to work harder (and utilize more channels of communication) in order to leave an impression in the minds of clients or prospects in today's world, where they are bombarded with thousands of individual marketing messages in any given day. The fact is, you cannot focus solely on internet marketing, or social marketing, or buzz marketing, or print marketing— you have to do it all.

So how do you make sense of it all? How do you prioritize your marketing investments when it comes to limited resources like time and money? How do you construct communications that work to reinforce not only your message of the moment, but also your brand?

First, you need to be aware of all of the tools available to you. Then, just like you choose certain tools to complete specific styles for clients, you need to decide which communications tools you will use based on the specific campaign, overall marketing goals or business problems you want to address.

You can think about using communications like you think about using products behind the chair. You need to know which products to use, how much of each to use, and when it is most effective to apply each one during the styling process. In other words, you have to determine which types of communications you will use to support a given campaign, how 'much' or how many of each type that you will use, and when you will use each one. Just as in the use of styling and finishing products behind the chair, you don't want to 'weigh down' your audience with an overload of communications; but you also don't want to use too little to achieve your desired result.

This is why establishing multiple channels of communications and creating a habit of engaging in regular, routine communications with clients and prospects is crucial. Once you have established channels of communication and grown your lists of contacts, you can then use these channels to expand on regular communications in order to support special initiatives, build more brand awareness and capture more client and prospect mind share.

For instance, imagine that you want to hold an event for clients to teach them about the basics of makeup application to create special looks for the upcoming holiday season.

Scenario 1: You do not really have many channels or a regular schedule of communications, but you throw an announcement up on your web site and put a sign by your makeup display, and maybe another one in the window or by the cash register. You mention the event to a few clients here and there, but otherwise you wait to see if anyone is interested enough to come.

Scenario 2: Now, let's say that you have already established multiple means of communication with clients and prospects, have implemented a communications plan, and you know of all of the tools available to you. So you send an advance, preview notice via e-mail to the businesses that you regularly partner with, to businesses located near yours who have a lot of female employees and customers, to large employers or civic groups in your area who have significant numbers of women (or teens and tweens) that fall within your target market, and to your most engaged and loyal clients. You let invitees RSVP via easy web form or e-mail reply.

You put an announcement in your regular e-mail newsletter and on your web site (again, with response via easy, instant online form or e-mail RSVP). You order and send out a targeted mailer to 500 likely prospects in your community, including individuals in local media, known fashionistas, civic and business leaders. You send a copy of your mailer and e-mail to leaders of local youth, college and young adult groups.

Your event features a charity aspect which will be facilitated by a donation cover charge, and so you send a copy of a 1-page press release to local radio stations, newspapers, city magazines, and civic or business leaders likely to be interested in helping raise support for this charity. You add a task to your calendar for a follow up press release to be sent to all of these same individuals following the event along with photographs and an event summary.

You add a link to the online event registration form to your Facebook page, and you plan to put teasers for the event on Facebook, your blog (and any other social media sites) twice a week until the event occurs. You add a task to your calendar to follow up after the event by putting photos from the event on Facebook as well as posting results and highlights.

You create a window and waiting area display with several example "looks" that you will be teaching at the event. (These can also be used on your web site, Facebook page, blog site, and in mailers and e-mail pieces promoting the event.)

You create special offers for the event as a way to incentivize RSVPs or encourage attendees to bring friends with them. You make the special offers available to attendees via your e-mail newsletter, direct mail, web site and Facebook.

At the event, you use special cards that you had printed for the occasion to collect contact information at the door for all attendees. Everyone who turns in their contact card receives a free sample (or goodie bag) including a flyer or postcard-sized sheet listing the "looks" that will be taught at the event and a list of the products that will be used for each. You pre-package sets of the products used for each "look" and sell them at special event-only pricing. You use the contact cards to draw winners for door prizes throughout the evening; door prizes that include products used to create each of the event "looks", a gift card and special bounce-back offer for the salon. You planned ahead, and you have staff on hand ready to take appointment bookings at the event.

Immediately following the event, you add the contacts to your e-mail and mailing database and you send a thank you to all attendees via e-mail with a summary of the looks they were instructed in, a list of products used and a special offer redeemable in-salon if they come back to purchase any of the remaining pre-packaged sets. You also include a list of open appointments that you have in the coming two weeks along with an incentive for them to book an appointment if they are new to your salon and information about your referral rewards. You send a special thank you via a personal e-mail or note card to the clients who brought new guests with them to your event, along with a reward redeemable at their next appointment.

You use your web site, your e-mail newsletter and your Facebook page to post pictures from the event, links to a downloadable PDF file containing a list of the "looks" and the products and tools used to create them, and you extend an offer to anyone who missed out on the event to come in for a complimentary demonstration (or to have one at their next appointment).

If all you really engage in when it comes to client communications are incoming phone calls to book appointments, you are missing out on some really powerful ways to build business and engage more deeply with your own clients. You are missing out on holiday and seasonal sales. You are failing to create a significant role in the lives of your clients when it comes to being a resource for their gift and discretionary personal indulgence dollars.

It sounds like more "to do" and it is. But it is through the use of planned, robust communications that business is built, new clients are gained, and buzz, viral marketing, and referrals occur. The very fact that it can seem like there are a lot of moving pieces is why it is crucial for you to know which tools are at your disposal, how they work best, and when to use them. That is why you need to establish a regular schedule for on-going communications as well as a plan that you can deploy any time you need to help support special campaigns or events.

Some of the basic tools that are (or should be) at your disposal:

- Business Cards (general)

- Business Cards (with client referral or rewards form)

- Business Cards (with seasonal or new client offer)

- "Ask Me About" titled product or event display/station talker cards, celebrity-endorsement "As Seen In" display sheets and shelf talkers

- Reminders (via phone, text, e-mail or direct mail per client's preference!) Appointment reminders have been shown to significantly reduce no-shows and rescheduling.

- Doctor and other offices use "intake forms" all the time. Create your own client "intake" or update form (or ask the client to re-verify their information verbally at each appointment) and include a question asking for their preference when it comes to appointment reminders.

- Note Cards (blank)

- Note Cards (thank you, sympathy, congratulations and birthday)

- Postcards (direct mail or use as bag stuffers, handbills, station talkers)

- Postcards (stacks to be placed in the break rooms of local large employers, your business park, schools, etc.)

- Signage (both for inside and outside of the salon or spa)

- Merchandising

- Flyers (direct mail, post as PDF online, bag stuffers, business-to-business offers, event handouts)

- Press Release template

- Invitations

- RSVP return mail and/or online forms

- Menus (general)

- Menus (special menus for events, special occasions, or specific service groups such as bridal or corporate events)

- Menus (pre-sold series purchase opportunities)

- Menus (combination menus featuring your offers as well as those of your business cross and cooperative marketing partners)

- Web site

- E-Mail (personal)

- E-Mail (marketing, such as Constant Contact—you don't want to send bulk marketing messages from your personal e-mail account for many reasons)

- Facebook (and/or other social sites, most if not all are free to use)

- Blog (free to set up and use on sites like blogger.com)

- Rewards, Loyalty and Referral Program support materials

Once you have identified all of the tools at your disposal, it is time to decide how and when to use each of them, how to use them together, and it's time for you to set up a basic, manageable schedule of communications tasks to perform each month.

If the event scenario presented earlier seemed overwhelming, remember to start small. Break down tasks until they are achievable given the time that you can devote to them, what you still need to learn in order to use them, or to those that you have the resources to complete (for instance, you may not yet have a resource to help you develop a web site; put that on your list of things to do!)

If you are the only one performing these tasks, it's unrealistic to try to create a web site, a Facebook page, start an e-mail newsletter and launch a direct mail campaign all in the same month. Create a list of what you have and what you want to add to your communications tool box. Prioritize the list of what you want, and focus only on the top one or two items at a time until you have incorporated them, then move on to the next.

And along the same vein, don't create a schedule for yourself that would exhaust a marketing team of 10 people; it's unrealistic to commit to updating your web site and Facebook page multiple times each day while you are simultaneously sending out reminders to all your clients and—oh yes—also working behind the chair. Creating an impossible 'to do' list will leave you feeling exhausted and defeated; it's like starting an exercise routine after years of inactivity by running a 26 mile marathon; it just ain't gonna happen!

Be patient. Cut yourself enough slack so that a missed goal doesn't end in complete system failure, but simply a renewal of your next goal. And solicit help. If you already put in 8-10 hour days on top of your personal, family and social life, you can't add hours of additional communications work to your own plate each week.

Delegation and out-sourcing is the name of the game if you want to develop a highly effective, robust communications program. Since employee buy-in is critical to the success of your marketing program overall, as well as that of individual campaigns, employee participation and ownership of specific communications responsibilities would seem both to be a logical expectation as well as an effective means of creating more buy-in. When staff assist in the promotion of an event or of the business overall, they will naturally have a bigger emotional stake in the results.

Some employees may choose to take on responsibilities in areas they enjoy and in which they are proficient; others may need encouragement or incentives to step out of their comfort zone and learn something new. Or you may have individuals within your client base who work in a related field, work from home or are students that would love either to pick up some part time work or would trade for services with you.

My point is, I know you did not go to cosmetology school to spend your time updating a web site or Facebook page, creating an e-mail newsletter or spending your time and money investing in the tools needed to create custom, professionally-designed salon or spa-branded marketing materials. I know that you want to spend your time behind the chair performing your art, creating. I know that you want to invest your time and money in technical and platform education, not learning how to build a web site. I know that time spent working on operational tasks vs. time spent working behind the chair impacts your revenue, profitability and income negatively. I know, I know, I know!

If marketing activities leave you feeling like you are trying to drive a car with four flat tires, or you think that it might actually be preferable to be slow-roasted over an open flame—rather than giving up on business and marketing operational tasks that you know need to be done, use the creativity you were gifted with. Use it to create rewards for yourself either for doing them, or for finding a way to farm it out in trade or pay.

Find a way, or as Tim Gunn so often says on the TV series 'Project Runway' "Make it work!"

It seems especially appropriate in this instance, since when he says this, he it is in the context of telling a designer to accomplish all that they have to do in order to be successful, in order to win, on a short deadline and with a limited budget. So it is an appropriate phrase for you to keep in mind when it comes to those aspects of running your business that you may dread, or for which you simply do not have enough time. You do not have to do everything yourself, but you must "make it work" when it comes to executing all of these tasks, one way or another, in order for your business to be successful.

Here's my suggestion for a manageable schedule with some basics to build on:

1st Monday or Tuesday monthly, basic:

Send e-mail newsletter featuring the current month's promotions, new products, contests, events, and results and highlights from any events occurring the prior month.

Ensure that your merchandising and signage is in place throughout the salon or spa for the month's new promotions, contests and events.

1st week, supplemental:

Change your window display.

Put a blurb on Facebook about new promotions, products, contests and events.

Seek out and firm up plans with marketing and events partners for coming promotions.

Seek out one new business to cross market with.

2nd Monday or Tuesday monthly, basic:

Begin marketing for the next specific major event or seasonal promotion/s.

2nd week, supplemental:

Post a blurb on Facebook about what is coming during the next season, or another tease for current promotions and events.

Write a press release for your next event and/or a follow up press release for recently held events or charitable endeavors.

Order any salon-branded promotional collateral, products or tchotchkes you need for the next event or seasonal promotion.

3rd Monday or Tuesday monthly, basic:

Send a 'last chance' e-mail or postcard/letter noting any soon-to-expire promotions and previewing the next month's promotions, contests and events.

3rd week, supplemental:

Check your remaining stock of business cards, appointment cards, referral rewards and gift certificates, order any supplies that need to be restocked.

Post a blurb on Facebook featuring one of your employee's favorite local places (a date-night or girl's night out destination, a local tourist or recreation attraction, a favorite bar or restaurant, a must-shop boutique, etc. And it's even better if this is one of your cross marketing partners!)

4th Monday or Tuesday monthly, basic:

Plan and finalize your schedule of tasks looking ahead 3 months at a time. Include information from distributors/manufacturers so that you can plan to support the launch of any new products. Identity businesses that would make desirable marketing partners for events and promotions in the coming 3 months.

Last day of month:

Take down any expired signage and break down expired promotions.

Ensure that your contact lists have been updated with any new contacts from forms, events or contest entries.

End of month, supplemental

Finalize contests/draw winners and award prizes.

Post a Facebook blurb with a summary of the month's activities and highlights.

Some major holidays to incorporate into your schedule for promotions, events, and salon-displays/decorating:

- Early-to-Mid January: Valentine's Day promotions should be in full swing for the February 14th holiday.

- Mid-February: While love is in the air, highlight your bridal packages and begin to book appointments for the upcoming wedding season. Better yet, work with other businesses to hold a bridal fair or sponsor a bridal directory.

- By the end of March: Mother's Day promotions should be underway.

- Mid-April: Prom and Graduation services, packages and promotions need to be in place.

- By the 3rd week of May (just after Mother's day), Father's Day promotions need to be rolling.

- By mid-May: Wedding and Bridal services, packages and promotions should be highlighted from now until July.

- Early July: It might seem like school just got out, but it's time to launch back-to-school promotions.

- End of September: Begin working to capture client's gift dollars for the upcoming holiday season.

- October-December: Focus on holiday merchandise sales—some salons or spas do more than 25% of their annual retail sales during the holiday season.

- End of December: January and New Year promotions.

Marketing 101: How to use the tools

Business cards

Business cards (like all other collateral) should be a reflection of your brand. Make the investment needed to ensure you have a professional, custom design that relates to the personality of your business. The business card is universally recognized and used; think of it as the best 2 x 3.5 inch billboard you could ever have! It should be memorable, accurate (no crossed out phone numbers or hours, please!), professionally designed and professionally proofed. Business cards cannot work for you when they are sitting in a drawer; make it your goal to give them away as fast as possible, instead of hoarding them so you don't have to reorder. Finding an affordable printer for business cards is not always easy; click the link on the Resources page of my web site at www.12monthsofmarketing.net for a quote, referral, design help or other assistance.

While this will sound obvious but it's still true; the more places to which your business cards go, the more people will know about you. And the easier and more rewarding it is for someone to contact you, the more likely they are to do so.

Give them away 2 at a time (so they can be shared):

- Person to person
- In thank you notes
- In gift baskets
- With gift certificates
- At the point of purchase
- In merchandising displays
- As bag stuffers
- On stylist stations
- Exchanged (cross marketing) for display in other businesses—your marketing and event partners, businesses located near yours, businesses owned by friends or family, businesses with services that compliment yours or with whom you share target markets
- Given out with treats at Halloween, or with cookies or chocolates at Christmas and for Winter Holidays
- Handed out at city events, street fairs, holiday parades
- Included in payments to local vendors
- Left with tips at local restaurants and bars
- On the community bulletin boards still found in many supermarkets
- Send a set of 25 cards along with a specially-created offer designed specifically for local retirement living centers, local golf clubs, civic clubs, local churches, large employers, schools, school districts, hotels/motels, or hospitals, etc.

What should always be on your business card:

- Your name and salon name

- Business address

- Phone number best to call to make an appointment

- Alternate or special-purpose phone number or message line

- Web site address

- E-mail address

- Facebook, Twitter, blog site and other social media page identifiers

Ensure that your business cards will be kept by adding creative value to the card itself:

- Calendar year or half year at a glance (to be replaced at the beginning of the next year or half year)

- Weights and measures conversion, or a ruler

- Tips and tricks for hair or makeup

- Rewards / punch card

- A bounce-back offer or special "code" word for offer or continuing price point

- Design cards to double as a bookmark

- Put a "fortune" or inspirational saying on it

- Hand write a compliment on it for the recipient, or write your alternate / personal phone number on it

Salon or Spa-Branded, Custom-Designed Note Cards

Sometimes we behave as though we believe that clients should be thanking us for the services we provide (in exchange for money) to them. The reality is, we should be thanking them for their patronage, the first time and every time. Your clients have lots of choices; in fact, there may literally be hundreds of other stylists or estheticians in your city they could choose to support through their patronage.

Note cards, and specifically thank you notes, postcards or even thank you business cards (maybe with a great inspirational quote on it) should be one of the staples of your personal marketing toolbox; one that you use daily.

Personal notes may be one of the most underrated forms of marketing when it comes to brand and relationship building even though it is one of the easiest to implement. Once you get the hang of writing a quick note to someone, it won't seem like such a chore. It will be uplifting for you to remember the high points of your day and extend a word of encouragement to others. Beyond the 'thank you,' here are some of the events that might trigger a note from you to a client, co-worker, vendor, consultant, friend, etc.:

- To say goodbye to a client who is moving away, going off to college or leaving on a military deployment (or to encourage a military spouse or parent)

- In sympathy or to say that you're thinking of someone due to the death of a loved one, job loss, divorce or separation, etc.

- To encourage someone who had a bad day

- As a personal invitation to an upcoming event or promotion

- Included as a note of congratulations with a special offer in your gift or charity auction baskets

- Congratulations for events such as a new baby, new job, promotion, new home, new marriage or engagement, graduation, awards, accomplishments, marathons, significant weight loss or other self-improvement

- 'Thinking of you' or 'miss you' notes to clients you have not seen in more than 60 days

- As a thank you to your children's teachers, or as a thank you to the principal or other leaders of local schools or district offices

- As a thank you to your business marketing partners, businesses near you and/or those who participate in cross or cooperative marketing with you

- As a get well / feel better soon, or other card of encouragement

- To extend employee appreciation, compliments or kudos

- As a note to city hall, a local politician or civic leader

- To communicate with the owners of local businesses

- As a thank you to local charity organizations, animal shelters, community services or volunteers

- As a thank you to someone who made your day, to a co-worker, or to a client for loyalty or referral

- As a thank you / new client welcome

- Holidays—Christmas, Thanksgiving, New Year, Valentine's Day, etc.

- To acknowledge milestones such as birthdays and anniversaries

Or create and use Postcards or Flyers for:

special offers	thank you cards	holiday greetings or offers
holiday gift ideas	invitations	reminders
events	miss you cards	congratulations
birthdays	anniversaries	referral rewards program / status
announcements	bag stuffers	moving, new location, or change of address or phone number
renovating	open house	bounce-back offer after event
station talkers	shelf talkers	contests
product knowledge	seasonal tips and tricks	special group offers (like for teachers, schools, students or large groups of employees

Menus

Keep your menu up to date. As is true for all for collateral, when a menu has become obsolete due to changes in pricing, phone number, address, staff, services offered or anything else that renders it inaccurate, do not cross out and write in the correct information. It sends so many negative messages to your customers! It says that you don't care how you present yourself, it points out to the client that they are paying more for the same services, it suggests that your business is struggling to the point that you cannot afford to replace your paper collateral.

One way to keep your menu from becoming obsolete is to list prices at a starting point followed by the words "and up." Such as:

- *Hair Cut, Blow Out and Style, 45 and up,* or
- *Hair Cut, Blow Out and Style starting at 45*

This allows for changes in pricing, and it makes it possible for individual stylists who may charge more than beginning stylists to do so, or for you to set pricing based on length and volume of hair, the length of time of the service, etc. It gives you the flexibility to charge appropriately for each service.

You may have noticed that I did not use dollar signs in the examples above. This is because in restaurant industry surveys it was found that customers spent more and ordered foods costing more when pricing appeared without dollar signs. Seeing a dollar sign apparently triggers negatives we associate with spending money in ways that plain numbers do not. And my personal opinion is that visually, cleaner is better. It's unnecessary to add the dollar sign; we know that in the U.S. we pay in dollars and cents for services, and I assume that the same holds true for the denominations used in other countries as well. Dollar signs ($) are different from our letters and numbers; notice how the sign jumps out compared to the other characters in this sentence.

You should develop a menu for every day services, but you may also want to develop special menus for:

- wedding and bridal services
- tourist, traveler, hotel/motel guests (*continued next page*)

- corporate or retreat services

- special buying groups, such as teachers or employees of large corporations

- graduation, homecoming and prom

- birthday parties, bridal or baby showers

- special occasion makeovers

- holidays

- gift idea menus

- product catalog/brochure with cocktailing recipes

- pre-sold series

- bundled services

- menus to be given out in businesses partnering with you for cross or cooperative marketing

- special menus for the employees of businesses near you or with which you partner for cross or cooperative marketing

- joint menus of offers with your cross and cooperative marketing partners

Consider including a policy and preferences on tipping. While it may feel a bit awkward to talk about it, you may be providing answers to questions customers were too embarrassed to ask. It might help clients to understand that when they pay for a service, that money is not necessarily going into their stylist's pocket. Many people are not aware of all of the costs that go into running a salon or spa as a whole, let alone the variety of ways that salaries and commissions might be structured. Few would understand what it costs a stylist to work at a salon or spa as an independent business owner or booth renter.

Include information about your products and why they are superior to other products—why you chose them, who can most benefit from their use, and how to use them. Since menus often go home with clients, including product knowledge can help to reinforce your messaging behind the chair and provide a reminder to the client as they consider future product and gift purchases.

Other take home pieces you might create for clients include bookmarks, bounce-back offers and bag stuffers. Think about choosing one retail product to feature each month and creating a print piece to go home with clients, to contacts in the mail and via e-mail, for shelf talkers and station stalkers, and to receive spotlight attention on your web site and Facebook page.

When you create a new menu, ask your graphic designer to provide you not only with print-ready files for professional printing, but also with a PDF (portable document format) to be set up as a link on your web site, Facebook page, blog site or e-mail marketing pieces. Depending on size, your PDF will probably also be something that you can (personally) e-mail to clients, prospects, new hires, etc. When you publish a new menu, be sure that you update all of the electronic versions of your menu as well as replacing the print versions.

More menu ideas:

- Create a special menu of "starter services" (or a new client offer) and have it printed on refrigerator magnets; mail them to people moving into new homes in your area, local businesses and prospect contacts collected at events.

- Add value to your menu to ensure it is kept by clients; a year at a glance calendar, school year calendar, list of holidays and observances, styling tips and tricks—anything appropriate to your audience that turns it into more of a keepsake.

- Once a year (and any time it is updated) mail or e-mail your service and product menu to your entire contact database. This can be a good way to reconnect with clients you may not have seen in a while or with prospective clients who may now be looking for a new salon or stylist, and can be a way to make clients aware of services they may not have known you offered, or may not have tried before.

- Subscribe to new move-in mailing lists and send a copy of your menu to new residents or to residents living in neighborhoods representing your prime demographic market or ideal clients.

- Include a copy of your menu as a bag stuffer.

- Distribute copies of your menus at local holiday fairs, job fairs, college and career fairs and to large employers in your area.

- Have your designer help you create a larger display version of your menu that you can frame and hang or have printed on a banner or professional sign.

Web site

You can have a web site that does not break the bank, is still well-designed and (most importantly) is effective when it comes to getting your business found online; a web site that does it's real and most important job, which is getting the client or prospect to book the appointment. In fact, this should be the top priority you have when developing your web site or making changes to it—a priority that overrules other goals where there is conflict of purpose or over-complexity caused by too many competing messages.

Many businesses make the mistake of designing a 'corporate brochure' type of web site full of self-congratulatory, "ain't we great!?" statements, or one that contains so much information that the consumer doesn't know where to start (and usually doesn't). Web site content that is not designed to take the viewer on a logical journey, that does not compel the viewer to make the appointment, and that does not highlight only the top 3-4 most important things prospects or customers would be most interested in knowing is probably wasted space from a marketing and business-building point of view and may be so convoluted that it works against that number one goal: Getting the appointment booked.

The *single most important thing* your web site can do is get the client or prospect to book the appointment. And this is made possible by search engine optimization and your content, because more people will *see* your web site if your site is designed in such a way that it gets found online.

Your web site should be a reflection of the brand of your business. The client should get the same "feeling" about your business whether they are visiting your salon in person or online. Your web site helps to create expectations, is a promise of service and begins to set the mood for a new client; after that, your in-salon experience needs to deliver on these promises!

Try to set aside your own personal preferences when it comes to the design of your web site. Try to remember that color, font, and image preferences are just that, preferences. They are subjective. It's more important for your web site to "feel" like the experience in your salon than it is for a designer to create something that you enjoy looking at. If you are working with a skilled designer, be willing to trust some of their recommendations, or at least bring in one or two objective third parties to weigh in with second opinions on areas that you do not feel sure about. (And conversely, it is also true that your designer may have recommendations based on their own preferences—again, this is where bringing in a couple of trusted, savvy business associates can help to choose direction.)

Be concise. The more you dilute the purpose of your web site (which is to get the appointment booked), the more you detract from its effectiveness. Just as you cannot be all things to all people, your web site should not try to tell everyone everything that anyone could possibly want to know about your business. You have just a few seconds to capture your reader's attention; do you really want them scrolling through a bunch of disclaimers and details trying to find your address and phone number? If you do plan to include areas of high text content, consider dedicating specific pages to them or include them as linked downloadable PDFs rather than as web pages.

Prioritize. Knowing that the primary responsibility of your web site is to get the reader to book an appointment, design the journey through your web site with that in mind. Your business phone number and address should be prominent and 'above the fold' on your landing page (if not every page). Your web site could:

- Give your site visitor reasons and the information needed to make it easy to book an appointment
- Give people a reason and an easy way to subscribe to your communications
- Give customers reasons to more deeply engage with your business and to purchase additional services and products from you
- Be a reflection of your brand
- Be easy to navigate
- Be concise
- Be visually stimulating and engaging, be provocative
- Lead the viewer on a logical journey beginning with what would (probably) be what is most important to them
- Be kept up to date
- Change on a regular basis; your web site should show enough 'signs of life' that it does not look like you built it 3 years ago and haven't touched it since
- Contain relevant, interesting content—the kind of content is relevant and interesting to your target audience and customer base

As the internet and the software used to create and maintain sites has evolved, it has never been less expensive or easier to build and update a web site, all on your own if that is your only option. And since it is so easy, it should also be easy for you to update and change your web site frequently so that you can use it strategically to support your most important goals. Here are some of the ways that you can make your web site work for you beyond what should remain the primary purpose (getting the viewer to make an appointment and purchase from you):

- to increase the perceived value of your business by showcasing the most important benefits you provide to customers

- highlighting the unique credentials, talents, skills and expertise possessed by you and your staff in order both to show the benefit to the customer as well as create a desire for prospective clients to want to be part of what you have to offer

- beyond service appointments, to give people additional reasons to come to your business; such as, to purchase gifts for others, support charitable and community causes, or attend events

- to increase client engagement, pull customers more deeply in through education, common interests and causes

- content that will help improve your site's standing in web search results

- creating a sense of "we"; in other words, to help your customers more closely identify with you and your staff, with the causes you support, with other local businesses and resources and resources within your community

- to provide links to and from community and charity resources

- promoting "buy local" consumer education and initiatives

- recognizing the accomplishments of staff, customers, local civic and community leaders, etc.

- conducting surveys and collecting information

- promoting seasonal campaigns or bi-monthly promotions

- selling gift certificates (or even products) online

- promoting web-exclusive offers, coupons or code word savings programs

- gauging customer interest in potential new products or services

- sharing links to businesses with which you cross or cooperatively market in order to increase your value to them as marketing partners as well as to support your joint initiatives

Facebook, Blogs and Social Media

Due to the frequency at which Facebook, blog and other social network applications change, it does not make sense to include step-by-step instructions on how to set up accounts here. The best way for you to become familiar with Facebook, a blog site like the one I use (blogger.com) or any other social marketing and networking site is to set up a personal account before you set up a page for the purpose of promoting your business. This will give you an opportunity to see how to set up your page, and to see how each application works as well as to see how other companies are using it to help build business.

Try not to think about your Facebook, blog or other social media site primarily as a sales medium. Using social media as a forum for hard sales efforts is the quickest way to lose your following and alienate your "friends."

It's not a contradiction to say that you can and should use your social sites to let your followers, friends and fans know about special promotions and events; in fact, you can even create Facebook-only, blog-site only or other social site-only offers, hold contests and conduct virtual events. But those communications should be an organic part of the greater relationships and conversations you are having online with customers, prospective customers and other followers.

> Using social media for **hard sales** is the quickest way to **lose** your following.

Social network site posts and updates should be approached as if they are conversations you are having with people one on one in your living room (rather than your business). Speak to followers in your posts, messages and responses like you are speaking with friends and family. Be relevant, be entertaining, be interesting, be provocative; stimulate thinking about what it is that you do in a way that relates to people personally.

Even more so than with your web site, your social network sites need frequent attention and updates if you want them to benefit to your business. The good news is that you do not have to be a prolific writer in order to create and maintain these sites; your posts or entries will often be limited to a sentence or two in length.

If you want people to pay attention, join, read, "like," and otherwise follow your sites, while your posts can be short, they need to be interesting and relevant to your target audiences. You can talk about more than just your business or area of expertise; this is a forum where people expect and want you to be personal over and above your professional objectives. This is a forum where you should communicate conversationally and with personality.

In addition to business topics, other things you might post about could be:

- Quotes—inspirational, funny, poignant, profound—this is an area where what speaks to you will probably speak to others

- Statistics; statistic-based facts relative to beauty, health, fitness, fashion or that are humorous, profound, location-based—there are many possibilities, just be interesting!

- Personal anecdotes (nothing that you would not want your mother, most straight-laced client or an employer to read!)

- "Did you know?" type of questions about common hair or skin care challenges, conditions and product solutions

- Community information and links

- Links to beauty, health and well-being articles and information, or on related topics such as fitness, men's or women's health, kid's resources, nutrition, etc.

- Events and follow up on events with photos and highlights

- Kudos, thank yous and recognition of accomplishments

- Tips and tricks for the season, for special occasions, or on special topics

- Introduction and overview of new products and services

- Service and/or product of the month spotlight

- Facebook, blog, or other social site-exclusive offers, coupons or contests

- Site-only immediate-response offers; such as, "the first 5 people to comment below will receive..."

- Reminders about expiring offers and teasers for new things coming soon

E-mail

Trying to run an effective e-mail campaign without e-mail addresses is like trying to invite people to your wedding without addresses. The invitations are printed and sealed, sitting there on the desk all beautiful and ready to go; but until you address the envelopes, they won't go anywhere!

Make it your goal to collect 100% of your client's e-mail addresses. Every event, promotion or contest should include basic data collection for clients and prospective clients. Your web site should have a form for e-mail sign up. Ask every client for their e-mail address and permission to include them in your e-mail communications at every appointment. And if you are collecting e-mail addresses, enter them into your contact database and ensure that they start receiving communications as quickly as possible.

I know this sounds basic, but believe it or not, there are still many people in the salon and spa service industry who say they are afraid they will "annoy" their customers if they ask them for e-mail addresses. Some assert that (unlike most U.S. consumers, and contrary to all recent studies which say the opposite) *their* customers are "not on e-mail" or do not want to receive e-mails.

Maybe there are a few people in your clientele who will ask not to be contacted by e-mail; but building your e-mail contact database is the only way for you to use e-mail communication to build business. Allowing negative feedback from one or two people to limit your ability to communicate with all of your customers is foolish!

And using it as an excuse is just lazy. If you are looking for an excuse because you simply do not want to make the effort, you need to come up with a better reason.

In today's society, most people expect to be contacted by e-mail and many prospective as well as current clients will want to be on your e-mailing list. It is permission-based from end to end; people give you permission to e-mail them, so they want and expect you to do so. Once they receive the e-mail, there is still no coercion. They have the ability to open the e-mail or to save it for later or delete it without even reading. They have the ability to print it or to forward it to a friend. They have the ability to unsubscribe from your e-mailing list at any time. Your readers have all of the power in the e-mail relationship; all they want from you is interesting, relevant and compelling content!

In order to keep your e-mails out of the junk e-mail folders and to keep your readers—well, reading—here are a few guidelines for using e-mail:

- Be as personal as possible. Even when you are sending a message out to all of your contacts, write as though you are speaking to just one person.

- Make sure that all content is relevant to the customer, and is written from a customer-centric point of view; remember, it is not about what is good for you, it is (only) about what is good for the customer. What's good for your customer *is* what's good for your business. If you write about your business as though you believe that your customer's primary interest is in your bottom line, it won't take long for them to delete your e-mails, stop opening them or unsubscribe altogether. And once you lose your customer's trust in this area, it will be difficult to regain it.

- Keep messages brief and readable in a quick sitting.

- Keep e-mail addresses private; when sending a personal group e-mail, put the e-mail addresses in the "BCC" (blind carbon copy) field, not the "TO" field where they can be seen by others. Better yet, utilize an e-mail resource such as Constant Contact (www.constantcontact.com) to manage your lists and conduct your mailings. Utilizing an e-mail marketing service will also help prevent having your personal or business e-mail black-listed as spam and gives you the ability to manage your contact database and quickly, easily send e-mail messages to all or targeted groups of subscribers.

  There is a link to Constant Contact on the Resources page of www.12monthsofmarketing.net, and as of the time of this writing, you can try their services out for free. Contact me if you need assistance creating your account or building a template to use for communications, or if you are interested in outsourcing your e-mail communications and would like a quote for services.

- Be yourself. Even your e-mail communications reflect the brand of you and your business in imagery and language.

- Include inspiration, insight and humor. If something you heard about touched or inspired you, chances are it will inspire and engage others.

- Be protective. If you would not want to read it about yourself, don't write it about someone else. Never, ever share the personal information of staff or clients without permission, even if you are sharing good news.

- Before you hit 'send,' re-read what you have written at least twice; read it out loud to see if it sounds like something that you would say.

- Ask a peer to proof-read any communications before sending out to groups of clients for language, branding, tone and as your back up to prevent dissemination of any inappropriate information.

When crafting communications for *any* purpose, focus on the positive of what you do offer and provide (not on what you don't do or sell). Be honest and communicate what is necessary, but try not to focus on the disclaimers of your offers, the negative parts of your policies, or on exclusions or limitations. Speak in positive terms even when you are conveying policy, such as your policy regarding children in the salon.

As an example, rather than saying, "leave your kids at home!" (which could be off-putting to customers even if they never brought kids with them to an appointment), state something that they can relate to in a more positive way, such as your intent to create a customer-focused experience for each client, a pampering escape from their everyday life and responsibilities, etc., and that children need to be supervised by someone over the age of 14 if they need to be in the salon during your appointment.

And again, be concise. Your e-mail messages should be brief, with each item being no more than just a few sentences. People skim e-mails, looking for headlines or pictures which catch their eyes. If you do need to send something with large text content, place it at the bottom with a link or as a separate web page or PDF with a link in the e-mail such as:

[click here to read more]

Send new subscribers a welcome e-mail message as quickly as possible, and set up a regular schedule of communications to keep your business in the forefront of their minds. If you provide readers with interesting and relevant content, they will look forward to receiving your communications; and (for those still terrified of sending e-mails to their customers) remember that no matter how often you send e-mails, the power of opening them and the choice to read them (or not) will always reside with the recipient.

If you are just beginning to do e-mail marketing, try setting a goal for yourself to send one e-mail each month to your total e-mail database. Think of it as your business newsletter, a chance to let customers know what is new, what special offers, events, contests and promotions you have for them in the coming weeks, which offers are about to expire, and to share highlights about what happened during the previous few weeks. In harmony with your social networking communications, include your product or service of the month spotlight feature (you can use the same for both).

Once you publish your e-mail newsletter, put a link on your Facebook, blog or other social networking site to the web version of your e-mail message so that people who have not yet subscribed can also read what is, essentially, your monthly e-newsletter. Place a link on your web site to your most recent e-newsletter.

Are you beginning to see how all of these tools can work together to help support your brand and your marketing messages in order to help you break through the clutter? In an era when people are bombarded with thousands of marketing messages every single day, creating brand and messaging consistency and giving your clients multiple ways to receive your messages greatly increases the chance that your information will get to them. They might receive an e-mail newsletter, postcard, see your Facebook post and receive a bag stuffer at their appointment each highlighting the same special offer or spotlight product or service—and all without you having to deliver so much as a single sales pitch from behind the chair!

By doing this, you will build brand awareness and gain mind share with clients and prospects so that by the time you actually sample or demonstrate the featured product or service at the client appointment, or as they pass by the display, they will already have been exposed to information about it and will already have an idea of how it can benefit them. By the time you invite them personally to an event, they will already know what it is and which of their friends might also be interested in attending.

Now that you have (hopefully) overcome the objections or fears you may have harbored about e-mail marketing and you are excited to get started, here are a few ways that you can put e-mail to work for you:

- Appointment reminders

- Sending directions and contact information

- Thank you notes (personal)

- E-Newsletters (short for Electronic or E-mail Newsletters)

- Promotional service or retail offers for clients

- Event announcements and reminders

- Collecting RSVPs and taking reservations

- Appointment inquiries from your web site

- Cooperative marketing and advertising with your business partners

- Extending recognitions, kudos, and congratulations

- Invitations (mass or personal)

- New subscriber welcome

- New client welcome, thank you reward, and/or menu of services

- Featured product and/or service of the month

- Special promotions

- E-mail exclusive offers (use a code word for these to help you track response)

- Highlighting community resources or worthy causes

- Increasing awareness of your business as a gift resource

- Personal birthday, anniversary or other special occasion greetings

- To extend special offers to large employers, seniors, schools, students or other special groups

- To send referral rewards or rewards status updates

- Announce contests or winners

- To conduct customer surveys or collect information about customer preferences, interests, etc.

September Promotion Ideas

Focus not only on what you are communicating to clients but on whether you are taking advantage of all the ways at your disposal to do so. Set up a plan and a manageable schedule to help you coordinate all of your communications to ensure that they all reflect the brand, messaging and "feel" that you want to convey, and so that you are using them in concert in order to maximize their impact.

September Month-Long Observances

September is Classical Music Month and National Piano Month

Partner with local music studios and piano teachers for cross marketing; extend local music teachers a special offer and/or seek nominations for the best area music teacher for a gift card and pampering product reward. Extend a special offer to all nominees and to those who nominated them.

Create a gift basket with gift card and pampering products and a favorite music album or a musical movie and promote it to clients as a gift for music teachers, dance instructors and other music professionals.

Add pre-recital and pre-performance hair color, styling, manicure and/or makeup services to your menu. Add post-performance de-stressing massages or other services to your menu.

September is Fall Hat Month

Design and purchase a salon or spa-branded fun hat for fall retail. Purchase salon or spa-branded "beanie" hats for winter and holiday retail sales, gift-with-purchase, to incentivize purchase of men's products or services, or as employee or client gifts.

Create a "no hat needed" hair styling and product promotion featuring a new celebrity-inspired, easy-to-manage hair style and your favorite finishing products.

September is Better Breakfast Month

Partner with your favorite breakfast spot for cross marketing or a special cooperative event or offer; partner with a local radio station for a live breakfast broadcast at your favorite venue in support of a local charity. Or provide a surprise breakfast for your staff.

Hold a special event or donate a portion of sales in September to support your local school's breakfast or hot lunch program.

Animals have Hair, Too!
The Truth about Cats and Dogs

September and October are a national focus months for pets and there are probably hundreds of pet owners and animal lovers in your clientele, and thousands more in your greater community. Partner with local veterinarian practices, groomers, pet shops or boarding facilities for cross or cooperative promotions and events.

According to the Humane Society (humanesociety.org), 39% of US households own at least one dog, and 34% of US Households own at least one cat. A significant number of those households, in both cases, own more than one pet.

This is a significant area of opportunity when it comes to networking, cooperative and cross marketing with local veterinarians, dog groomers, pet stores, breeders and kennels. You share similar demographics for 'ideal client' markets and many pet care providers have very loyal followings. Some are already even engaged in regular print and e-mail marketing. You also share values because you are all concerned for the health, well being, and appearance of your clients. Create open house events, pet receptions, off-leash park tailgating days and other opportunities for cross-promotions.

Some salons have already realized that they have an opportunity to expand retail sales by carrying pet shampoo and care supplies; it's a great opportunity to expand your retail in pet care and fun or salon-branded pet supplies such as food and water dishes, brushes, pet (lint) rollers, etc. Bringing this kind of one-stop convenience to the pet owners among your clientele is also a natural extension of 'what you do' in bringing quality products clients can trust to meet the needs of their pets when it comes to skin and fur care.

If you love animals yourself, post a bulletin board in your business in September to hold pet pictures, starting it off with one of your own. Ask people to bring in photos of their pets or submit them to you online via your web site, Facebook page, blog site or e-mail in order to save a percentage or dollar amount on the retail pet products they purchase (and/or their people hair care products, too.)

For a charitable aspect, add an event to support your local animal shelter with dollars or by encouraging (or even facilitating) pet adoptions to good families. You can offer to post pictures of local shelter animals in the salon or online, provide applications, and create a special offer for clients who adopt a shelter pet in September (and for all your pet-loving clients).

Man and Beast Grooming Package

Reach out to attract clients among area pet owners by partnering with a local groomer who has the ability to provide mobile services to come to your location and provide pet grooming while your clients receive their services. It will take cooperation and coordination ahead of time to co-book your pet-loving clients.

Partner with the groomer to create a package which will be offered to their clientele as well as yours, offering a dollar or percentage off services occurring simultaneously and accompanied by a second bounce back offer if they pre-book their next service appointment (within 4 weeks for men, 6 for women, and as prescribed by the groomer for pets!)

If clients love this, partner with the groomer for joint people-and-pet service hours on an on-going basis.

Shelter Me

Create a special offer for clients who adopt a shelter pet this month. To facilitate the opportunity for clients, partner with your local shelter to create an in-salon event to pair clients with adoptable pets on a Saturday. Publicize in advance through newspapers and community resources and post on your supermarket or community center bulletin board.

Food 'N' Shelter

Contact your local shelter to find out if there are items they need and accept as donations and offer clients a free add-on service or discount when they bring these items in or make a cash donation to the shelter. Create awareness for the shelter as well as your business; at the end of the month, write an article about this effort as a press release for print in your local newspaper and submit it along with testimonial from the shelter as well as a picture of a four-legged shelter friend that tugs at the heart. If possible, create an on-going discount to extend to pet-lovers in conjunction with support of the shelter, and ask the shelter to provide patrons with a copy of your offer.

Retail Opportunities

A growing number of salons are carrying professional retail items for pets including shampoo and other hair care products: toys, collars, bowls, brushes and other supplies. It's an area where you can experiment with little risk; if you don't want to buy in products yourself, partner with a local veterinarian or groomer and offer to give them shelf space in return for commission on items sold. Your clients will appreciate the convenience of not having to make a trip to the pet store. And don't forget the bling! Collars, dishes and holiday pet-wear make great impulse buys and gifts.

Pet Owners Paradise!

If you brought in retail products for pets, give pet owners a discount on retail purchases for their pet when they purchase retail products for themselves. Or, in conjunction with a groomer, extend an on-going discount for dual pet-and-owner grooming bookings or product purchases.

A Picture's Worth a Thousand ... Pennies

When your client brings in a picture of their pet that makes you say "awwwww..." give them a thousand pennies— or Ten Paws ($10)—off service or retail purchases totaling $50 or more.

September Week-Long Observances

The Third Week of September is National Assisted Living Week

Extend a special offer to the residents of local assisted living, retirement living communities, nursing homes or senior centers. Provide services in-home for seniors in your area who may not be able to travel to appointments. Help coordinate group or small group transportation for seniors to your salon or spa on a given day each week or each month.

Hold a workshop at a local senior center for senior skin and hair care, nail care (pedicures are especially important for seniors) and distribute or sell samples, travel or retail-sized products as well as bounce-back offers.

The Fourth Week of September is Build a Better Image Week

Partner with a motivational speaker or life coach for a seminar and cooperative offers; building a better image involves work on the inside and the outside, and people who feel like they look their best are more confident!

September Holidays and Observances

September 6 is Read a Book Day

Commit to reading at least one book for business or personal development before the end of this year, or commit to reading one every month. If you need a place to start, try some of the books listed at the bottom of the main page of my blog at www.savvystylist.net.

In anticipation of upcoming holidays, think about adding tasteful gift-quality books about love, friendship, photography, landscape, points of local interest, etc. to your retail offerings. For a list of some gift-suitable books visit my web site at www.12monthsofmarketing.net and click on "Resources."

Add coffee table or gift books to your retail offerings or to your waiting area. Pair gift books with coordinating blank gift cards and gift bags to make gift-giving easy for clients (and don't forget signage and scripting that suggests the addition of a salon or spa gift card!)

September 10 is Swap Ideas Day

Create a support network among peers such as other salon or spa professionals and/or other small business owners. Schedule monthly meetings for this group to share challenges and ideas as well as to create cross and cooperative marketing initiatives.

Create a charity-benefit swap event with cover charge where clients can bring-one, take-one of items like jeans, jewelry, books, home accessories or some other category.

Why should Starbucks have all the fun? Create a reading area within your business (or in cooperation with another nearby business) with a book swap library on an on-going basis for clients. Add a coffee or tea offering; if demand corresponds, partner with a local vendor to bring in a small selection of sandwiches or cookies to sell.

Add a "Swap Ideas" question and answer section or an electronic 'bulletin board' to your blog or Facebook page where clients can ask one another questions or get information about local resources such as tourist points of interest, shopping centers, repair or renovation resources, etc.

Give Away a Fortune

Purchase spa or salon-branded fortune cookies or create a custom fortune cookie line with your own favorite inspirational quotes and messages. Gift a fortune cookie with purchase for clients, serve them at the end of an event or make them available in the waiting area.

Include a few occasional random offers or freebies in your fortune cookie messages like bounce-back offers or to give away samples of new products or services that you want your clients to get excited about.

Branded, custom fortune cookies could be a great product to distribute in cross-marketing efforts with other businesses, to utilize at events or just to create some excitement at the cash register.

September 16 is National Play Dough Day

Purchase salon or spa-branded play dough from a promotional products vendor and make it available for retail sale, gift-with-purchase or as incentives for clients to book their children's appointments when they book their own.

Purchase play dough or silly putty for children to play with when clients must bring children to appointments.

September 19 is Talk Like a Pirate Day

Included because it's my daughter Sarah's favorite! On 'Talk Like a Pirate Day,' let staff dress in pirate garb for the day and tell clients to "walk the plank" instead of saying goodbye. Create a special pirate punch and snack for clients. Place a 'treasure chest' at your point of purchase displaying seasonal retail gifts for purchase and gold-wrapped chocolate coins for client treats.

Hold a happy hour for the pirates among your clientele, or hold a joint event at a local bar or restaurant complete with 'fishy' food and games.

Extend an offer for a free kid's haircut when booked at the same time as a parent's appointment with the idea of encouraging your clients to bring their children to your salon or spa rather than frequenting some of your more generic, walk-in style salon competitors.

September 20 is National Punch Day

Create a special punch or sangria recipe to serve to customers. Hold a contest and solicit client's favorite punch recipes. Hold a punch tasting event for entrants and reward the winner with a gift card and prize basket. Reward all entrants with a bounce-back offer that packs real punch!

Give double punches on client's reward punch cards for appointments or for retail purchases made on this day, during this week, or during the whole month of September.

Partner with a kick-boxing aerobics instructor or an actual boxing gymnasium for a cross or cooperatively-marketed event or offer.

September 21 is World Gratitude Day

If you are not in the habit of writing thank you notes to at least your most faithful clients, start today. Commit to writing at least one thank you note each day (or one to each client, if possible).

Thank your staff for their work and acknowledge special talents or personality traits with a personal note left as a surprise sometime this month. A spirit of gratitude tends to be contagious, spreading not only to those who receive the note, but putting the sender in a more positive state of mind as well. Plus, acknowledging and rewarding behavior you want more of tends to bring more of the same!

Purchase salon or spa-branded note cards for thank you notes.

Design and purchase one-of-a-kind blank cards, thank you note cards or boxed sets of cards to add to your retail offerings. Be sure that your blank notes are near your gift card display and sized appropriately so they can be easily paired by guests for gift giving.

September 22 is Business Women's Day

Invite business women to drop off a business card as entry in a special drawing where the winner/s will receive a gift card and prize basket, or create an on-going drawing for a free haircut or other service (or product) for local businesswomen each month.

Hold a happy hour for the business women among your clientele featuring a guest speaker, live music, business fashion show or some other area of interest or fun for busy working women.

Join your local Rotary, Merchant's Club or Chamber of Commerce and get involved in networking to build the strength of your city's businesses. If your city has a 'buy local' campaign; get involved, if not, start one! Extend a special offer to members of your Chamber of Commerce, City Hall, Tourism Board and other city offices.

September 28 is Ask a Stupid Question Day

Hold a contest for your clients to find out which one can ask the most creative, thought provoking, funny, profound—or even stupid—question. Post question entries online and in the salon for public vote.

Create a 'Frequently Asked Questions' section on your web site with answers to clients most common skin or hair care questions or conditions that commonly occur. Suggest services and products that can reduce and repair the effects of aging on hair, scalp and skin. Suggest products that can extend the life of hair color or protect hair from breakage or chemical damage. Create signage for the salon and post some of the most compelling questions/answers in the salon, as station talkers, etc. Asking questions can be a great way to stimulate retail product sales—and that's never stupid!

September 30 is National Mud Pack Day

Create a special offer around relevant services and products clients can use at home to pamper, moisturize, repair and restore the skin. If you do not usually carry skin care products, purchase a point of purchase display with a special serum or cream wrinkle-reducer for lips and eyes, a cooling eye gel or another similar product for retail sale.

If you do not offer spa or skin care services, partner with a local dermatologist, esthetician or spa for a joint event or invite a local esthetician to demonstrate services to your clients in the form of mini-services or samples and other 'in the chair' demos throughout the month. Extend a special offer to their clients.

September 30 is Healthy Aging Month

September is Healthy Aging Month—an ideal time to promote anti-aging and reparative hair care, skin care, or makeup products and services. Or partner with a local esthetician or dermatologist to provide healthy aging retail promotions, events and education to your clients.

September Planning and Tasks

Order retail products from manufacturer's September-October, November-December and Holiday offerings to support your promotions for October and continuing through to the end of the holiday season. The more sales you capture in October and November for holiday, before shoppers focus on traditional retail outlets, the better!

Think outside the box and try some new point of purchase and impulse buy items and displays for the holiday season. Ask some of your favorite clients to participate in a survey or small group and run some of your ideas past them relative to expanding your retail to include items suitable for holiday or year-round gift giving.

Use messaging in displays, postcards, newsletters, and station talkers to speak specifically and clearly to customers about the items you are suggesting for gifts, including gift certificates themselves. Partner with local boutiques, wine shops, coffee shops, gift shops, artisans, etc., for combined holiday-suggestive point of purchase displays and combination offers. Purchase salon-branded novelty, party, hostess and gift items.

Develop marketing and promotional materials for events, retail promotions and contests going out through December. Early planning is vital to a successful holiday season, especially since you might only see clients twice from October to December. Plan now for your complete slate of October, November and December events and promotions. Choose a charitable endeavor to support during the holidays like adopting a family, shelter, pet shelter, or children's services, etc., that will speak to your customers emotions and help fulfill their desire to give to others in the community.

Communicate in September

Items to include in your e-mail or print newsletter, web site, Facebook and blog posts and in direct mail communications this month:

- September and October events and promotions; save the date for major holiday events or sales you will be holding

- September contests and August winners

- Extend your August back-to-school efforts by suggesting 'care package' items for college students; continue to suggest retail products and gift certificates as gifts for teachers and coaches

- Promotions expiring in September, new products coming for October and holidays

- Last minute openings on the books

- A spotlight product, service or staff member of the month

September Calendar / Suggested Communications and Tasks Schedule

SUN	MON	TUE	WED	THU	FRI	SAT
1st week of Month						
1st of September—Merchandise for September						
1st of September—Begin collecting entries for September contests						
			Order from manufacturers retail promotions for products to support October - November marketing plans; design related signage		Send September Newsletter with coupons, announce contests and winners, new products and services coming events, openings still on the books, events and promotions	
2nd week of Month						
			Order event supplies, postcards, collateral, gifts and salon-branded items for October, November and December contests		Write press releases for any events/results reporting or future events / charitable focus	
3rd week of Month						
			Finalize, review and lay out plans for October - November - December events and promotions		Send September "last chance" promotions and openings on the books e-mail and/or direct mail	
4th week of Month						
Last day of September—Take down any September-only promotions						
Last day of September—Draw September contest winners						
			Design and select salon-branded holiday wear and items for holiday retail		Send October focus e-mail / direct mail	

September Worksheets

$_____ Retail Sales Goal

Promotions_____

_____

_____

_____

_____

$_____ Avg. Retail/Client

$_____ Retail Sales Results

$_____ Service Sales Goal

Promotions_____

_____

_____

_____

_____

$_____ Avg. Service/Client

$_____ Service Sales Results

$_____ Event Revenues Goal

Events _____

_____

_____

_____

_____

#_____ Attending Event/s

#_____ Apts/Booked at Event

$_____ Event/s Sales

$_____ Total Event/s Results

$_____ Charity/Fund Raising Goal

Charity Events _____

_____

_____

_____

_____

#_____ Attending Event/s

#_____ Apts/Booked at Event

$_____ Charity Event/s Sales

$_____ Total Charity Results

September Marketing Summary

Marketing Partners: _____

_____

_____

_____

Marketing Collateral Needed (or Used): _____

_____

_____

_____

Other Efforts:

#_____ Number of Clients New to Salon

%_____ Client Retention Rate (90 days)

Retention Efforts: _____

_____

or % _____ Clients Re-booked at Appointment

$_____ Gift Certificate Sales

#_____ Contacts added to marketing / e-mail database

october

make over
your events

Holding events is a natural way to enhance business in the salon or spa to entice and reward customers for being part of your community, as a means of gaining new referrals and contacts, and in order to bring clients to a more deeper level of engagement with (and loyalty to) your business. While most salon and spa owners want to hold events, some are truly too busy to properly plan and execute events, some do not understand the advance work needed, and others misgauge customer interest, lack necessary resources or space, cannot get employee 'buy in,' or simply come up with a great idea at the wrong time or with too little time to execute—any one of which can seriously undermine the potential for success of any event.

In any case, successfully executing events that meet specific goals is going to come down to that four letter word: Plan.

One of the most frustrating problems when it comes to marketing is when you get a great idea for an event but you realize that you needed to have come up with the idea weeks earlier in order to execute it. It has happened to me, and this has probably happened to you more than once when it comes to events for special occasions like Valentine's Day, Mothers Day or another holiday or for seasonal focus themes such as graduation, prom, or bridal: You or your team came up with a great idea or you were told or read about an event held by another business that you would love to repeat. But since the idea came too late to execute or the holiday or observance has already passed you by, you mentally file the idea away, promising yourself that you will do it when the next chance comes around. However, when the next opportunity arrives, that idea is buried down deep under the weight of the passage of time and the busyness of your daily grind.

To begin to make over your marketing when it comes to events, commit to making three small but fundamental changes:

1 - No more filing ideas away "mentally."
Carry a small notebook with you—keep it in your purse, your briefcase, backpack or car, and keep one on your reception desk, night stand and kitchen counter—so that you always have a place to jot down your good ideas, no matter where you are.

2 - Set up an idea file.
When you see something in print or online that sparks a great event idea, drop a copy into your file. When genius strikes and you record a great idea in your notebook, drop a copy into your idea file. When you attend an event that inspires you, keep souvenir programs, pictures, clippings, etc., and—yep, you guessed it—drop them into your idea file.

3 - Set aside a monthly, scheduled block of time.
Set aside a specific block of time on the calendar every month to review your idea notebook and files against opportunities that will arise in the coming months. Don't wait for 'spare time' that may never come. Like any other 'exercise,' if you don't make this a monthly, mandatory "appointment" for yourself, you will probably never get around to it.

During this time you set aside each month, think at least three months ahead in order to anticipate and plan promotions. That means that if today is your October planning session, you are finalizing any last details for November's promotions and events, you are beginning to execute preparation work for December's and you are laying out a general plan for January. Thinking out at least three months ahead will help ensure that you don't miss any more opportunities and will give you the time you need to garner employee enthusiasm and buy-in, to identify potential marketing and event partners, to delegate responsibilities, and will provide you with enough time to properly market your event or promotion.

Working backward from your desired event date, add tasks and deadlines to your marketing calendar where they make the most sense in order to marry the new tasks into your basic communications schedule and to lay out event preparation responsibilities. This will help to keep your time line and tasks manageable and practical in light of regular work, other responsibilities, staffing, etc. Defining tasks which need to be done ahead of time will also make it easier to enlist help, delegate and share responsibilities with others. Having a written time line, including assigned responsibilities, will give you the ability to stay on target, to quickly make up missed tasks, and to hold staff accountable.

Depending on the complexity and scope of a given event, you may need more time or less to execute an event from preparation through to post-event activities, but you can still use the general suggestions below to help set up your schedule:

7 Questions to answer before setting a date

1. What is the goal of your event? Most, if not all of the activities incorporated into your event should support your main goal in one way or another.

2. What would characterize the ideal attendees for this particular event?

   a. Who in general will be invited?
   b. Who will be specifically targeted with invitations?

3. What will happen at the event? What will happen to help you reach your goal that is customer-centric and persuasive enough to (a) entice people to attend and (b) to do what you want them to do?

4. When will the event be held?

    a. Date/s

    b. Beginning and End Times

5. Where will the event be held? You may actually need to answer this question before #4 above as your location may dictate both your date and beginning and end times. Alternately, if the date of the event is more important than the location, the date you choose may limit or dictate your event location. In other words, you need to determine whether the place you want to hold your location is more important than the date, or vice versa.

    a. How many people do you expect to attend?

    b. How much space do you need to hold activities?

    c. What will be the flow of the basic event time line and the flow through your space?

6. Assign responsibilities: Who will do what?

7. What will happen after the event?

Notice how far down the list actually setting the date, time and place occur; that is because the questions you answer prior to these will greatly impact when and where your event will take place. All too often we come up with event ideas and calendar them based on free weekends or slow days (in other words, what works best for you) when in reality, your event goal and what would be most convenient for your ideally-desired attendees should dictate the answer to those questions. Your event should be held at a time most conducive to their schedules and at the place most likely to entice them to come and facilitate your goal.

The Goal

The event itself is not the goal, unless your (only) goal is to assemble people in one place. Setting specific goals for your events will help you as you sift through all of the possible variables; who to invite, what will happen at the event, and who will be responsible for what.

You may actually have more than one goal for an event; if so, prioritize all of your goals in their order of importance so as to help as you make other decisions and plan the event itself. If you try to accomplish too many different things with one event, you may end up with an event that feels as fragmented as your competing goals. If you find yourself in this scenario, consider breaking up your goals into multiple events or limiting them to the one or two most important goals, rather than trying to accomplish all of them at once.

Here are some event goals and tactics which may help to support them:

- To gain clients new to the salon, try
    - meaningful, compelling bring-a-friend rewards or incentives
    - adding a strong social components to event activities
    - inviting clients likely to have friends, co-workers or family that have characteristics of your ideal attendees
    - working with partnering businesses to extend your reach to additional prospects
    - targeting large pools of individuals in organizations within your community whose employee, client or patron base has characteristics of your ideal attendees (large employers, schools, community groups, charity supporters, seniors, etc.)

- To launch new products or services, try
    - incorporating sampling and demonstrations into your event
    - inviting manufacturer's representatives, educators or other expert presenters to help
    - giving away samples and making stickered "Try Me" products available (such as setting up a "skin bar" with products and experts to help apply or teach application techniques)
    - inviting 'pioneers' and influencers among your clientele—people who like to be the "first" to do something, who would enjoy exclusive access to a new product or service, or who would be likely to build buzz among their friends and family about your products or services
    - inviting those of your clients who are the most engaged and enthusiastic about other services or your business as a whole

- To sell through retail products, try
    - inviting clients who most often purchase retail products from you
    - inviting clients who have asked questions about your products or products used during services
    - extending an event-exclusive offer, incentive or special event-only pricing; communicating benefits and adding value
    - featuring celebrity and expert endorsements and recommendations
    - creating specific instructional use, cocktailing and application tip sheets to send home with products

- To sell pre-sold services or packages of services, try
    - inviting your most enthusiastic, appreciative and engaged clients
    - creating a true client-appreciation event
    - incorporating demos, mini-services and sampling into your event
    - inviting expert presenters and industry celebrities and incorporating customer testimonials
    - promoting exclusivity, being part of the "in crowd," emphasizing that offers are only for invited clients, and inviting clients who would most appreciate V.I.P. status
    - inviting people who are likely to be able to afford to purchase packages of pre-sold services and/or products
    - inviting people who would appreciate the convenience of pre-booked services and/or savings over time by pre-paying

- To increase client engagement, try
    - using demonstrations and sampling to get clients connected with services and products they have not previously tried
    - bringing in marketing / event partners in order to become the facilitator to bring other resources directly to your clients
    - incorporating a customer survey
    - holding a focus group event
    - creating an event to take attendees on a journey through multiple touch points of your business (or through all services)
    - inviting attendees that share common interests, support common causes, or might be likely to make a social connection
    - holding a combination social event / mixer with demonstration and/or sampling
    - incorporating contests with prizes and door prizes into the event that feature several of your products and services
    - ensuring that staff on hand are educated about products and services, or inviting expert presenters to communicate how your products and your business improves the lives of your clients

Who Should You Invite?

Think beyond answering "everyone," because 'who' should be invited to your event and the people on whom you should expend extra effort and energy when it comes to inviting people should be specifically related to your goal. If your primary goal is to attract new clients, then focus specifically on inviting prospective clients— individuals outside of your current client base—as well as on the clients in your current base who would be most likely to bring a friend (in your desired target market) to your event.

If your goal involves selling big ticket packages of services and products, then you need a strong invitational push to existing clients, and specifically to your most loyal, enthusiastic clients—those clients most likely to want to move to the next level of engagement with you, who are the most likely to be able to afford, or who would be most likely to commit themselves to the services that you or your business provides over an extended period of time. Identify clients who would be motivated by convenience, value or inclusiveness and by the personal V.I.P. attention represented by becoming a 'club' customer or purchasing a series of pre-paid and pre-booked appointments, and focus your energies on enticing them to attend the event.

Even if your event is general enough (like an Open House) to be marketed to 'everyone' in your contact database via e-mail, your web site, direct mail invitations, salon signage, word of mouth, etc., you should still identify clients and prospective client types that you would most like to draw to your event based on who would be representative of your ideal overall client base and target markets. To improve event results and increase the likelihood of meeting your goals, target specific individuals or groups with additional and with more personal invitations. For instance, if your goal is to increase sales of makeup or manicure/pedicure services, extend additional, personal invitations to those among your client base who would be more likely to use those services or products. Incentivize clients who fall within your ideal target markets to bring friends to your event. Extend special invitations via hand-delivered flyers to local businesses whose employees or whose customers fall within your desired target markets. Mail, e-mail or hand-deliver invitations to civic groups, church organizations, or other organizations whose members fall within your desired demographics.

What Will Happen at the Event?

In order to draw people to your event and meet your goal, what happens at the event itself must be customer-centric. If you sent out invitations saying something to the effect of, "gee, things are slow for our new stylists, could you please send some clients our way?" you can expect a return of zero in your investment, and you might even lose a few regular clients in the process. Just as with all of your marketing, what will entice individuals to attend and to bring people with them and what will persuade them to facilitate your goal when it comes to the sale of services or products is *what is in it for the client* (not for you). The activities held during the event must entice, entertain and benefit the client, and the way that you craft messaging for your invitations must be centered around the benefits, possible prizes, samples, demonstrations, education, social connections, etc., for the client.

If your goal is to bring in new clients by way of client referrals (clients bringing friends or family to the event), then your event should be populated by activities that facilitates the interaction of people who are likely to enjoy one another personally and socially.

If you want to sell more makeup and increase your makeup product and service client base, don't discount your cosmetics; instead, hold a skin bar happy hour complete with wine tasting or cocktails. Bring in a professional party planner, chef, caterer, or other expert to give tips to guests on how to make and present party fare or cocktails. Teach them how to create party makeup looks at home. Pre-package coordinating makeup selections for sale at the event at event-only pricing.

Turn up the music. Give away door prizes with salon or spa-branded gifts, samples and a bounce-back offer. Guide guests on a journey through service area stations that includes ample sampling and a chance to play with makeup and skin care products. This journey might also include hair and scalp analysis, scalp massage, hair color consultation, mini manicures, etc.; all of which are accompanied by short, written "prescriptions" for recommended services and products.

Create star-quality goodie bags for everyone who attends with samples plus branded products like nail files, compacts, lip balms, hand sanitizers—the types of items we all like to keep around in purses, backpacks and cars. Make sure every goodie bag includes one or more bounce-back offers from your business and encourage your marketing partners to give you samples, tchotchkes, gift certificates and/or special offers to include as well. Packing value into your event will help clients justify out-of-pocket cover charges or expenditures at the event.

At each station, give participants a brief 1-2 line written "prescription" so that when their journey through the salon or spa is complete, they have several product and service recommendations to choose from when it comes to booking their appointment or selecting products for purchase. Once an attendee has visited all of the stations, reward them with a retail product gift, salon or spa-branded product, or with a gift card redeemable at their next appointment.

Hold door prize drawings throughout the event to keep people there. Bring in partnering businesses to extend the reach of your events in terms of invitees and to add additional items and offers to goodie bags and prizes. Work with partnering businesses to help share costs and responsibilities and invite their employees and their employees' families to participate. (Their employees and families may be 'ideal' prospective clients, too!)

To help persuade people to attend and participate, add a charitable cause to your event and donate the cover charge or a portion of proceeds to a local worthy cause. Invite employees from the charity and their patrons to attend the event. Adding a charitable cause also gives you a compelling angle for garnering press coverage; generate a press release before and after the event to submit to local news publications, radio stations and civic organizations.

While it might be tempting to dilute your focus by promoting retail product or service sales other than within your main goal area, the more that you keep the focus of activities, talking points and sampling related to specific goals, the more successful you will be in meeting them. Create focused merchandising areas and keep the spotlight on them. Let the follow up appointment or the next event become the forum to expand the client's exposure to other retail areas.

No matter what activities your event will feature, you should have a plan to collect the contact information of all attendees either through a check in or check out process. Contact information cards can double as entries for door prizes or contests, for prizes to be awarded after the event, etc. You can have these cards printed up on postcard or even business card size stock, asking attendees:

- Name

- E-mail address

- Phone (optional)

- Mailing address

- New to salon/spa?

- How they heard about the event (this will help you track the effectiveness of how you marketed as well as to know who among your clientele were motivated to bring guests to your event, and who should be thanked)

Set the Date and Time for the Event

You might instinctively want to schedule your event for a date and time that works best for your business, for you, or your staff, or you might limit yourself to times that your salon would normally be closed. But again, when deciding on the best date and time for your event, the goal and especially the client—those people you most want to attend—should be your primary consideration.

If the goal for your event is meant to be appealing to working professionals, a weekend evening or weeknight after work might be best. However, if you want to draw stay at home moms, you might want to hold an event when most kids are in school, or during an evening when they might want and be able to get out of the house. Consider whether you might be infringing on work, leisure or family time. In consideration of the demands on the lives of your regular clients and especially those you most want to attend, you might want to schedule an event during times that they would normally book their appointments. This consideration might even lead you to create a full-day event or a week-long extended lunch hour event where clients can come at their convenience and meet up with friends; or as a weekday happy hour afternoon-to-early-evening occasion so that people can meet after work, before other evening commitments.

If you are working well ahead of time, and if you are using e-mail, your web site, your Facebook and social network sites fairly interactively, you might even consider letting your contacts tell you what types of events they would be most interested in and when they would be most likely to attend. Ask about the types of events to which they would be most likely to bring a friend. Ask clients about which charities they would feel good about supporting by way of donations or cover charges. In addition to cutting out some of the guesswork, you will also be creating tacit awareness, acceptance and even preliminary commitment to your event, before it has even been planned!

Where will the Event be Held?

There are many good reasons for you to default to holding events right in your salon or spa, not the least of which is bringing clients and prospects into the heart of your operation, fully marketing all of your products and services to them and having all of the tools and equipment on hand that you need to do great demonstrations and provide on the spot services and bookings. But for those of you who are independent professionals, booth renters, or are otherwise space-limited, this might not be an option. Plus, if you are holding a large event or one in partnership with one or more other businesses, it might not be practical to hold your event in your salon or spa due to space constraints.

But the lack of space, or lack of enough space does not have to be a show-stopper; that is one of the reasons it is important for you to build working marketing and event partnerships with other businesses and with professionals like party and event planners who can help connect you with local facilities that can accommodate larger events. Noting (again) that your primary considerations must be for your goal and your guests, here are some things to take into account when choosing the best location for your event:

- proximity to and convenience of your target audience / invitees

- attractiveness and appeal of location to your invitees

- ability to stage and accommodate all of the activities you want to include

- other businesses willing to co-sponsor the event and their facility needs

- total numbers of people invited, anticipated to attend, initial RSVPs, etc.

- media, dignitaries or celebrities you want to invite

- presentations or demonstrations you want to conduct

- public address (P.A.) system, music or other sound system needs

- tool and equipment needs

- food and drink regulations

- safety regulations

- parking needs

Once you have chosen a venue, think about how attendees will flow through event activities and space, as well as where you will stage activities. Do not forget that you may need space for jackets or other personal belongings, space to stage activities, storage space for supplies and equipment, space for demonstrations, consultations, mini services, a retail product "Try Me" bar or station, sampling areas, retail (and retail storage) sales area(s), places for speakers or presenters to work, crowd seating, food or beverage station and/or seating, holding or resting area, rest rooms, microphone and public address (P.A.), music and sound system needs, space where drawings will be held, appointment bookings will be taken, where various 'stations' will be, how people will flow through a multi-station event, a place to check in and collect contact information, what they should do when they are finished, how they will check out, where to stage goodie bags, etc. There is a lot to consider! Your plan for the event as well as the number of people you anticipate will attend should give you an idea as well for how to answer the final question.

Who will Do What?

Adequately staffing your event and planning for set up, take down and cleaning is another key component for your event plan. Too few people to help will mean exhaustion for you and your team, and a poor impression for guests who may then be subject to an event flawed by long waits, hurried or inept demonstrations, uptight staff, inadequate information about what to do next—certainly not the atmosphere of luxury, expertise and confidence that you hope to instill!

Alternately, over-staffing could also result in a negative impression; if guests perceive you expected a larger turnout, they may feel that your event was not 'the place to be' after all. Be sure that you have a plan for either eventuality; if too few people RSVP or attend, have a holding area "behind the curtain" for extraneous staff, have alternate responsibilities for them or simply send some home. If more people come than anticipated, (first, jump for joy! and then,) be sure that you either have additional staff available on call who can arrive quickly or that you have a plan to change the flow of the event, the number or duration of demonstrations, the ability to quickly set up more stations or additional chairs, etc. Since few events ever run completely as planned, contingency planning needs to be a regular part of your event planning process.

What will happen after the event?

In the post-event euphoria and exhaustion, it can be easy for activities like clean up, debriefing staff and following up with contacts to slip through the cracks; the latter two of which are crucial if your goal was to build for the future. Approach it this way: Until post-event activities are completed, the event is not over.

Plan for time and personnel needed for "take down" of event activity areas, clean up, return of the facility to regular operational setup, return of any rented or catering equipment, and for the return of unsold retail products, tools and equipment to your salon or spa (or its regular location in the salon or spa). If your event is held in-salon, incorporate a plan to return your facility to a business-ready state both in planning and in assignment of responsibilities (unless you are looking forward to doing it all yourself!)

Set up a meeting time with staff (and/or your event partners) 2-3 days following an event in order to debrief and to be sure that follow up activities are on track. Talk about what went right and what went wrong, but if any one aspect of the event went particularly poorly, don't allow anyone to become the brunt of criticism. No event will ever go perfectly and people do make mistakes; regardless of any mistakes made, you want to be sure that your staff know their input and assistance was appreciated. Make it your goal as a team to honestly address problems with the goal of learning from them for future events—without throwing anyone under the bus. After all, no one is going to want to help with the next event if they felt terrible after the last one. If something did go seriously wrong, or someone on your team behaved in a way that was truly out of line, address it privately rather than humiliating them publicly.

As soon as possible (or as soon as promised) after an event, add contacts collected to your database (and share them with marketing event partners, if appropriate). Send out a "Thank You" e-mail or direct mail communication to all attendees. Send a confirmation to anyone who booked an appointment at the event, who purchased a pre-paid series or package, or who ordered products from you for future delivery.

Schedule a series of follow up offers and communications to be sent during the 6 weeks following the event. First, because your best chance to cash in on the impression made by your staff and your business will be when the experience is fresh and foremost in the minds of attendees, and second, to establish long-term awareness of your business in their minds by creating additional interactions. If your event included an opportunity to purchase a pre-sold series or package, extend the offer or another version of that offer to attendees for a limited time, and do the same for any product or service offerings made at the event.

Gain feedback from attendees for future events and gauge potential interest in your services and products through surveys taken either at the event itself or in one of your follow up communications. Ask for contact information (unless you intend for the survey to be confidential) so that you can match up attendee' areas of interest to future promotional offers or provide other requested follow up.

A sample post-event survey might include some of the following questions:

- Demographics and identifiers:
  - o attendee name
  - o e-mail address
  - o gender
  - o age range (such as, 10-18, 19-24, 25-34, 35-44, etc., this can help as you analyze trends in different age groups and as you try to target specific offers to clients)
  - o zip code (to see if your attendees are clustered in certain neighborhoods; this can help to design targeted marketing to those neighborhoods in the future)

- Event information
  - o how did you hear about the event?
  - o did you come by yourself or with a friend, if with a friend, who?
  - o what was your favorite part of the event?
  - o how would you rate the facility? (you can ask about specific areas as well, such as cleanliness, décor and furnishings, rest rooms, food, music, seating, lighting, check in, check out, etc.)
  - o which products (or services) most excited or intrigued you? why?

October Promotion Ideas

Identifying and defining measurable goals for each promotion you run can help as you try to think of ways to incentivize clients to purchase the product or service, or to attend your event. Set goals for each promotion you run in terms of the number or dollar amount that you want to sell through (or a limit on the number available); then work to create promotions that are compelling enough to get your customers to buy them. Following the promotional period, measure results relative to each of the goals that you set. Analyze what worked and what didn't work, and use this information as you plan future promotions.

October Month-Long Observances

October is Adopt a Shelter Dog Month

Hold an event, donate a percent of sales or take donations for your local animal shelter; sponsor or hold an event to facilitate pet adoptions. Revisit the idea of adding pet-themed items to your retail or partnering with a mobile groomer for an event or for an on-going cooperative marketing offer.

October is Clergy Appreciation Month

Extend a special offer to church employees and/or volunteers.

October is Long Range Planning Month

Set aside at least one full day in October to review or create a systematized, measurable and trackable long range plan and set personal goals. Set aside a day or weekend to talk about the mission and goals of your business, to get employee buy in and to create a blueprint for the coming year. Put your plan on paper and give copies to a mentor or trusted friend; review progress at least quarterly in the coming year. Include your distributor sales consultants or a marketing professional for additional resources and expertise or invite other salon professionals to help you with ideas.

Visit www.12monthsofmarketing.net and click on 'Resources' for a one-page outline for a long range planning workshop.

October is Breast Cancer Awareness Month

Hold a cutting event for Locks of Love (www.locksoflove.org) or hold a cut-a-thon to support local cancer patient facilities, the City of Hope or a local Susan G. Komen 3-Day Walk for the Cure team. Organized charities can provide you with support and a wide range of ideas for fund raising. Check with your tax professional to be sure that you structure your fund raising efforts appropriately to ensure donors contributions (and yours) are tax-deductible.

As a team, choose to donate proceeds from one day of services and sales in October to a national or local breast cancer charity or services organization. Charitable giving guidelines prohibit dictating a donation amount, but you can give clients a "suggested donation" amount; most will meet and exceed this, and you can let all clients know that their donations are welcome (whether they have an appointment that day or not). Seek out a corporate or individual sponsor to match donations. Write a press release before-hand to publicize the event, and afterward to present results and use Facebook, your e-mail newsletter, blog and website to help publicize before and afterward.

There may be a cancer treatment facility near you to which you would be able to donate products and/or services for patients or family members who are staying nearby. Or adopt a local cancer patient for a year of services (or a caregiver) and let employees and clients help by taking donations for holidays, birthday, anniversary and other special occasions in the patient's life during the year.

Color a World Without Cancer

Hold an in-salon contest and invite clients, their children, the children of employees, or even invite a local elementary school to participate in a coloring or art contest titled, "Color a World Without Cancer." The winner/s will be chosen from entries to receive a free cut and color in November. All entrants should receive a special cut and color offer from you. Write a press release and send copies of finalists work to your local newspaper for added awareness.

Purchase special pink and pink ribbon products and tools to add to your retail offerings in October. Design and purchase a unique awareness-messaged t-shirt, tank top, mug, water bottle or other salon or spa-branded tchotchke for retail sale before October, with proceeds or a portion of each sale going to a national or local cancer charity.

October Week-Long Observances

The First Week of October is Customer Service Week

Extend a special offer to receptionists, administrative staff, retail sales people, customer call centers, hotel concierge, restaurant hostess and wait staff and other customer service professionals in your area.

The Third Week of October is Massage Therapy Week

Create signage and use your e-mail newsletter and other communications to tell clients about the benefits of the massage therapy services and/or related products that you offer. If you don't yet offer massage services, partner with an independent massage therapist to introduce your clients to their services or to reward clients with mini-massages during appointments.

Create a special offer for free mini-massage add-ons to increase awareness of your massage services and pamper clients during services. Treat your employees to massages. Partner with physical therapists and create offers cross-marketed to their rehabilitating patients.

Create menu options and extend special offers to individuals in physically demanding professions, such as those in health care or construction jobs.

October Holidays and Observances

October 5 is Do Something Nice Day

There are people in our communities who do something nice just about every day. Take nominations for local heroes and work with your cooperative and cross marketing partners to create one or more generous prize packages. Reward do-gooders in your community with a great prize package, publicize your event online and with press releases to local radio stations, newspapers, etc.

Come and Get It Day!

Send out a note via text message, e-mail or Facebook and let the first 5 (or however many you desire) people that text or e-mail back, or answer your Facebook question "come and get it" in the form of a free product, service or other prize. Everyone who responds should receive a special bounce-back offer and/or product sample or salon or spa-branded tchotchke.

October 7 is 'Be Bald and Be Free' Day

Hold a "Cut-a-Thon" or a complete "Shave Off" hair event to benefit Locks of Love (www.locksoflove.org), a local cancer charity, in support of a 3-Day Walk (Susan G. Komen) team, or to be donated to the City of Hope. Solicit donated stylist services as well as donations from patrons for the event. Involve your marketing partners to make the event even bigger. Write press releases before your event to increase awareness and afterward to report results. For more ideas on how to use charitable events and fund raisers to build business, read the June Chapter of Volume I of 12 Months of Marketing for Salon and Spa.

October 10 is Universal Music Day

Partner with local music studios, instructors or dance studios for cross marketing. Extend a special offer to music instructors, music store staff, music or dance studios and school music teachers and volunteers. Create a menu options for music students, teachers, band members or directors for hair color, styling, makeup, manicure or complete makeover services prior to performances, competitions and recitals.

Hold a special music-centric happy hour in the salon or spa. Purchase albums of local artists for retail sale in the salon, client thank you gifts, or for contest prize basket inclusion.

October 11 is 'It's My Party' Day

Extend in-salon or in-spa party services to groups of women or to teens / tweens for birthday parties or sleepovers. Create a menu of party services and recommended retail products. Add pre-party services and makeovers to your menu.

Partner with a party planner or with independent party-style sellers (jewelry, kitchenware or jeans party retailers, etc.,) for cooperative or cross marketing. Create a flyer or postcard that independent party sellers can give away at the parties they hold in your local area along with product samples, branded lip balms or other tchotchkes and a special offer.

Partner with a party planner and/or caterer to create a party planning class for clients. Teach basic bartending, host/hostess duties, tablescaping, party decorating, how to make gourmet appetizers, etc. Demonstrate your party hair, manicure and makeup services and styles.

October 12 is Cookbook Launch Day

Solicit the favorite recipes of employees, clients or both and generate a print or online cookbook for your community.

Work with a caterer or dinner preparation business for cross or cooperative marketing. Hold a joint event for clients in the form of cooking classes.

October 15 is Bring Your Teddy Bear to Work Day

Host a drive for clients to bring new stuffed animals and toys into the salon or spa in return for a discount or thank you gift. Donate toys to Toys for Tots (the annual U.S. Marine Corp holiday drive), a local children's hospital or another charity.

National Boss's Day is in October

Promote the gift of services and products best suited for gifts on Boss's Day. Purchase special greeting cards appropriate for giving with this gift to bosses, or to bosses and/or co-workers throughout the year. Create a Boss's Day gift basket.

Create a menu of corporate services (such as mini-massages, professional presentation makeup and hair styling or touch ups, manicures or pedicures) which you could perform at conferences or meetings. Promote these to local event planners, sales and other executives. Provide a menu to companies that have regular corporate travelers of the services you can provide for their guests and send a copy of your menu to local hotels and motels.

Add options to your menu for job seekers prior to interviews or for individuals with professional promotion opportunities, performance reviews, etc.

October 19 is Evaluate Your Life Day

Partner with a local gym, life coach, weight loss expert, etc. to provide consultations and recommendations to clients and/or employees. Create cross-marketed offers that can make the lives of all of your clients better.

With the holidays coming, gear messaging toward preparing for holiday parties and events and for getting ahead of anticipated New Year Resolutions. Partner with a trainer and create cooperative offers specifically designed to show off clients at their best during the upcoming holiday season.

October 22 is Make a Difference Day

Working with a local church or senior center, create a list of cleaning, maintenance and other household or garden assistance for local seniors. Work as an employee team and/or solicit client volunteers to help perform tasks. Publicize efforts with a press release to local radio stations, and newspapers.

Celebrate afterward with volunteers and reward them with a gift card, salon or spa-branded tchotchke, samples or retail products and a bounce-back offer.

Leave a New Client gift card, product samples, salon or spa-branded lip balm, hand sanitizer or lotion, a copy of your menu, and/or a special offer with each of the seniors that you serve. Extend a special offer or send a supply of New Client gift cards to the staff of the senior center.

October 23 is iPod Day

Let clients enter a special drawing at their appointments from now through the holidays for an iPod. Or purchase iTunes cards for prizes, to be added to prize or holiday baskets or to add to your retail gift selections in the salon or spa.

Purchase a supply of iPods or other MP3 players for customer use during service appointments; preload each with different styles of music so that clients can listen to their favorites under the dryer, during a massage, straightening, texturizing or other services.

Mother-In-Law Day is in October

Create a special appointment block for clients to come and have appointments with their Mother-in-Law or sell special greeting cards for sale now and through the holidays for gift giving to them along with spa or salon gift cards.

Create a special Mother-in-Law's gift basket that includes a certificate for service. Use signage to make suggestions for service and product gifts that clients should purchase for their Mother-in-Law; or create a special Mother-in-Law's bundle of services and/or products.

Animal Lover's Day is in October

Turn your salon into a pet owner's paradise stocked with pet coat-care products plus pet "bling" like special collars, leashes, bowls, etc. Give pet owners a break when they purchase items for their own personal use as well as for their pet.

Partner with a local groomer for cross or cooperative marketing. Hold an event or create a recurring schedule with a mobile groomer on site so pet owners and their pets can receive services at the same time.

All Popped Up

October is National Popcorn Poppin' Month, so give each client a bag of freshly popped popcorn, a bag of kettle corn or a sampling of your favorite popcorn flavor. Partner with an equipment rental company and promote their business while renting a machine for the month (at a free or discounted rate). Or sell popcorn or bags of microwave popcorn with proceeds going to your favorite cancer charity. Work with local merchants to stage a cross-marketed sidewalk popcorn sale or special charity fund raiser event.

October 30 is Candy Corn Day

Fill a glass container with candy corn and hold a contest for entrants in-salon and online to guess how many are in the container. The winner could receive the candy plus a gift card, spa or salon-branded goodies and samples. All entrants should receive a special bounce-back offer.

Set up a number of cups or glasses on a table or shelf and give clients a chance to toss candy corn into them standing at a distance. Designate special cups through the use of color dots (or some other marking); if the client gets a candy corn into one of these cups, they win a special prize. Base the number of candy corn throw tries on expenditures, such as one candy corn per dollar spent at appointment. This could be a month-long event. You can also adapt this for other holidays, like candy hearts for Valentine's Day, jelly beans for Easter, etc.

Halloween

In partnership with businesses near you, host a safe trick-or-treating event for children and include a bounce-back offer and spa or salon-branded tchotchkes as well as treats from you.

Purchase salon or spa-branded candies or create special goodie bags to go home with clients during October; include a special Halloween day, week or month-long offer or a special offer for the children of customers who might be going to one of your competitors for salon services.

Working with the businesses you partner with for cross or cooperative marketing, hold a Halloween costume party for clients or for employees at a local bar or restaurant. Extend a special offer to the employees and families of businesses with which you partner.

October Planning and Tasks

Select from manufacturer's retail promotions to support your November, December and Holiday goals, events and promotions. Design and print (or order) marketing and support materials needed for coming events and promotions.

Capturing holiday sales ahead of the big retail push that will be underway by Thanksgiving is imperative if you want to have healthy holiday season sales; discretionary dollars designated by your customers for gift giving will disappear quickly once Thanksgiving hits.

Planning for Holiday and November-December should be nearly complete, and you should be publicizing and gearing up for a strong holiday push or a major event in November. Make sure all of your cross and cooperative marketing partners are on board and that their employees have scripts for making gift certificate and retail gift suggestions to clients. Consider an internal incentive or contest to ensure that your marketing partners and their employees focus on supporting your shared sales goals and event initiatives.

Communicate in October

Items to include in your e-mail or print newsletter, web site, Facebook and blog posts and in direct mail communications this month:

- October, November, December and Holiday events and promotions
- Strong messaging to promote sales of gift certificates and products you offer that would make ideal holiday and hostess gifts
- Promotions expiring in October, new products coming for the holiday season
- 'Save the date' announcements for holiday events
- Announce September contest winners and October contest opportunities
- Last minute openings on the books
- A spotlight product, service or staff member of the month

October Calendar / Suggested Communications and Tasks Schedule

SUN	MON	TUE	WED	THU	FRI	SAT
1st week of Month 1st of October—Merchandise for October 1st of October—Begin collecting entries for October contests						
		Order signage, event supplies and promotional materials for November - December promotions			Send October Newsletter with coupons, announce contests and winners, new products and services coming events, openings still on the books, events and promotions	
2nd week of Month						
Set aside time for long range planning; create marketing blueprint for next year		Order in gifts, salon-branded items, impulse buy and other items for November-December			Write press releases for any events/results reporting or future events / charitable focus	
3rd week of Month						
Begin marketing for holiday		Finalize, review and lay out plans for November - December - January events and promotions			Send October "last chance" promotions and openings on the books e-mail and/or direct mail	
4th week of Month Last day of October—Take down any October-only promotions Last day of October—Draw October contest winners						
		Order event supplies, postcards, gifts and salon-branded items needed for November-December promotions			Send November focus e-mail / direct mail with strong holiday gift suggestion and messaging	

October Worksheets

$_____ Retail Sales Goal

Promotions_____

_____

_____

_____

_____

$_____ Avg. Retail/Client

$_____ Retail Sales Results

$_____ Service Sales Goal

Promotions_____

_____

_____

_____

_____

$_____ Avg. Service/Client

$_____ Service Sales Results

$_____ Event Revenues Goal

Events _____

_____

_____

_____

_____

#_____ Attending Event/s

#_____ Apts/Booked at Event

$_____ Event/s Sales

$_____ Total Event/s Results

$_____ Charity/Fund Raising Goal

Charity Events _____

_____

_____

_____

_____

#_____ Attending Event/s

#_____ Apts/Booked at Event

$_____ Charity Event/s Sales

$_____ Total Charity Results

October Marketing Summary

Marketing Partners: _____

_____

_____

_____

Marketing Collateral Needed (or Used): _____

_____

_____

_____

Other Efforts:

\#_____ Number of Clients New to Salon

%_____ Client Retention Rate (90 days)

 Retention Efforts: _____

_____

\# or % _____ Clients Re-booked at Appointment

$_____ Gift Certificate Sales

\#_____ Contacts added to marketing / e-mail database

november
make over
your network

Throughout this book I have recommended that you partner with other businesses for many events and promotions, so maybe this chapter should have come earlier, but I think that it's right where it needs to be. Because if you have been working to build, improve and expand all of the business and marketing components presented up until now, you have strengthened and fortified your business and yourself as a professional, whether you are an independent owner, lease or booth renter, or you lead a full service multi-station salon or spa. Your business now has a lot (more) to offer other businesses in return for the additional exposure and marketing reach that they can provide for you.

Since it's true that everyone needs a haircut of one kind or another, chances are that you are already indirectly connected to many other businesses, civic and community associations, charities, and a wide variety of other organizations. Each of your clients represents hundreds of other people; families, social and professional acquaintances and other groups. In other words, you should not have to go very far to find some great marketing and event partners.

If you have not done so already, it is time to start thoughtfully identifying and persuading other businesses to partner with you for marketing on a regular basis. It's time for you to begin to help advocate for and give support to one or two community service organizations or charities on a regular basis. It's time to join your city's Kiwanis Club, Rotary or Chamber of Commerce. It's time for you to begin to make your presence known to local leaders and for you to plug in to your city government so that you can influence the laws, regulations and taxes that will impact your business for years to come. It is time for you to participate in groups with other local business leaders for networking, brainstorming, problem solving, inspiration and personal development.

While this may sound like yet another overwhelming, time-consuming set of new responsibilities, remember that as with any other long term project, you only need to take one step at a time. Plus, these will be some of the most important things you can do to ensure the growth and profitability of your business now, and it's sustainability into the future.

Plan to develop and maintain a presence in city and local leadership organizations— and know that you don't have to do it all yourself! As your business grows, the best thing that you can do to ensure success into the future is to develop other leaders within your business; people who can extend your presence and the influence of your business by serving with you or on your behalf within some of these organizations and by attending trade and professional conferences. Your time is already at a premium; by developing other leaders in your business, you can extend the influence of your business beyond your own time constraints. More importantly, creating opportunity and mentoring others is the best legacy you can leave. Those people who continue after you, born and nurtured within the industry under your care, extend your influence into the future. And isn't this the true definition of art—that which endures into and shapes the future?

Partnering with other businesses for shared marketing and events makes sense. When you cross market with other businesses, you extend your marketing reach by hundreds (if not thousands) more prospective clients at a very low cost; perhaps as minimal an investment as the cost to purchase and place business cards, flyers, display sheets, or your menu of services in the waiting area, on the tables of, or at the point of purchase of other local businesses. And it's not just about exposure to their clients; by presenting your business to their customers, they are also giving you their unspoken (or even spoken) endorsement.

And there is more to be gained by working with other businesses in this way, there is also a shared sense of community and destiny—the realization that you are not just in this by yourself, not limited only to your own resources or creativity. So often as entrepreneurs, small business owners, and independent professionals we feel that we need to be brilliant, creative, self-sufficient—and that we have to "do it all" on our own. To share resources, shelf space, contacts, to brainstorm together to solve problems, to entice more people in your community to spend dollars locally, to actually work together to create a greater sense of community among your customers—when we feel this shared sense of destiny with others, we work even harder to ensure the success of everyone.

Every promotion or event that you hold has the potential to be attractive to some other business in your area for sharing marketing outreach and costs. But how do you find them?

The most logical place to start building alliances may also be the simplest and most convenient; namely, those businesses located nearest yours. Other alliance possibilities probably exist among your friends and family, and an avenue you may not have considered, among your clients themselves.

When building these working relationships, let businesses know up front who else you are working with. This will help you avoid misunderstandings and will keep you out of situations where you might make commitments to businesses who may compete directly with one another.

Cross marketing with other businesses can provide you with continuous exposure to new prospects. The businesses with which you choose to cross market should have a client base that overlaps with major segments of your own client base, or should represent target markets that you would most ideally like to attract. The same holds true for businesses you include in cooperative marketing or event activities. And remember that when you endorse other businesses by allowing them marketing access to your clients, you are, in effect, recommending that your clients do business with those companies, so your endorsement should only be given to those businesses that you truly endorse.

Cooperative Marketing

For the purposes of this book "cooperative marketing" speaks to marketing activities that you do in cooperation with other salon or spa professionals or with other businesses. It is implied that contacts will be shared to a central source for coordinated marketing or advertising campaigns. You can craft offers that work in conjunction with one another such as a "Get in Shape" package that includes a certain set of your services in combination with the services of a fitness center or instructor, or create separate offers to be offered to the clients of all participating business.

Cross Marketing

Whereas cooperative marketing is working together, cross marketing is crossing over to market to someone else's clients and marketing their services or products to yours. The main benefit to participants is an expanded base of specifically targeted prospective clients; optimally these clients will share many of the traits you would find in your largest demographic target markets. You should still use a central source for marketing so that you do not violate your clients trust by giving their contact information away to another business; or you can simply trade marketing materials for distribution to one another's clients in print or e-mail communications or displays.

Some of the items you might cooperatively share or trade for marketing space within other businesses include:

business cards or brochures	Facebook or blog posts
web site links	e-mail newsletter inclusion
retail space	press release inclusion
lobby or client waiting areas	charity endeavors
break room or lunchroom space	real or virtual bulletin boards
point of purchase displays	

One additional benefit of both Cooperative and Cross-Marketing is the implied endorsement of the businesses you partner with. Since you are—essentially—recommending that your clients do business with your marketing partners, expose your clients only to those businesses that will treat them as good as you do!

Marketing Partnerships

Your marketing partnerships will be most effective when you choose partners in context of specific promotions or events, and in relationship to your business, the nature of your clientele and your business goals. For the purposes of this book, when the words 'Partnership' or 'Marketing Partners' are used, it refers to an informal partnership (rather than a legal or formal one). While there may be instances where you want to detail responsibilities in writing, most partnerships will be demonstrated in cooperative work together with verbal agreements, trust, and the benefit of the doubt.

Purposefully seek out and establish partnerships with businesses that have something you want (and want something you have) to create leverage and win-win scenarios. Here are some additional considerations to keep in mind when considering businesses you might partner with:

Ideal client base—business partners whose ideal or main types of clients share some of the same characteristics or demographics as your ideal clients, such as geographic location, income or home ownership, gender, age, children, disposable income, charitable interests and activities

Social basis—partnerships or suggestions from among your current clientele, your family, friends, acquaintances, co-workers or former co-workers, etc.; partnerships whose businesses are represented by some of your current clients

Proximity—partnerships with businesses that are located near yours

Contact lists—partnerships with independent sellers who already have large client and prospect lists, they are typically familiar with your community and surrounding areas, and they may also have a sizeable sphere of influence in the local community

Networking—participate in civic organizations in your community such as your city chamber of commerce, rotary, business roundtable and other social civic organizations

Avoid sharing your contacts with other businesses outright. Whether you have a privacy policy or not, most of your clients believe that they are only giving you their contact information (and permission to communicate with them) and no one else. They will not mind if you endorse other businesses through shared marketing, but they will find it objectionable if you give their information away.

You can honor client trust by agreeing up-front that all businesses participating in cooperative marketing, promotions or events will provide their contacts to a central source or individual. This company or individual will utilize the contacts appropriately for a campaign or marketing activities occurring for an agreed-on period of time, but will not release the contacts to the other businesses involved. This applies both for cooperative and cross marketing campaigns.

The Schmuck-Factor

On more than one occasion, I have been approached in the mall and complimented on my personal style only to feel completely "shmuck-ified" mere seconds later when the sales pitch from a independent cosmetics seller came on the heels of what I thought was a genuine compliment. The last time that happened, while I still felt the shmuck factor, I did strike up a conversation with this person that was more helpful and it led to an "a-ha" marketing moment: Independent sellers have contact lists, have events know-how, think creatively and are more than open to working partnerships. What's more, their contact lists are likely to include some of your ideal client demographics.

So seek out partnerships for promotions and events with independent sellers—but avoid the shmuck-factor when it comes to your marketing techniques!

Partnerships In Context

Building even just one cooperative or cross marketing partnership can bring new clients to your business and make both businesses more profitable. So building partnerships with several businesses and using them in context with themed promotions, holidays, events and charity fund raisers can make a huge difference in growing your business, growing your client base, engaging and retaining clients, increasing retails sales and building for the future. When created in context, business partnerships can maximize your exposure to your ideal types of prospective clients and give you the means to fill up your events and your books. Partnerships give you the ability to create bigger events and promotions than you could do on your own and reduce your expenses because costs for events and campaigns are shared.

You don't have to partner with everyone.
But partner with someone.

Can't think of where to start? Start with a list of 12. List of set of 12 different kinds of businesses in your community that represent different groups of your target clientele (for instance, a wine shop, a boutique clothier, a candy or chocolatier, a community bank, a dog groomer, an animal charity, a senior center, etc.) Or, simply make a list of the 12 (non-competing) businesses closest in proximity to your location:

> For each of the 12 businesses on your list, make a list of 3 possible promotions or events you could imagine working on together;

> Write down the names of the next 12 months beginning with the next calendar month beginning about 8 weeks from now;

> Match up the business with which you want to partner with the month when one of the ideas for cooperative promotions or events you thought of would make the most sense; then,

> Approach the owner or manager of that business and suggest the cooperative marketing effort you want to run with them.

Prime Candidates for Partnerships

Shared Contacts • Shared Leads • Shared Costs for Shared Events • Promotions • Packages • Charity Fund Raising

Solo Artists:

- Instructors: Fitness, Jazzercise, and Exercise, Personal Trainers, Dance and Martial Arts Teachers, Music Teachers, Academic Tutors
- Handymen, Landscapers, Yard Care
- Independent Realtors, Insurance Agents,
- Animal Trainers, Groomers,
- Skin Care or Cosmetics Estheticians, Massage Therapists,
- Wedding, Party and Event Planners, Caterers, Interior Designers
- Freelance Graphic Designers, Marketing, Advertising and Public Relations Professionals,
- Independent Sellers, Home-Based Business Owners
- Musicians, Bands
- Promotional Products Vendors, Silk Screeners
- Artists, Woodworkers

Homeowner's Services:

- Housekeeping Services
- Home Repair and Renovation: Flooring, Windows, Roofers, HVAC (Heating and Cooling)
- Appliance Repair and Sales
- Builders
- Community-Based Banks, Financial or Lending Services
- Facilities: Hotels and Motels, Banquet and Event
- Facilities
- Restaurants, Bars and Wine Shops, Wine Tasting Rooms
- Senior Living and Activity Centers, Apartment Complexes, Subdivision and Suburban Community Centers

Retail:

- Boutique Clothing, Gift, Art, Stationers and Bookstores
- Dry Cleaners
- City Merchants (Downtown) or Retail Merchants in closest proximity
- Wine Shops, Vitamin or Natural Supplement Stores

Studios and Practices:

- Gymnastics, Fitness, and Martial Arts Studios, Sports Practice and Coaching Facilities,
- Gentlemen's Clubs, Sportsmen's Clubs and Organizations, Smoking Rooms,
- Music or Dance Studios
- Realty Offices, Insurance Offices
- Veterinary Services, Kennels and Grooming Services
- Dentistry, Cosmetic Dentistry and Orthodontists,
- Cosmetic Medical and Surgical Services, Specialty or General
- Medical Practitioners, Chiropractic Services, Naturopathic Services
- Manicure-Pedicure, Spray Tan, Massage Therapy and Spa Services

Networking Organizations:

- Women-Owned Businesses, Business-to-Business, Chamber of Commerce, Downtown Merchants

Civic, Social, and Community Organizations:

- PTA (Parent-Teacher Association - each school has their own school PTA board and meetings)
- School District Offices, Private and Public School Offices, Teacher's Unions
- Scouting Organizations, Church Groups,MOPS (Mothers of PreSchoolers)
- City Rotary, Chamber of
- Commerce or Merchants Associations
- Theatres and Theatre Groups
- Music and Arts Performance Facilities, Organizations, and Performers
- City Hall, Law Enforcement, Emergency Services and City Services Offices,
- City or County Parks and Recreation Offices and Activities
- Community Charitable Service Providers:
- Charities usually have large contact lists and run regular campaigns!

Potential Candidates for Partnerships

Using Fund Raising to Build Business

You can choose to support one or any number of charities in your community through themed promotions or events, but it may be more beneficial for you and for the charities you most want to support if you select just one or two organizations to support on a regular basis. When considering your options, why not choose to benefit organizations that have directly impacted your own life? You will express yourself the most honestly and persuasively when speaking to issues you understand personally. Plus, you will receive the most personal satisfaction when you help support causes you genuinely believe in.

A few years ago I attended a salon event that had added support of a popular charity to their event in order to extend an additional reason for their customers to come to the event and to support its goals. At the end of the event, when the time came to write the check to the charity, it seemed apparent while watching the math (deducting costs from proceeds, to determine what amount would go to the charity) that the salon owner did not genuinely intend to benefit the charity.

I saw firsthand the damage that shorting the charity did to personal and professional relationships. As someone who had helped to facilitate the evening and donated a significant amount of my own time and money, I felt betrayed as well.

I share that only to say this: If you do not genuinely desire to support a charitable cause, don't add one to your event only to mislead your customers. You can benefit your business while also benefitting a charity, but this is one more important reason why it is desirable for you to approach this area with the goal of developing a long-term, on-going relationship with a specific charity or cause/s that you truly want to benefit.

While in most cases I recommend that you put the desires of clients first in decision making, in the case of supporting charitable causes or local social service organizations, I suggest that you choose those you most desire to benefit out of your own passions or personal experiences. If you do not have a personal passion in this area, then you can reach out to employees or customers to choose causes based on their experiences. You can also choose to provide support for customers or community members who have personally experienced tremendous loss or have personal need.

Here are some ways that you can benefit charities while building business:

- Events or marketing promotions with all profits* going to charity (*usually this means net proceeds after costs)

- Events with all proceeds going to charity (costs are donated)

- Events with a cover charge going to charity

- Events or marketing promotions with a percentage of overall or specific product/service sales going to charity

- Events where you solicit donations or a portion of sales and promise to match the donation up to a certain amount, or acquire a corporate or individual sponsor willing to match donations up to a certain amount

- Feature information in your communications about your charity, its needs, and how it benefits others on an on-going basis to help build awareness, or as build up to a specific event or marketing promotion

- Product or service of the month with proceeds or percentage of sales to charity (or a certain dollar amount for each unit sold, etc.)

- Donate actual products or services to a charity, to patients or their family members, to care givers, to the employees of the charity, etc.

- Hold a cut-a-thon, massage-a-thon, polish-a-thon, etc., accepting donations for the charity in lieu of payment for services and encouraging contributions from all clients, corporate sponsors, advertisers, etc.

- Treat someone in need to 'queen for a day' treatment

- Create a 'make over a hero' program where clients can nominate someone in the community who deserves some special pampering (and create bigger prize packages by working together with other businesses to create a bigger program)

- Adopt a family (or an individual) for a year or another specified time period, for a specific service, or for a series of services

- Honor the employees of one charitable organization each month with a prize package, set of gift products, service coupons, etc. Work in conjunction with marketing partners in order to create larger prize packages.

However you decide to do the math after an event, remember that the more you whittle down the portion designated for charity, the more that it will appear that the event was not as much for the charity as it was for you. Hold yourself accountable by setting a minimum donation amount and by telling your clients, employees and marketing partners how much money was raised for the charity following your event or promotion.

In the weeks leading up to your event or promotion, plan to send a series of press releases to local newspapers, magazines, radio stations, local and national offices of the charity, city hall, and other media highlighting your chosen charity and the work that it does as well as how your business plans to benefit them.

- 6 weeks before event / promotion—send a general press release with "more details to follow"

- 3-4 weeks before the event / promotion—send a second press release with more details and a compelling reason for people to support the charity and your event

- 1 week before the event / promotion—send a full press release

- After the event / promotion—send a press release including one or two of the best photos and summary results

City, Civic and Leadership Organizations

While participating in city, civic and local leadership organizations requires that you commit precious time and resources, they also provide great contacts for your business not just for networking and to connect with prospective clients, but also for your own personal development. Plus, being involved in these organizations gives you opportunities to influence local regulations and taxes. Networking in city and civic groups also helps to bring together local, independently-owned businesses that can work together to develop community awareness of the benefits of buying from local, independently-owned businesses and the formal development of "Buy Local" merchant groups.

Chamber of Commerce

Chambers of Commerce exist to represent the interests of business and might include economic development consultants and committees or local tourist and visitors bureaus, and membership is voluntary. Since they are generally populated by members of city government, local politics and special interests, they can also wield influence that may (or may not) coincide with what is best in general for local businesses. It is important for you to know how your local Chamber of Commerce works, how it is connected to local governing agencies, who belongs to it and who is influential in decision making, and—if you can—to participate, especially if you can help improve the overall business climate of your city, influence urban development, and impact the regulations and taxes which impact your business.

In addition to a Chamber of Commerce, you city may also have other committees on which you can participate or provide recommendations and input; some examples include arts commissions, tourism boards, transportation committees, human services, parks and recreation, planning committees, visitors information centers, street fairs, city celebrations, parades, historical foundations and others.

Chambers of Commerce often have multiple networking and civic service meetings, luncheons, business directories, new business services, after hours mixers, breakfasts, grand openings, ribbon cuttings, golf outings, even civic mission trips. Usually they work closely with city government to promote the interests of business in your city, including investing in the infrastructure (roads, transit, parking, parks, etc.) needed to help attract more visitors to your city, and more shoppers to your city's businesses.

Close cousins of the Chamber of Commerce are local Optimist/Soroptimist, Rotary and Kiwanis clubs. These are service organizations made up of business and community leaders who voluntarily give of their time, abilities, money and other resources to help others in their communities and around the world. Clubs like these make significant contributions to meeting needs locally, but they have also provided meaningful support to the victims and rebuilding efforts following major catastrophes (such as Hurricane Katrina in 2005 and the earthquake in Haiti in 2010). Members have opportunities to work on local, national and even international projects.

Generally, these clubs meet weekly and hold several social and networking-friendly events throughout the year, participate in city street fairs, parades and festivals, and their members are usually personally invested in supporting the economic health of the local business community. For more information about these organizations and how to find clubs near you, visit their web sites:

Rotary—www.rotary.org

"Rotary International is the world's first service club organization, with more than 1.2 million members in 33,000 clubs worldwide. Rotary club members are volunteers who work locally, regionally, and internationally to combat hunger, improve health and sanitation, provide education and job training, promote peace, and eradicate polio under the motto Service Above Self."

Kiwanis—www.kiwanis.org

"Kiwanis is a global organization of volunteers dedicated to changing the world one child and one community at a time. Our members develop youth as leaders, build playgrounds and raise funds for pediatric research. We help shelter the homeless, feed the hungry, mentor the disadvantaged and care for the sick. Working together, members achieve what one person cannot accomplish alone. And along the way, club members share friendship and laughter. Located in 80 countries, Members stage nearly 150,000 service projects and raise nearly $107 million (US dollars) every year for communities, families and projects."

Optimists—www.optimist.org

"Optimist International is an association of more than 2,900 Optimist Clubs around the world dedicated to "Bringing Out the Best in Kids." Adult volunteers join Optimist Clubs to conduct positive service projects in their communities aimed at providing a helping hand to youth. With their upbeat attitude, Optimist Club members help empower young people to be the best that they can be. Each Optimist Club determines the needs of the young people in its community and conducts programs to meet those needs. Every year, Optimists conduct 65,000 service projects and serve well over six million young people."

Soroptimists—www.soroptimist.org

"Soroptimist is an international organization for business and professional women who work to improve the lives of women and girls, in local communities and throughout the world. Almost 95,000 Soroptimists in about 120 countries and territories contribute time and financial support to community–based and international projects that benefit women and girls. The name, Soroptimist, means "best for women," and that's what the organization strives to achieve. Soroptimists are women at their best, working to help other women to be their best."

Opportunities abound for you to participate in professional organizations in order for you to both give and receive help personally and professionally. In addition to business-building through networking, it is easy to see that your participation can also provide you with the ability to influence city government, planning and transportation issues as well as the rules, regulations, laws and taxes that directly impact your profitability and the way that you do business. Your participation will directly help these organizations and the local community members that they serve, and you can also be a conduit of information and connection for your clients to their city and civic organizations, community events and local causes. You can even help lead efforts in your community by gearing your charity-benefit events to support club service activities and projects.

Buy Local Campaigns and Merchant Groups

And one more option for you to consider when it comes to making over your networking: Retail revenue and profits for all businesses (and especially for small, independent professionals and stores) have been negatively impacted—in some cases drastically so—in all of our communities during the last few years of economic recession and the so-called recovery. Most small businesses have few 'rainy day' funds or resources to draw on; scores of businesses have closed down, and many are barely hanging on.

In response, "Buy Local" organizations and initiatives have sprouted up nation-wide in efforts to draw more consumer spending to locally-owned independent businesses and away from national and international chain stores. Part of the consumer's willingness to buy locally in increasing numbers, even if it sometimes mean paying higher prices, stems from the educational efforts of local chapters which are usually comprised of local, voluntarily-participating businesses and civic leaders.

"Buy Local" campaigns facilitate dissemination of information to community residents about how large a portion of each dollar they spend remains to benefit the local community when they shop at local, independent businesses rather than at national chains headquartered elsewhere.

According to a 2002 study published online by AMIBA (the American Independent Business Alliance) while only $13 of every $100 spent at a national retail chain store "stays" in the local community, when spending that same $100 at an independently-owned local business, $45 out of $100 "stays" right in the community. Plus, local merchants spend a much larger portion of their total revenue on local labor, they keep more of their profits in the local economy and they provide strong support for local artists and authors, charities and other businesses, creating further local economic impact.

Organizations like AMIBA benefit participating members in several ways. They provide members with merchandising, signage and information to be used to provide public education within a community about the specific social, economic and cultural benefits that local independent businesses provide. They provide members with cooperative purchasing, branding, marketing and resource-sharing opportunities so that they can better compete with big, national chains. Members, together, have a stronger voice to be able to make impacts to local and state politics. And they empower citizens to be able to help to guide the real economic future of their own neighborhoods and cities.

While most of these types of organizations were initially founded to promote local shopping, many have gone on to leverage their group power to influence government policy in their communities. Many also choose to incorporate support for other principles into their campaigns, such as promoting "green" and sustainable business practices.

These organizations exist in many cities and often utilize resources provided by advisory non-profits like AMIBA (www.amiba.net). This is not necessarily intended to be an endorsement for AMIBA; there are several similar non-profit companies providing these types of services. I am simply familiar with it due to the existence of a local chapter and the involvement in that group of some close friends.

November Promotion Ideas

With almost a full year under your belt when it comes to making over your marketing, think about your promotions in terms of how you can extend your marketing reach beyond the walls of your own business, and beyond your marketing contact list, to reach out to prospects among the client base of your marketing partners, other local businesses, your city's civic organizations and other community groups.

November Month-Long Observances

November is Military Family Appreciation Month

Use your web site, Facebook page, blog site and e-mail to extend a special offer to local military members and their families or host a military family open house. Send a copy of your offer to the newspaper of your local military base for inclusion in updates to military families, or send a stack of offer cards, business cards and/or your menu to the offices of military family service organizations. 'Adopt' a local member of the military (or a spouse) for free haircutting, massage, manicure or another service for a year.

If you do not live near a military base, extend a special offer to all Veterans in your community and take copies of your offer, business card, menu and manufacturer's samples to the office of your local V.A. (Veteran's Administration) or other Veteran's organization.

Take nominations from clients or contact your local military base and 'adopt' a military family or service member and provide salon or spa services and/or needed food or gifts for them for the holidays through the end of the year.

Create military care package product baskets for retail sale containing a product mix perfect for military members based in dry, hot climates (like the Middle East) or other typical military environs. Include foil packettes and other samples and products that will travel or ship well. Hold a contest and award one or two of the baskets for free as well as selling these in your retail mix.

Host a holiday care package or holiday greeting card event and invite clients and community members to come and write a thank you note and solicit drawings from children, and/or solicit donations and gifts suitable for sending to troops overseas during the holidays.

Have a Beautiful Holiday Season

In early to mid-November, have some fun and jump start holiday sales by holding a Holiday Shop in-salon or cooperatively in a marketing partner's space. Clients will focus mainly on shopping at malls and department stores beginning around Thanksgiving; getting sales ahead of that holiday will make a big difference.

If you cannot hold a Holiday Shop event in your salon or with a partnering business, contact local churches and schools to find out about participating in their holiday bazaars. If you participate in an off-site event, be sure that your kiosk includes more than just gifts and gift certificate sales. Have copies of your business cards, menus, contest entry forms for data collection and ads for coming events and promotions displayed for clients to take or used as bag stuffers. Bring a travel kit and do free mini makeovers, mini manicures, quick style fixes, sample skin and hair care products, etc. If you are a stylist, schedule a succession of 2-3 models to come so that you can show attendees your style and demonstrate use and benefits of products that they can purchase from your kiosk.

Feature a new-client incentive in your materials to entice shoppers to give you a try before the end of December. Make sure all take-away materials have your contact information. Your in-salon Holiday Shop should be well-merchandised, from the outside in. Entice shoppers in from the outside through the use of store front areas and displays visible from the doorway. Make your event larger by partnering and cross-marketing with local businesses to reach out to multiple client bases in promoting holiday specials for all businesses represented.

Purchase non-traditional items that clients would be likely to purchase on their own or in conjunction with gift certificates (such as branded "bling" T-shirts and tanks, chocolates, candies, wine, candles, interior decor items, holiday dishes, gloves, hats, notebooks, pens, jewelry, lip glosses, skin lotions, etc.,) as well as traditional salon-type gift offerings like plush robes or terry hoodies, nail files, brushes, combs, hair accessories or hair or skin care travel products.

Just as you catered to prom-goers, brides and graduates in the summer, you can cater to holiday party-goers now. Partner with a local limo service, restaurants, and party destinations to create a package including a makeover or spa package prior to the event with a champagne or non-alcoholic sparkling cocktail to get things started.

November is National Jewelry Month

Partner with an independent jewelry seller or purchase jewelry wholesale to add to your point of purchase or regular retail offerings. Start with a seasonal display for the holidays that you will be able to modify and build on into the New Year through Valentine's Day, Mother's Day, the summer Wedding Season and back again into the fall/winter Holidays.

And don't forget Tweens and Teens; add a point of purchase jewelry display stocked with seasonal items that younger clients (or the children of clients) would enjoy as well. Make it obvious to the moms, dads, aunts, uncles and grandparents in your clientele that these items would make great gifts for holidays throughout the year, or as acknowledgements for special events like birthdays, music concerts and recitals, sports awards, academic achievements, etc.

November is Inspirational Role Model Month

Take nominations and select a winner at the end of November to receive a free service in December along with the individual who nominated them. Make sure all entrants and all those making nominations receive a special promotional offer and create recognition flyers or even a press release to honor some of the most special stories.

November Week-Long Observances

The Second Week of November is National Hunger and Homeless Week

During the holiday season, raise awareness for local shelters, missions, and other charitable food and housing providers. Extend a special offer or give branded tchotchkes as thank you gifts to clients who donate money, food, or clothing to these charities.

Donate a portion of sales from product or service sales in November to a local shelter, mission or charitable grocery or meal provider.

Publicize efforts and raise awareness within your community with press releases submitted to local radio and news stations/reporters as well as local newspapers and city magazines.

The Third Week of November is National Game and Puzzle Week

Hold a game night at a local bar or restaurant, or sponsor a teen game night and invite local church or other youth organizations to attend for fun, games, manicures and makeovers.

During November, let clients have fun by solving puzzles or participating in 'Shower' style quizzes and games in the waiting area or in the chair; hold a contest for speed and/or accuracy or create your own salon or spa game with client rewards.

For a 'Salon Shower Game' that can be played by clients or by employees as a product knowledge training exercise, write down a list of your top 20 products, and a list of the specific benefit each provides, additional or secondary benefits such as vitamins, SPF protection, aromatherapy, and/or each product's intended use) and then reorder one of the lists randomly and see whether your clients (or your employees) can match up the product with its characteristics.

Create a special word of the month (such as 'turkey', 'pumpkin' or another seasonal word) and any time a client says the word, give them a chance to drop an entry form in a fishbowl for a drawing to be held at the end of the month. Create a gift prize basket with pumpkin, cloves, spice or another aromatherapy lotion, candle, etc., plus a gift card redeemable at their next appointment. Include a second gift certificate for your client to give a friend, co-worker or family member who would be a new client to your salon to help spur client referrals.

November Holidays and Observances

November 1 is Sandwich Day

Partner with a local caterer to provide mini-sandwiches as a treat for clients and extend offers for holiday catering and party makeovers. Provide a special offer to extend to the caterer's clients for pre-holiday party makeovers at your salon or spa. With a local caterer, create a cooperative offer for holiday party services or a corporate event package that can be added to your regular menu and your hotel / motel, city tourism and corporate services menus.

November 3 is Men Make Dinner Day

Create a package for men which includes either a dinner prepared for pick-up or catered by a catering marketing partner plus a gift card for your salon or spa so men can treat their special someones to a dinner and some pampering.

Work with a dinner preparation company or caterer to create a cooking class for bachelors (or bachelorettes) who want to improve their day-to-day cooking skills or to help them prepare to cook for parties or the holidays.

Partner with a local restaurant to create a makeover and a meal package to market for date nights in November or all year long. The 'Cheapskate Dates' featured in the February Chapter would also make great promotional options for Men Make Dinner Day.

November 8 is Parents as Teachers Day

Home-schooling support groups exist in most communities; contact local home-schooling consortiums and tutors to extend a special offer to their parents and families.

November 10 is Area Code Day

Have some fun! Use the numbers of your area code to create a special offer for services and/or products. If you live in a multi-code urban area (like the Seattle area where I live) you can use more than one local code to create special offers; for instance, a "206" might include a pre-sold package of two hair color highlights at $6 off each while a "253" might be a pre-sold package of 3 haircutting appointments sold at $25 each and a "360" could be $3.60 off any 2 retail products.

Loosen Up, Lighten Up Day in November

Hold a skin bar happy hour focused on helping clients "lighten up" complexions by freeing skin from buildup and reducing the effects of stress and environmental damage and how to "loosen up" wrinkles. Partner with a caterer or restaurant to provide light refreshments and give clients the recipes for this light party fare.

Partner with a local gym or fitness trainer for cross marketing or a cooperative "loosen up, lighten up" weight loss and makeover promotion to prepare for the holidays which includes a skin/makeup consultation and set of pre-selected makeup palette products.

November 15 is Clean Your Refrigerator Day

Partner with local cleaning services or professionals for cross or cooperative marketing.

Partner with a nutritionist to create a client event (inviting their clients and yours) that teaches how to clean the "bad stuff" out of our refrigerators, how to prepare delicious, healthy and nutritious meals for Thanksgiving or the December holidays and information about detoxifying, cleaning and caring for hair and skin. Discuss the relationship between diet and healthy hair and skin. Set up a hair, skin or makeup bar for clients and give quick holiday hair and makeup demonstrations or mini-touch ups to attendees.

Create bag stuffers and include nutrition tips and information about the connection between elements of diet (such as hydration, anti-oxidants, etc.) and healthy hair and skin in your e-mails and Facebook posts in November and throughout the holiday season.

Partner with a party planner to hold a workshop for clients on how to set a beautiful holiday party table. Invite their contacts as well as your clients to attend and extend a special offer to all invitees. Create door prizes that include place setting elements such as napkin rings or wine glass charms as well as holiday hair or skin 'glitter' or glow products, manufacturers samples, and a gift card redeemable at a future appointment. Make sure that one person from each client base (the party planner's and yours) wins. Collect contact information at the event and extend a special offer to all attendees after the event. Send a post-event e-mail with photos from the event and party planning tips to all of your contacts.

Boutique-quality, unique or beautiful napkin rings and glass charms would make a great addition to your retail during the holidays and as hostess or girlfriend gifts all year long. During the year, hold happy hours or girlfriend makeup or blow dry parties. Incentivize attendance with wine and chocolate and use collector-quality glass charms or napkin rings as door or contest prizes, as well as for retail sale.

November 20 is Beautiful Day

Hold a "Beautiful Holidays" open house or holiday fair in conjunction with independent sellers (jewelry, party supplies, clothing, accessories, kitchenware, giftware, etc.) and invite all clients as well as the general public to attend.

Pre-package holiday makeup kits to be ready for sale in addition to regular makeup products, nail products, etc. Book appointments, give hair and makeup demonstrations, mini-manicures and pedicures, and sell holiday gift items as well as your salon and spa home care retail products.

Make this event bigger and combine resources with your marketing partners for communications and the event. Create 'goodie bags' with branded tchotchkes and samples from all participants to give to all attendees. Collect contact information for all attendees and be sure that you add them to your contact database. Extend a bounce-back offer via handout at the event as well as a follow up e-mail or direct mail offer.

November 25 is Shopping Reminder Day

Hopefully you have been working to create awareness among your clients of the great gift options you offer during the holidays; and hopefully you, yourself, are developing a mind set beyond hair and skin care products when it comes to your retail offerings. Send a special "Holiday Shopping List" or "Gift Wish List" to your clients in November that features your best options for gift giving for various recipients (i.e., a gift basket and/or specific product and service suggestions for men, for teens or tweens, for women, for co-workers, for moms or sisters, etc.)

Becoming a true gift resource for clients will mean more frequent client visits, more gift card sales and more referrals. Build a bigger role for your business in the lives of your clients!

Humane Society Day is in November

Extend support to your local Humane Society or animal shelter by helping promote or even facilitate pet adoptions. Reward pet adopters with a special incentive upon proof of recent pet adoption.

Hold a wine tasting for pet lovers with the cover charge being donated to the Humane Society. Purchase animal-themed wine glass charms for the event and make these available for sale along with other pet-themed supplies, pet grooming or coat-care products.

Contact your local animal shelter to find out if there are items they need and accept as donations, and offer clients a free add-on service or discount when they bring these items in with them to their appointments or provide you with a receipt showing that they made a recent cash donation to the shelter. Write a press release to publicize your efforts and raise additional community awareness and submit it along with testimonial from the shelter and a picture of a four-legged shelter friend that tugs at the heart.

Create an on-going discount to extend to pet-lovers in conjunction with support of the shelter, and ask the shelter to provide patrons with a copy of your offer.

A growing number of salons are carrying professional retail items for pets including specialty pet-care shampoo and other hair care products: toys, collars, bowls, brushes and other supplies. It's an area where you can experiment with little risk; if you don't want to buy in products yourself, partner with a local pet store, veterinary office or groomer and offer to give them shelf space in return for commission on items sold. Your clients will appreciate the convenience of not having to make a trip to the pet store.

Don't forget the bling! Collars, dishes and holiday pet-wear make great impulse buys and gifts. Add a charitable aspect to support your local Humane Society and designate a percentage of proceeds from the sale of these items to be donated to this charity or a local animal shelter or animal emergency services provider.

Extend a special offer to all pet owners. Cross market with local animal groomers, mobile grooming service providers, veterinarians, and pet shops. If you brought in retail products for pets, give pet owners a discount on retail purchases for their pet when they purchase retail products for themselves. Or in conjunction with a groomer, extend an on-going discount for dual pet-and-owner salon service and grooming bookings or people and pet dual-product purchases.

Like parents with kids, pet owners have regular extra expenses—so give them a break! In another data-collection focused contest, allow clients to provide their contact information and that of their friends-who-own-pets and draw a winner at the end of the month for a free hair cut or another service, or reward them with one of your pet-themed retail items. If you are partnering for cross marketing with a groomer, your contest award could feature a free cut for both owner and pet! Extend a special offer to contest entrants and all pet-owning clients after the drawing.

November 27 is Flossing Day

Partner with a dental practice for cross marketing and create a holiday dental hygiene tip sheet for clients (such as the effects of and how to minimize staining by wine, how to freshen your breath at a party without a toothbrush, etc.) Stock salon or spa-branded (or generic) 'flossers', disposable pre-loaded toothbrushes, mints or gum at your point of purchase as 'must-haves' for the holiday season for the car, pocket or purse.

Beating the Holiday Blues

Many members of your community do not have holiday parties or family events to attend; consider providing volunteer services at a local shelter or senior center and make opportunities for service or donations available to co-workers and clients.

The Monday after Thanksgiving is Cyber Monday

Make every Monday a "Cyber Monday." Utilize your web site, Facebook, Twitter, text messaging and/or e-mail communications every Monday during the holiday season to let clients know about holiday specials, gift giving ideas, open appointment times, holiday charitable drives, etc. Populate your communications with holiday party ideas, quick and easy recipes, hair, skin and makeup tips and tricks, photos showing great holiday looks, and other holiday-related information.

Make Cyber Monday part of your marketing habit and utilize technology on set Mondays throughout the year to extend cyber offers and information to your readers all year long.

November Planning and Tasks

Choose from manufacturer's bi-monthly and holiday promotions to support your goals and events for November-December and into the New Year. Purchase any last retail products needed for Holiday or November-December events and promotions. Even though these months will be hectic, set aside some time and begin to plan for January and February. Design and print (or order) marketing or support materials needed for coming promotions through the holidays and into next year.

Communicate in November

Items to include in your e-mail or print newsletter, web site, Facebook and blog posts and in direct mail communications this month:

- November, December and Holiday events and promotions

- Last minute openings, plus any extended hours for the holiday season

- Suggestions for holiday makeovers and holiday season hair care or styling, makeup, nails and skin care

- Tips for making a holiday look last all through an event from setting makeup or hair to staying hydrated, getting enough rest, and pampering services needed before-and-after holiday events

- Gift bundles, partnered promotions

- Specific ideas for gift giving

- Remind clients that your gift cards make great gifts, and for whom they would make the best gifts in terms of teachers, family, friends, co-workers, etc.

- Promotions expiring in November, new products coming in December

- A spotlight product, service or staff member of the month

November Calendar / Suggested Communications and Tasks Schedule

SUN	MON	TUE	WED	THU	FRI	SAT
1st week of Month 1st of November—Merchandise for November 1st of November—Begin collecting entries for November contests						
		Order from manufacturers retail promotions for products to support December - January marketing plans; design related signage			Send November Newsletter with coupons, announce contests and winners, new products and services coming events, openings still on the books, events and promotions	
2nd week of Month						
		Order event supplies, postcards, collateral, gifts and salon-branded items for December contests			Write press releases for any events/results reporting or future events / charitable focus	
3rd week of Month						
		Finalize, review and lay out plans for December - January - February promotions			Send November "last chance" promotions and openings on the books e-mail and/or direct mail	
4th week of Month Last day of November—Take down any November-only promotions Last day of November—Draw November contest winners						
		Order event supplies, postcards, gifts and salon-branded items needed for January promotions			Send December focus e-mail / direct mail with strong holiday gift messaging	

November Worksheets

$_____ Retail Sales Goal

Promotions_____

_____

_____

_____

_____

$_____ Avg. Retail/Client

$_____ Retail Sales Results

$_____ Service Sales Goal

Promotions_____

_____

_____

_____

_____

$_____ Avg. Service/Client

$_____ Service Sales Results

$_____ Event Revenues Goal

Events _____

_____

_____

_____

_____

#_____ Attending Event/s

#_____ Apts/Booked at Event

$_____ Event/s Sales

$_____ Total Event/s Results

$_____ Charity/Fund Raising Goal

Charity Events _____

_____

_____

_____

_____

#_____ Attending Event/s

#_____ Apts/Booked at Event

$_____ Charity Event/s Sales

$_____ Total Charity Results

November Marketing Summary

Marketing Partners: _____

_____

_____

_____

Marketing Collateral Needed (or Used): _____

_____

_____

_____

Other Efforts:

#_____ Number of Clients New to Salon

%_____ Client Retention Rate (90 days)

Retention Efforts: _____

_____

or % _____ Clients Re-booked at Appointment

$_____ Gift Certificate Sales

#_____ Contacts added to marketing / e-mail database

december
make over
your new year

To make over the (next) New Year, you need to do something that you are probably well-suited to do. As a professional in the salon or spa, you are already creative and already a believer in the power and necessity of continuing education. You already believe in yourself and your ability to build something special in the pursuit of practicing your art. You have a vision not only of the business that you can build, but also the good that it can enable you to do.

To make over your next New Year (and the next, and the next) will take all of these things that you already believe in, and something more. It will require you to be open to doing all of the things that you do in your business in new ways, in ways that some other professionals in your industry resist. It will require you not only to accept but to actually embrace the reality that the future of your industry will look radically different than its past. It will require that you embrace changes that need to happen in any and all aspects of how you do business, both relative to your clients (and how you serve and relate to them) as well as in manufacturing and distribution.

As formerly distinct lines disappear (such as in how distribution is done, and where professional products are available for sale), it will require you to be more open-minded and creative when it comes to retail sales and services.

As clients continue to gain access to even more information, it will require you to be that much more transparent in your dealings with them. You will have to work even more creatively to build and sustain your role in their lives as an expert, and to provide them with convincing evidence that you are positively impacting their lives; not just in improvements to their appearance, but also in how you impact their lives socially and professionally.

You will have to build the perception of real, meaningful value in the lives of your clients by finding new ways of meeting their needs. And you will have to discover new needs, wants and desires in their lives to fulfill.

In the future, salons and spas will need to align themselves with other personal care providers, service organizations and retail stores or may even need to provide some services off-site in order to better meet the time demands of busy, working professionals, working parents, etc.

To make over the next New Year—for years to come—you must not just be willing to accept radical change. To truly succeed; you must be willing to lead change.

So make over... everything!   It's going to be a great year!

December Promotion Ideas

December Month-Long Observances

December is National Bingo Month

Sponsor a bingo tournament for a local senior center or hold a bingo tournament in-salon for youth or senior groups. Create a bingo-style contest or rewards card for clients.

Create a "BINGO" set of 5 products for clients bundled at a special price or reward clients for every 5 products (or services, or combination of products or services) that they purchase in December.

Create a special 'Bingo' contest in conjunction with partnering local businesses where clients receive a free gift or entry in a drawing for free service (and/or prizes from other businesses) in January if they visit each of the businesses on a card or flyer. (Credit for this idea goes to Celia Bender, a self-employed marketing professional, who employed this contest as part of a regional "buy local" campaign effort in Enumclaw, Washington.) Make sure that all entries, from all businesses, make it to your print and e-mail marketing contact database and receive special offers for the New Year.

Many Bingo-loving seniors may feel left out during this time of year. Partner with a local senior center to host a holiday Bingo Tournament, enlisting business partners to create special prizes designed to bring seniors into the salon and into your partners' businesses.

Holiday and New Year Parties

Partner with local limo, shuttle, hotel, or related services to offer clients special packages including mini-makeovers or blow out and styling plus transportation to or from their big holiday or New Year's party.

Host or provide mini spa or makeover services for corporate holiday parties where you will also have the opportunity to sell retail products, collect contact information, and follow up with a special offer for January.

December is Write a Friend Month

Purchase specialty blank greeting cards, holiday cards, or stationery/note card sets for retail sale. Add a holiday greeting card display to your point of purchase or general retail with one-of-a-kind saucy, spicy, elegant (etc.) cards that clients cannot find anywhere else.

Purchase or create a special holiday card to send to clients. Express your appreciation for their patronage and best wishes for the new year. Sign each personally. Include a business card that also contains a special holiday or New Year offer, or that features a special sentiment or wish for the New Year.

Capture this moment in the life of your business with a staff photo and create a beautiful, zany, or otherwise one-of-a-kind holiday greeting to be used in printed cards, online and/or in advertising during the holiday season.

If your client gift budget is $0, you can still give a meaningful gift to everyone on your list, including clients and staff. In 2009, inspired by a popular religious book and group study, Dawn Taylor, the owner Salon Bella Dea in Auburn, WA, wrote a personal letter to her clients telling them how they have impacted her life over the years. She thanked them not only for their business, but also thanked those clients who knew her parents and had prayed for her mom while she was battling cancer, for all that she feels that she learns from her clients, and how much she appreciates them entrusting her with their hair.

She said that the idea behind her letter was to tell people what she would want to tell them if she knew she had only a short time left to do so. Without being morbid, the result was a letter written to people telling them they have impacted her life in ways they might not even know, inspiring them to continue to make a personal difference in lives where they can, never knowing how much even a small act of kindness can mean. The gift she gave to her clients was nearly free, but priceless!

December Week-Long Observances

The First Week of December is Cookie Cutter Week

Partner with an independent kitchenware seller for cross marketing or sell cookie cutters during the holiday season. Hold a cookie baking or decorating contest. Collect and share staff or clients favorite holiday cookie recipes online, on bag stuffers and in your e-mail newsletter.

Or create a cookie recipe collection book to have printed to give to clients during the holidays or to sell as a gift book as part of your retail offerings next year.

Purchase boutique-quality or salon or spa-branded cookie cutters to use as ornaments for your holiday tree and/or to give one to each client as a holiday thank you gift when they come in to your salon in December.

The Second Week of December is National Handwashing Week

Purchase salon or spa-branded hand sanitizers as gifts for clients, gift-with-purchase or for retail sale.

Purchase beautiful, guest-quality hand towels as client gifts, gift-with-purchase or for retail sale along with branded hand sanitizers, hand soap, boutique soap dispensers or soap dishes, scented candles or incense burners, etc.

The Fourth Week of December is 'It's About Time' Week

Plan now to help clients and employees develop and meet their New Year Resolutions by partnering with a fitness, weight loss, counseling, life coach, home or office space organizer or another expert for cross or cooperative marketing offers.

Add a quirky or fun inexpensive digital watch or personal alarm clock to your impulse buy and gift offerings; purchase salon or spa-branded digital watches to gift to clients or their children.

Build Business Right Under Your Nose
(with what's right over your head)

So often we overlook some of the simplest, most obvious ways to grow that are right under our nose, or in this case—literally—right over our heads.

Here are 9 ways to use the roof over your head to build business (adapted from my blog at www.savvystylist.net):

- Does your business 'share' a roof with other businesses? Partner together with the other businesses located in your business park, building, mall or immediate locale to hold a special holiday open house or sale event.

- Exchange and display the web site links of the businesses with which you share a roof on your web site, your Facebook page, in your newsletters, etc.

- Extend a special offer to all the employees who work in other businesses near yours (and their families).

- Extend your own employee discount to the employees of local businesses on an on-going basis or for a limited time.

- Create a special offer for all of the customers of the other businesses who share a roof with you and ask them to display your offer, hand out your bag stuffers, or include your offer in their mailings, newsletters, on their web site, etc.

- Partner with local roofing, construction, and home renovation businesses for cross marketing.

- Partner with local home repair or renovation professionals to hold a special 'how to' class or workshop for your clients on a particular do-it-yourself project (or create a series of classes).

- Partner with local companies that provide home renovation or repair services or appliance sales/repair services for cross marketing.

- Extend a special offer to your landlord or employees of the management company that owns your building.

December Holidays and Observances

December 4 is Santa's List Day

Set up a drop box during November and December for the children of clients and the public to drop off letters to Santa. Publicize your Letter to Santa drop off promotion on Facebook, your blog, and in your e-mail newsletter. When children drop off a letter to send to Santa, give each a small salon or spa-branded yo-yo, hacky sack, candy bag, watch or alarm clock or some other toy along with a bounce-back offer for mom or dad.

'Adopt' a local needy family (preserving their privacy) and as staff, donate a day of proceeds or have staff or clients donate items needed to help this family have a "Merry Christmas."

Or be "Santa" to a local individual or family and gift year long haircuts (or another service) for the New Year to a local family struggling with cancer or another illness or a severe personal setback (such as a house fire or burglary). Or donate a year's worth of hair or skin care products, etc.

Say thank you and extend holiday greetings to your most valuable clients in some special way and extend your brand by gifting branded travel mugs, t-shirts or tanks, unique nail files or other creative, buzz-worthy, low-cost items. Sell some, too!

December 5 is Bathtub Party Day

Create a Bathtub Party gift set with boutique-quality or spa or salon-branded gift towels, bubble bath and room spray, personal fragrance, and/or candle for retail sale, for gift to your best clients, for gift-with-purchase or for gifts for staff.

Partner with a hot tub/spa seller for cross marketing. Recommend hot tub-appropriate products to clients and create a tip sheet for the hot tub seller's customers about post-hot-tub skin care plus a bounce-back offer.

December 6 is Mitten Tree Day

Set up a "Mitten Tree" to collect donations of mittens, hats, coats and other cold weather gear to be given to a local charity, social services organization or a needy family. Or partner with a charity or social service organization and host a "giving tree" where clients can choose to purchase specific items to donate to a local needy child or family. Write a press release to publicize efforts and help solicit additional donations. Thank those who donate with a gift card, sample or retail product, salon or spa-branded tchotchke and a bounce-back offer.

Purchase unique and/or beautiful cold weather accessories for addition to your holiday/impulse-buy retail offerings. Or purchase spa or salon-branded cold weather accessories such as scarves, beanie hats or headbands for gift-with-purchase, client gifts, prize baskets or employee gifts.

December 12 is Poinsettia Day

Send a poinsettia or other holiday arrangement to a local senior center, school, charity or church. Or purchase poinsettias as holiday gifts for your employees.

Partner with a floral supplier for cross marketing, and/or sell miniature poinsettias in your salon during the holidays.

December 18 is Bake Cookies Day

Partner with a local caterer or bakery to provide cookie treats for clients or to create cookie gift packs for your staff, VIP clientele, to send to a charity, to city hall, the teachers at your local school, a business to whose employees you wish to extend a special offer, etc.

Purchase pre-wrapped snack cookies to sell in the salon during the holidays or year round, or to offer to clients during appointments.

Work with a nutritionist to create a collection of healthy cookie recipes and ingredient substitutes so that clients do not have to choose between indulgence, health or their waistline during the holidays. Hold a workshop to teach healthy cookie cooking or include cookie nutrition tips on bag stuffers, Facebook posts, and in e-mail marketing.

Hold a contest and have clients bring some of their favorite homemade cookies in to the spa or salon to have a "Cookie Tasting." Use a points system for both taste and design and reward winner/s with a gift card, branded goodies or other rewards. Extend a special offer to all participants.

Create a larger cookie-tasting event with other businesses in your area or hold your event with a partnering bar, restaurant, coffee shop or other business. Collect contact information at your events and extend a special offer to all participants.

Create an online cookbook or share cookie recipes from staff or clients on your web site, your Facebook, blog or other social media site or on bag stuffers. Include a special bounce-back offer with a cookie-related code word.

Purchase cookie-fragranced (preferably spa or salon-branded) room sprays, sachets, candles or other items for retail sale, gift-with-purchase or for client gifts for the holidays.

Demonstrate to clients how to use fragrance sprays with their blow dryers at home to quickly diffuse cookie scents in their home to give the illusion of fresh-baked cookies to their guests (also ensuring that clients will experience the same illusion in your salon or spa during their appointments!)

December 30 is Make Up Your Mind Day

The New Year is coming! Make up your mind as a business owner to analyze each and every aspect of your business from a client-experience point of view. Obtain resources and support for your own renewal and re-energizing, both for yourself personally and for your business. Create a plan to help support staff development in technical as well as personal areas.

Map out your plan for next year's marketing, promotional, charitable and other initiatives. Create a list of businesses that you want to partner with, and a list of businesses/organizations to which you want to extend special employee or patron offers in the New Year.

Partner with fitness, nutrition, weight loss, motivational, counseling, coaching, organizing and other professionals for cross marketing in order to connect your clients with more resources in their community.

Create and host in-salon support groups for clients to help them meet their New Year Resolutions and goals.

Out with the Old, In with the New (scene stealers)

This year will be over and before you know it, you will find yourself setting out on a new year. Take some time in December to evaluate the past year and make professional as well as personal New Year Resolutions for the coming year. You may be planning to open your own salon, expand, become an educator or platform artist, enter a competition, publish your work, select new products, or you might simply need to update your pricing and services.

No matter what your goals, putting them on paper and noting the steps required to reach them will help you to avoid procrastinating and take the first step. Sharing your goals and your time line with a trusted friend or mentor can also help you to feel more accountable toward them.

Take stock of the last year, analyzing initiatives, marketing efforts, events, and cross-marketing partnerships against your goals. Take note of any unexpected benefits from the programs you ran, what worked well, what you enjoyed the most, problems you did not anticipate, or where you fell short in efforts to market, promote or create buzz around your promotions.

Consider speaking to a few key customers about what type of programs or packages would induce them to take action. Asking a few trusted clients to participate in a focus group and garnering customer feedback on a regular basis can help you to construct more effective promotions and events, avoid unforeseen pitfalls and give clients what they really want from you as you continue creating a larger role for your business in their lives. Make adjustments to your annual marketing plan to prepare it for launch.

Plan now to help clients ring in the New Year (or say goodbye to the old one) with a special VIP customer reception held in-salon or at a local restaurant, wine, book or gift shop that is willing to partner with you for a cross-marketed event. Ideally, this reception will be exclusively for clients who are the most loyal and responsive to your events and promotions, rather than open to all. This VIP event should be for your most loyal clients, and especially those who are influential within their communities or within civic, political, corporate, or other mid to large-sized groups. Your goal is to create a loyal, locked in client base for the new year who will be likely to build buzz, refer friends, family and coworkers, and stay dialed-in next year.

At the reception, offer VIP-client-exclusive packages for 3, 6 or even 12 months, or offer packages that support cross-business promotions with the marketing partners you established this year. Create packages with compelling savings or add-ons; if working with other vendors, these packages should be cross-marketed to their clients as well as yours.

If you have created several strong marketing partnerships, hold the event in a venue large enough to accommodate a large number of clients and activities. Treat invited guests like the celebrities they are; provide them with a goodie bag to take home full of freebies and offers and provide a thank you gift to all clients who enroll in a membership or purchase a package.

Provide incentives for clients to bring a new guest with them to the event, or who refer new clients to your salon in January. And remember, you don't have to give away your services or retail products; salon-branded t-shirts, tanks, and other gifts make very reasonably priced but effective "thank you" gifts for your clients and extend your brand beyond the walls of the salon.

In December you will wrap up holiday sales and clean up on holiday party makeovers. Show your appreciation to clients with special thank yous, holiday messages and gifts.

Prepare for the New Year, including putting the finishing touches on your marketing plan. During the last week of December when you may be closed for the holidays or things are on the slow side, set aside time to take stock of where you are, how far you have come during the last year, and make New Year's (business) Resolutions. Set aside time to appreciate your mentors, co-workers and friends and celebrate the end of a great year – and the beginning of a promising new one!

As you plan for the New Year, take a step back to examine the experience provided to clients in your salon or spa. When was the last time that you truly viewed the experience from your client's point of view? It is not always easy to see things from their perspective. When you are there performing your role day in and day out, it can be easy to overlook details that might be escaping your notice simply because you have become accustomed to seeing them. One way to overcome this tendency is to actually analyze the client experience in a systematic way, from a non-traditional point of view.

Just as in theatre, the client experience occurs on a set. This set is comprised of the outside and inside of the salon, and scenes occur not only on set, but on the phone, on your website, by email, and any other touch point that your client has with you, or with any member of your salon, as well as within the salon or spa itself. The first step in improving the client experience, then, is to set the stage. As this year winds down, take your analysis of the client experience and create a new set for your salon for the new year.

Think of your salon or spa as a theater, with employees as main cast members and your clients as recurring characters. If you begin to view each client experience as a "scene" in your overall business script, you can pull apart different components in order to more properly set the stage for success.

Small indulgences, small moments of escape, small pleasures. When the stage is set it is easy to move toward incorporating small moments of indulgence to enhance the client experience. Look for ways that you can treat clients to moments of luxury, relaxation, aromatherapy and other sensory indulgences to enhance their experience, set your business apart from others, and keep them coming back for more. A dark chocolate you ask them to sample in the chair or at the point of purchase. A demonstration of how to use a room spray and blow dryer to diffuse fragrance at home. The gift of a genuine compliment and a sincere thank you to every client.

Draw other actors to your stage. Make a list of businesses in your physical proximity or who are connected to you through family, friends, or clients. Set out to contact each of these businesses to create cooperative and cross marketing opportunities to support your marketing goals during the coming year. For instance, if you want to hold a fashion show, partner with a boutique clothier, shoe store, caterer, wine shop, and an esthetician and show not only the latest fashions and accessories, but also demonstrate how to combine essential wardrobe elements creatively, how to create a seasonal hair and makeup look—all in a setting where clients can also bring friends to enjoy the event as well as some great refreshments. Invite your catering partner to share party planning tips or recipes (or use your fashion show event as a springboard for the next event—a Party Planning Workshop!) One good idea can be the seed to launch a series of events, drawing your clients into closer relationship with your business and resulting in new clients.

As you plan to write your marketing "script" for next year, create events and promotions for each month purposefully designed to create moments of (client) self-centered indulgence: wine and chocolate; a fashion show; mini-massages; a bridal fair; a demo on applying eye-shadow before they leave the salon; a workshop on personal development or empowerment; a charitable campaign, food or clothing drive to bring some of the simple pleasures of life to those less fortunate in your community—the possibilities are endless. View the value of promotions and services from the client's point of view—not the manufacturer's, distributor's, or even your own—and create messages that highlight the client-pleasure factor.

All that the end of a year means is that it is the beginning of the new one: Commit yourself to continual learning and improvement, and to the continual analysis and improvement of every aspect of the client experience; lather, rinse, repeat!

December Planning and Tasks

Choose from manufacturer's bimonthly promotions to support the promotions and events you have planned for January and February including New Year packages and Resolution-helping partnerships with fitness instructors or facilities, martial arts studios, jazzercise or dance studios and others.

Put final adjustments into your marketing and business plan for the first half of next year and ensure that your business partners are lined up to support your planned joint marketing and events to wrap up the old year and begin the new one.

Create a loyalty or rewards program for the New Year.

Plan a New Year's party for your business partners, co-workers and friends to say thank you and get the New Year off to a good start. Create a New Year's Eve party makeover package for clients. Purchase salon-branded items to help kick start efforts and events in the New Year.

Sketch out a plan for February events including a Valentine's Day gift and gift certificate push.

Communicate in December

Items to include in your e-mail or print newsletter, web site, Facebook and blog posts and in direct mail communications this month:

- Any promotions expiring in December
- Series or bundled packages available for purchase for the New Year
- Products or services whose prices are set to increase in the New Year
- Last minute gift and holiday ideas
- Holiday party ideas, makeover ideas and tips and products for clients to help ensure that their party look lasts until well after midnight
- Suggest that clients purchase spa services for gifts as well as for themselves during the hectic holiday season or as a reward for making it into the New Year
- January and February "Save the Date" reminders for events through Valentine's Day
- Last minute openings on the books and best time to book for holiday party preparation
- A spotlight product, service or staff member of the month

December Calendar / Suggested Communications and Tasks Schedule

SUN	MON	TUE	WED	THU	FRI	SAT
1st week of Month 1st of December—Merchandise for December 1st of December—Begin collecting entries for December contests						
		Order signage, event supplies and promotional materials for January - February promotions			Send December Newsletter with coupons, announce contests and winners, new products and services coming events, openings still on the books, events and promotions	
2nd week of Month						
		Order in gifts, salon-branded items, impulse buy and other items for January - February			Write press releases for any events/results reporting or future events / charitable focus	
3rd week of Month						
	Begin marketing for New Year	Finalize, review and lay out plans for January-February - March promotions			Send December "last chance" promotions and openings on the books e-mail and/or direct mail	
4th week of Month Last day of December—Take down any December-only promotions Last day of December—Draw December contest winners						
		Order event supplies, postcards, gifts and salon-branded items needed for January - February promotions			Send January focus e-mail / direct mail	

December Worksheets

$_____ Retail Sales Goal

Promotions_____

_____

_____

_____

_____

$_____ Avg. Retail/Client

$_____ Retail Sales Results

$_____ Service Sales Goal

Promotions_____

_____

_____

_____

_____

$_____ Avg. Service/Client

$_____ Service Sales Results

$_____ Event Revenues Goal

Events _____

_____

_____

_____

_____

\#_____ Attending Event/s

\#_____ Apts/Booked at Event

$_____ Event/s Sales

$_____ Total Event/s Results

$_____ Charity/Fund Raising Goal

Charity Events _____

_____

_____

_____

_____

\#_____ Attending Event/s

\#_____ Apts/Booked at Event

$_____ Charity Event/s Sales

$_____ Total Charity Results

December Marketing Summary

Marketing Partners: _____

_____

_____

_____

Marketing Collateral Needed (or Used): _____

_____

_____

_____

Other Efforts:

#_____ Number of Clients New to Salon

%_____ Client Retention Rate (90 days)

 Retention Efforts: _____

_____

or % _____ Clients Re-booked at Appointment

$_____ Gift Certificate Sales

#_____ Contacts added to marketing / e-mail database

appendix

acknowledgements

Pgs. 7-10, 'Everything is Marketing' by Fred Joyal, founder of 1-800-DENTIST
I recommend this book personally, not only for dental professionals, but for anyone in a service industry.

Pg. 17, 'Make Over My Hero' by Claire Koutsouros of Hair by Claire in Doylestown, PA, with thanks to Jessee Skittrall of Absolut Hair in Everett WA.

Pg. 84, 'Trombone Players Wanted' video series by author Marcus Buckingham
I recommend this video series personally, as a great training and development tool, usable by professionals in any industry, and a great resource as well for job seekers.

Pg. 278, Celia Bender, Chameleon Productions and Fee Mail, Inc.

Pg. 279, Dawn Taylor, Salon Bella Dea

with personal thanks to

John Schmidt, East Coast Salon Services based in Runnemede, NJ
(www.eastcoastsalon.com)

David Hanen, Founder, LOMA and Pearatin Hair Care products
(www.lomaforhair.com)

Sydney Berry and George Learned, Salon Services and Supplies, Renton, WA
(www.salonservicesnw.com)

John Busch, Lithtex NW commercial offset printing
(www.lithtexnw.com)

Jim Conway, American Solutions for Business
(www.americanbus.com)

observances cited

Some observances occur on the same day, or same day of the month (such as Thanksgiving, which always occurs on the 4th Thursday of November); however, some observances are set on new days each year by their founders. Check with the sponsoring organization for observances which may change from year to year.

observances, continued

observances, continued